"This incredible book is the comprehensive criminology of video games! It's a deep dive into what they teach about crime, violence, consequences, and games' ability to reify harms and solutions. Culture plays with rule breaking—use this book to understand the place and value of video games in understanding crime."

Jack Denham, *Associate Dean: Social Sciences, York St. John University*

"Extends the criminological gaze towards an immensely popular—yet strangely neglected—area of popular culture. The result is a series of fascinating and illuminating explorations of how video games reflect—and perhaps shape or contest—our common conceptions of crime, justice, transgression and pleasure. A fabulous contribution to popular criminology!"

Majid Yar, *Professor Emeritus of Criminology, Lancaster University*

T0372858

VIDEO GAMES, CRIME, AND CONTROL

Discussing the state of play in contemporary popular culture, specifically the role of crime and crime control in the video game medium, this book discusses the criminological importance of video games.

Pulling together an international group of scholars from Brazil, Canada, Sweden, the United Kingdom, and the United States, this edited volume analyzes a wide range of noteworthy video games, including Bioshock, Death Stranding, Diablo 2, Beat Cop, The Last of Us, Disco Elysium, Red Dead Redemption, P.T., Spider-Man, Spider-Man: Miles Morales, Star Wars Jedi: Fallen Order, and Grand Theft Auto. The book thus seeks to advance dialog on video games as important cultural artifacts containing significant insights regarding dominant perceptions, interests, anxieties, contradictions, and other matters of criminological interest.

Covering policing, vigilantism, different forms of violence, genocide, mental illness, and criminological theory, *Video Games, Crime, and Control* will be of great interest to students and scholars of Criminology, Media Studies, and Sociology, specifically those focusing on Game Studies and Cultural Criminology.

Kevin F. Steinmetz is a professor of criminology in the Department of Sociology, Anthropology, and Social Work at Kansas State University, USA. His scholarship cuts across multiple areas including cybercrime, criminological theory, racial inequality and criminal justice, gender and crime, as well as crime, criminal justice, and popular culture. He is the author of *Hacked: A Radical Approach to Hacker Culture and Crime and Cybercrime and Society*. His works have also appeared in prestigious outlets, including *The British Journal of Criminology, Theoretical Criminology, Critical Criminology, Crime Media Culture*.

Jonathan A. Grubb is the Military Domestic Abuse Senior Research and Evaluation Analyst for the National Organization for Victim Advocacy (NOVA). His research centers on the spatiotemporal clustering of crime, victimization of vulnerable populations, perceptions and attitudes of professionals working with victims of domestic violence as well as human trafficking, and arson within urban environments. Recent publications include *Crime TV: Streaming Criminology in Popular Culture* which utilizes modern television shows as a frame for understanding criminological theory.

Routledge Studies in Crime, Media and Popular Culture

Routledge Studies in Crime, Media and Popular Culture offers the very best in research that seeks to understand crime through the context of culture, cultural processes and media.

The series welcomes monographs and edited volumes from across the globe, and across a variety of disciplines. Books will offer fresh insights on a range of topics, including news reporting of crime; moral panics and trial by media; media and the police; crime in film; crime in fiction; crime in TV; crime and music; 'reality' crime shows; the impact of new media including mobile, Internet and digital technologies, and social networking sites; the ways media portrayals of crime influence government policy and lawmaking; the theoretical, conceptual and methodological underpinnings of cultural criminology.

Books in the series will be essential reading for those researching and studying criminology, media studies, cultural studies and sociology.

Corporate Wrongdoing on Film
The 'Public Be Damned'
Kenneth Dowler and Daniel Antonowicz

The American City in Crime Films
Criminology and the Cinematic City
Andrew J. Baranauskas

Video Games, Crime and Control
Getting Played
Edited by Kevin F. Steinmetz and Jonathan A. Grubb

VIDEO GAMES, CRIME, AND CONTROL

Getting Played

Edited by Kevin F. Steinmetz and Jonathan A. Grubb

Routledge
Taylor & Francis Group

LONDON AND NEW YORK

Designed cover image: gettyimages.com

First published 2024
by Routledge
4 Park Square, Milton Park, Abingdon, Oxon OX14 4RN

and by Routledge
605 Third Avenue, New York, NY 10158

Routledge is an imprint of the Taylor & Francis Group, an informa business

British Library Cataloguing-in-Publication Data
A catalogue record for this book is available from the British Library

Library of Congress Cataloging-in-Publication Data
Names: Grubb, Jonathan A., editor. | Steinmetz, Kevin F., editor.
Title: Video games, crime and control : playing cops and robbers / Jonathan A. Grubb and Kevin F. Steinmetz.
Description: First edition. | New York : Routledge, 2024. | Series: Routledge Studies in Crime, Culture and Media | Includes bibliographical references and index.
Identifiers: LCCN 2024015595 (print) | LCCN 2024015596 (ebook) | ISBN 9781032388090 (hbk) | ISBN 9781032388038 (pbk) | ISBN 9781003346869 (ebk)
Subjects: LCSH: Crime in video games. | Violence in video games. | Criminology. | Social control. | Popular culture. | Video games—Social aspects. | Video games—Psychological aspects.
Classification: LCC GV1469.34.V56 V53 2024 (print) | LCC GV1469.34.V56 (ebook) | DDC 794.8/4556—dc23/eng/20240407
LC record available at https://lccn.loc.gov/2024015595
LC ebook record available at https://lccn.loc.gov/2024015596

ISBN: 978-1-032-38809-0 (hbk)
ISBN: 978-1-032-38803-8 (pbk)
ISBN: 978-1-003-34686-9 (ebk)

DOI: 10.4324/9781003346869

Typeset in Sabon
by Apex CoVantage, LLC

As always, for Pamela, Elsie, and Alice.
—Kevin F. Steinmetz

To Delores, Tom, and Matt, each of you had a profound influence on my love for games, from playing Trivial Pursuit on holidays to exposing me to Nintendo games for the first time. Thank you for shaping my passion for gaming. And to everyone who identifies as a gamer, finding excitement, inspiration, dread, and solace across genres and methods of play evolving over the past half century.
—Jonathan A. Grubb

CONTENTS

CONTRIBUTORS

Colin Atkinson is a senior lecturer at the University of the West of Scotland. He conducts research on crime, policing, and security, and their representation in popular culture. Colin has a professional background in counter-terrorism intelligence analysis. His current favorite Star Wars video game is *Star Wars Jedi: Fallen Order*.

Jocelyn Booton has a master's in social work and love for research. She currently works at Wilfrid Laurier University in Ontario, Canada.

Breanna Boppre is a senior research associate in the Justice Policy Center at Urban Institute (United States). She is also a lecturer in the Department of Victim Studies at Sam Houston State University. Her work appears in numerous peer-reviewed outlets including *Justice Quarterly* and *Criminal Justice and Behavior*.

Andrea Corradi is an Assistant Professor in the Department of Criminal Justice and Criminology at Georgia Southern University (United States). Her research focuses on the examination of intended and unintended consequences of social control regarding security, extremism, policing, incarceration, and health.

Christina Fawcett is a genre, media, and monster theorist in the Department of English at the University of Winnipeg, Canada; her work explores villainous and monstrous spaces in video games, media, and young people's texts. Her writing addresses genre and cultural studies, monstrosity and trauma, embodiment, and identification.

Michelle Goodridge is the head, user and access services, the liaison librarian for game design and a contract teaching faculty member for game design all at Wilfrid Laurier University (Ontario, Canada). She has an MA in public history and a MLIS in library and information science.

Edward L.W. Green grew up in southeastern Kentucky and is a criminologist with research interests in the sociology of punishment, corrections, theory, and cultural production of crime narratives. He has over a dozen scholarly publications in journal articles and book chapters across various criminological topics. He is an associate professor at Roosevelt University's Department of Criminal Justice in Chicago, IL (United States).

Jonathan Grubb is a senior research and evaluation analyst for NOVA's DoD Domestic Abuse Victim Advocate (DAVA) Program. He has published more than a dozen peer-reviewd publications, edited volumes, and book chapters, commonly examining victimization of vulnerable populations as well as on perceptions of professionals working with victims of domestic violence and human trafficking.

Logan P. Kennedy is a tenure-track assistant professor in the Department of Criminal Justice and Criminology at East Carolina University, United States. His research examines protest policing and how crowd psychology drives police training in this area. His work appears in peer-reviewed outlets such as the *British Journal of Criminology*.

Steven Kohm is Professor of Criminal Justice at the University of Winnipeg, Canada. His research focuses on media, popular culture, and crime. He is co-editor of *Screening Justice: Canadian Crime Films, Culture and Society* (2017), and co-editor of *The Annual Review of Interdisciplinary Justice Research*.

Chris McDiarmid studied at Western University in the Bachelor of Arts program with a focus on film studies. He has worked for the Oshawa Public Libraries in Oshawa, Canada since 2005 and is an avid puppeteer and programmer. He is interested in fantasy and science fiction and is currently writing his first novel.

Michael Ouellet is a Ph.D. candidate in criminology and social justice at Ontario Tech University in Canada. He received his BA at Bishop's University in psychology and a master's degree at Wilfrid Laurier University in Criminology. He currently specializes in policing research.

Sarthak "Sar" Pal, a criminology graduate student at Wilfrid Laurier University (Ontario, Canada), has research interests in youth gang desistance, cybercrime, and corporate antitrust issues in Canada. He is also passionate about child and adolescent education and has a keen interest in cars.

Melissa A. Petkovsek is an associate professor of criminal justice & criminology at the University of Central Missouri, in the United States. Her background in neuroscience and psychology inform her research, which explores biological and social risk factors of antisocial behavior.

James Popham is an associate professor in the Department of Criminology at Wilfrid Laurier University in Brantford, Ontario, Canada. He holds a Ph.D. in sociology from the University of Saskatchewan and frequently publishes research about our interactions with digital media and its impact on society.

Chad Posick is Professor and Chair in the Department of Criminal Justice and Criminology at Georgia Southern University in the United States where he is also co-director of the National Youth Advocacy and Resilience Research Center. His research interests include victimization, statistical methodology, and biopsychosocial perspectives on behavior.

Shon M. Reed is a former Assistant Professor in the Department of Sociology & Criminal Justice at Old Dominion University. His research focuses on gender and crime, victimization, and gendered criminal justice responses to victimization. His work appears in peer-reviewed outlets such as Crime, Law, and Social Change, Child Abuse & Neglect, Feminist Criminology, Sexuality & Culture, and Sex Roles.

Sara Skott is Associate Professor in Criminology at Mid Sweden University, Sweden. Her research concerns different types and aspects of violence, including exploring violence through the lenses of Gothic and Ghost criminology. Her research also concerns the social construction and performative aspects of violence, including mediated constructions of violence.

Karl-Fredrik Skott Bengtson is conducting research in the field of psychology and English literature at Linköping University, Sweden. His main research interests concern the uncanny, nostalgia and in-depth character analysis. He has also explored different modes of communications and the relationship between depressive symptoms, autistic traits, and ambiguous scenarios.

Kevin F. Steinmetz is a professor of criminology at Kansas State University in the United States. His other books include *Hacked: A Radical Approach to Hacker Culture and Crime*, *Technocrime and Criminological Theory* (Routledge), *Cybercrime & Society*, and *Against Cybercrime: Toward a Realist Criminology of Computer Crime* (Routledge).

ACKNOWLEDGMENTS

Like all books, this one would not have been possible without help. First and foremost, we are deeply appreciative of our contributors. We are extremely humbled by their outstanding work and their diligence in the editorial process. We also appreciate our editorial handler at Routledge, Medha Malaviya, who supported us along the way. We also appreciate the support and insights of our friends and colleagues including Jordana Navarro, Joan Antunes, James Popham, Rebecca Stone, Edward Green, Carl Root, Brian Schaefer, Travis Linnemann, Don Kurtz, Cassandra Cross, and any others that we may have forgotten to include but appreciate, nonetheless. Kevin would also like to thank his wife, Pamela, who is—as always—a wellspring of love and support.

The subtitle of this book was chosen for three reasons. Two are obvious—"getting played" refers to getting manipulated, falling for a ruse, or being outright defrauded *and* gestures toward the fact that video games are objects of play. The subtitle thus represents both criminology and gaming simultaneously. It is also an homage to one of our favorite podcasts *Get Played* featuring Heather Anne Campbell, Nick Wiger, and Matt Apodaca. We thank them for their wit, humor, and the hours of audio joy they have brought us.

1

INTRODUCTION

Kevin F. Steinmetz and Jonathan A. Grubb

Criminology is a discipline preoccupied with the flow of blood, the rattle of steel bars, the cold snap of handcuffs, the capricious machinations of law, and the anguished cries of victims. To make sense of such serious issues, criminologists often turn to serious methods. Professional interviews, passionless surveys, and bureaucratic datasets are the bread and butter of our discipline. Yet, some criminologists recognize that crime and justice are not only serious but *entertaining*. The stories that capture the popular imagination are replete with dastardly criminals, violence, valiant crime fighters, corrupt systems, and victims to avenge. Such representations convey, produce, reproduce, and even challenge popular understandings of such issues. As a result, criminologists have turned to pop culture and media representations to understand views of crime and crime control held by creators, publishers, the public, and the like. The result is what Rafter (2007, p. 404) calls "popular criminology," a "discourse parallel to academic criminology and of equal significance." Involved is a constellation of ideas, beliefs, and explanations regarding crime, criminals, law enforcement, prisons, and related matters that exist among non-academic populations. Such a criminology's "audience is bigger" and "social significance is greater" as its influence is pervasive throughout society in shaping or representing the attitudes of many outside the ivory tower (Rafter, 2007, p. 415).

Criminologists have examined a variety of media to understand popular representations of criminologically-relevant subjects including television (e.g., Grubb & Posick, 2021), movies (e.g., Rafter & Brown, 2011), music (e.g., Steinmetz & Henderson, 2012), comic books (e.g., Phillips & Strobl, 2013), literature (e.g., McGregor, 2021), and others. An area of crime and media research largely neglected by criminologists to date, however, is video

DOI: 10.4324/9781003346869-1

games. This oversight may be a result of a tendency of some to disregard games as simply *play*. Such reasoning, however, is near-sighted. As famous horror author Clive Barker (2009, p. 2) once remarked, "It's easy to dismiss the stuff which gives people pleasure. We are so often guilty of assuming that the experience which provides pleasure is likely to be benign. The spectacles in the Colosseum were not benign."

Games are a significant medium in contemporary popular culture. The Entertainment Software Association (2022, p. 4) estimates that "65% of American adults and 71% of American kids play video games." Pricewater-houseCoopers (2023), an economic firm which regularly generates research and statistics for media industries, claims that total global video game revenue was likely to increase from $227 billion in 2023 to an estimated $312 billion by 2027. Video games are thus *serious* business. And like other media, crime, victimization, and crime control are central themes in video games (e.g., Kelly et al., 2020; Steinmetz, 2018). Games often allow consumers, for instance, to play as members of organized crime syndicates (e.g., *Mafia, Grand Theft Auto*), illicit hackers (e.g., *Watch Dogs*), police officers (e.g., *Resident Evil, SWAT, Crackdown, L.A. Noire*), and prisoners (e.g., *The Suffering, A Way Out*). They frequently feature criminal legal settings including police stations (e.g., *Resident Evil 2*), courtrooms (e.g., the *Ace Attorney* series) and prisons (e.g., the *Silent Hill* series). And the narratives of games are often driven by crimes like murder, theft, and robbery (e.g., *Max Payne, Murdered: Soul Suspect, Thief: The Dark Project*).

Video Games, Crime, and Control: Getting Played is an effort to take seriously the criminological importance of video games. It pulls together an international group of scholars from Canada, Sweden, the United Kingdom, and the United States who utilize their skills to excavate the depths of a diverse selection of popular and noteworthy video games like *Bioshock, Death Stranding, P.T., Diablo 2, Red Dead Redemption, LEGO: Star Wars, Disco Elysium, Spider-Man, Spider-Man: Miles Morales,* and *Beat Cop*. Involved is the curation of in-depth analyses that explore topics like criminological theory, policing, vigilantism, violence, genocide, mental illness, and intimate partner violence. By and large, these chapters consider video games as a reflection (warped or otherwise) of dominant cultural appetites, sensibilities, and anxieties, as well as a font of meaning from which audiences can draw ideas, values, perceptions, and even ideologies—in other words, it considers video games as a new frontier in the social construction of crime, criminality, and justice (Barak, 1994; Kappeler & Potter, 2006). In the parlance of cultural criminology, these chapters explore video games as "theaters of meaning" where the politics of crime and crime control play out in gamified form (Ferrell, 2013). They trace "the complex capillaries of meaning that snake through and around" (Ilan, 2019, p. 7) the production and consumption of video games to explore what such products can teach us about perspectives of crime and criminal justice, the formation of social reactions to crime in the late-modern mediascape, the intersections between play and power, and the complex relationship between reality and fiction where often art imitates life and life imitates art (Ferrell et al., 2015; Picart, 2021; Picart & Greek, 2003).

On the Shoulders of Giants

At this juncture, before we introduce the chapters that fill this volume, it is worthwhile to briefly consider the treatment of video games in criminology more generally. Though it constitutes a relatively nascent area, we identify two general trajectories of gaming research in the discipline. The first is what we might call behavioral and attitudinal studies. Scholars in this area investigate the relationship between video gaming and outcomes like aggression, violence, and desensitization to violence (e.g., Exelmans et al., 2015). Evidence on this matter is decidedly mixed. One commonly cited meta-analysis published by Anderson and colleagues (2010), incorporating 381 effect sizes from 130,296 participants, underscored exposure to violent video games was associated with significant increases on measures of aggression, aggressive cognition, and aggressive affect, regardless of whether a cross-sectional, longitudinal, or experimental design was used. A similar meta-analysis by Ferguson (2015), however, with 106,070 participants from 101 studies, highlighted that at most only minimal increases in aggression were associated with video games. Divergent findings in this line of inquiry are not surprising given limitations identified by researchers, including inconsistent measurements of aggression, issues with spuriousness, and the potential to confound aggression with competitiveness, as well as failure to incorporate pre-tests (Adachi & Willoughby, 2011; Ferguson, 2015). In short, violent video games *may* impact aggression—that said, their connection to violence is decidedly less clear.

While many studies in the area attempt to trace direct causal connections between video game playing, attitudes, and behaviors, a related body of research adopts a more nuanced perspective—one that views video games as an arena where controls are loosened and individuals are more free to engage in extreme, deviant, or otherwise salacious behaviors within games themselves. In this area of research, rather than view games as an engine of change in individuals, folks are viewed as already primed to behave in such ways and only need a domain lacking in restrictions, similar to the kinds of views offered by control theorists or critical criminologists influenced by Freudian psychoanalysis (e.g., Hall, 2012; Reiss, 1951). Consider, for instance, Atkinson and Rodgers's (2016) analysis of online pornography and video games. They argue that, counter to the narrative that Western societies are growing more peaceful over time, libidinal desires are finding alternative pathways for expression, specifically in the online and virtual realms. In this sense, it is not necessarily that video games cause violence but, rather, they provide an avenue through which otherwise violent energies might be expressed. In fact, it would seem, according to these authors, that such spaces provide relatively lawless zones that allow for experimentation with violent or extreme content and interactions. These "zones of cultural exception" are domains where "subterranean values are capable of flourishing relatively unchecked as the constraints of dominant values and social norms are rejected or loosened" and "excitement and engagement within these spaces can be experienced without feelings of guilt or repulsion" (Atkinson & Rodgers, 2016, p. 1299). Similar to Goldsmith and Brewer's (2015) notion of "digital drift," video games become sites whereby people can exercise their fantasies of, for example, assaulting sex workers, marauding villages, and killing folks with relative abandon free from judgment or consequence—an "interior world in which a kind of elective or temporary madness can be engaged, we can choose to go crazy, to take a kind of psychopathic holiday in which our everyday rules and conventions are fully suspended for the time that we are 'there', in the zone" (Atkinson & Rodgers, 2016, p. 1304).

Interestingly, in their follow-up analysis to Atkinson and Rodgers's (2016) essay, Denham and Spokes (2019) empirically test the idea that players will pursue wanton violence when given the means through which they can enact such fantasies. The authors observed 15 participants as they played *Grand Theft Auto V*, a game which explicitly gives players license to behave in criminal and violent ways. While the authors did observe that players would act out violent scenarios in the game, they also demonstrated prosocial behaviors within the game world or engaged in consumer-driven activity. In other words, the view presented by Atkinson and Rodgers is "problematized by complicated and varying individual player choices" which were more varied than would otherwise be expected under the "murder box" approach (Denham & Spokes, 2019, p. 751). As the Dude from *The Big Lebowski* would say, there are a "lotta ins, lotta outs, lotta whathaveyous."

The second trajectory of video game research—the one in which most of our chapters reside—is what we term cultural studies of video games. These studies examine how video games represent, create, and recreate narratives or construct and reconstruct the social reality of crime and crime control. Prior research in this area has established that video games, while perhaps a domain filled with playful excess, are also criminologically-relevant theaters of meaning (Ferrell, 2013). For instance, consider Fawcett and Kohm's (2020) analysis of *Batman: Arkham Asylum* and *Batman: Arkham City*. Like the comic books, these games tend to portray crime and villainy as a product of psychopathy and mental illness (Veitch & Steinmetz, 2018). Typically, such portrayals tend to cast criminals as dangerous others in need of indefinite confinement and rehabilitation. Yet, Fawcett and Kohm (2020, p. 283) note that these games also portray prisons as fundamentally flawed institutions marred by "brutality and profound injustice." They further argue that the games force players to grapple with this contradiction through interactive gameplay—that players simultaneously are required to use brutal violence against prisoners to advance in the game while also bearing witness to the corrupt and inhuman administration of justice by the system. The authors conclude their analysis by arguing that video games can communicate "both mainstream and critical ideas about crime and punishment" in tandem with one another which may "provoke dialog on critical issues in criminal justice" (Fawcett & Kohm, 2020).

In a related study, Steinmetz (2018) examined representations of prisons and punishment throughout the *Silent Hill* series. *Silent Hill* comprises one of the best-regarded horror franchises in video games and, like most horror media, its narratives and imagery make use of contemporary social problems to produce anxiety and dread in its audience. Steinmetz argues that the games are riddled with representations of retribution and confinement which interact with cultural anxieties that stem from vertiginous feelings of insecurity in both the Japan and the United States, countries grappling with increasing securitization and prisonization, especially in the 1990s and early aughts, the hey-day of *Silent Hill*. As Steinmetz (2018, p. 267) argues, "*Silent Hill* reveals an American-Japanese public imagination that clamors for respite from insecurity while also becoming horrified by the carceral 'Frankenstein's monster' it has created."

In a follow-up analysis, Steinmetz and Petkovsek (2023) consider representations of the police in the preeminent horror gaming franchise, *Resident Evil,* a series mired in zombies and other biological horrors as well as shadowy organizations. Like the *Silent Hill* analysis, the authors consider the horrific elements of *Resident Evil* as linked to shared cultural anxieties found in both the United States and Japan. The authors argue that the horror of policing, to borrow a phrase from Linnemann (2022), in *Resident Evil* is derived mainly through a tension between competing representations of the police. On the one hand, police are portrayed as "stalwart" or "ethical, professional, loyal, and capable protectors" and, on the other, as "fallible" or rife with "failure, hopelessness, and corruption" (Steinmetz & Petkovsek, 2023, pp. 163, 167). In addition to noting such representations mirror perceptions and values documented in real-world policing cultures, the authors argue that this tension works as a device for conveying horror because public anxiety regarding the police is mired in a similar tension. Police are often simultaneously marketed, by politicians and the police themselves, as the only institution capable of fending off crime and, yet, they are also conveyed as continually on their heels to contain the supposed criminal menace, typically portrayed in monstrous terms (Linnemann, 2022; Linnemann et al., 2014). The stakes involved in *Resident Evil*, which are immeasurably high, are said to justify extreme measures taken by officers and agents throughout the series to fight such monsters—that the "ends justify the means." The authors note that "such logic has been used" in the real world "to justify war crimes and atrocities perpetuated by US soldiers and intelligence agents in the wake of the War on Terror as well as street-level decisions by patrol officers and investigators" (Steinmetz & Petkovsek, 2023, p. 173). Thus, *Resident Evil* portrays the horrific implications of a policing ideology which attempts to "maintain an image of moral righteousness while being freed of legal accountability" (ibid.).

In another example, Skott and Skott Bengtson (2022) reach back into the vault to analyze the 2000 Nintendo 64 hit game, *The Legend of Zelda: Majora's Mask*. The game is essentially a "time loop" game in which the protagonist, Link, must work to reverse a curse set upon him in a world threatened by a moon—bearing is sinister face—which threatens to crash and destroy everyone and everything in three days' time. The gameplay involves link replaying these three days, continually experiencing the end of the world, multiple times until he solves the mystery of his curse and the world of Termina. They argue that "the game conveys a culturally imagined understanding of carcerality as a consuming, violent experience which not only renders individuals invisible, but socially non-living, stripped of identity, disrupted spatially as well as temporally" (Skott & Skott Bengtson, 2022, p. 595). In other words, the game reflects an ideology of positivity and imprisonment which excludes and renders individuals ghost-like—socially dead and forgotten, trapped in space and suspended in time.

These are only some examples of an emergent area of criminological analysis which take video games seriously as objects of cultural inquiry. Others include representations of violence, security, and rehabilitation in *Prison Architect* (Treadwell, 2020), right-wing domestic terrorism in *Far Cry 5* (Green, 2022), as well as an examination of anomie, general strain theory, and structural inequalities in *Cyberpunk 2077* (Steele, 2023). These studies, and others, have paved the way for the current volume and we are therefore indebted to these scholars for their contributions. Despite these inroads, however, more work is necessary. Given the immense growth and overall size of the video game industry and the saturation of the media in the social fabric, there is a need for criminologists to continue analyzing games as cultural texts to excavate the ideologies buried within. It is toward this endeavor our volume is committed.

Chapter Summaries

With this preamble out of the way, we can now introduce the reader to the various chapters contained herein. This book groups together nine noteworthy analyses of video games as cultural enmeshed within broader cultural and political contexts. These chapters cover significant ground. Some explore the relationship between games and criminological theory, probing deeper epistemic and ontological questions through the medium. Others use games as a way to ruminate on various crime problems, notably violence. Many, however, consider the relationship between video games, punitive ideologies, and narratives of crime control. Regardless of the subject matter, each chapter demonstrates how the reader can approach video games with an analytic eye.

Would you kindly read Melissa Petkovsek's analysis of *BioShock* (Chapter 2)? Rather than serve as a banal—though admittedly awkward—question to ask of the reader, "would you kindly" references a key phrase uttered in *BioShock* that, as revealed toward the end of the game, presents a fundamental challenge to the idea of player agency within video games. Petkovsek investigates the treatment of agency and choice within the context of *BioShock* and then relates these themes to similar philosophical disagreements within the discipline of criminology. Specifically, she considers the parallels in *BioShock*'s ruminations on agency and those endemic to the rapidly growing field of bio-social criminology. The result is an analysis of free will and determinism illuminating for students and scholars alike.

In Chapter 3, Kevin F. Steinmetz examines Hideo Kojima's masterpiece, *Death Stranding*, a game about a post-apocalyptic world mired in ghosts made of anti-matter, time-accelerating rainfall, ghost-detecting babies encased in glass tanks, and package delivery. Despite its weird story, characters, and imagery, the game is ultimately an exploration of themes fundamental to the modern human experience including connection, loneliness, and, of central concern for this chapter, *violence*. For Steinmetz, *Death Stranding* provides a deep meditation on violence and its consequences. While violence is an option available to players navigating Kojima's dystopian landscape, the game often discourages violent means through the careful structuring of game mechanics, imagery, and narratives. Players who attempt to use violence more than necessary will likely find the game unfulfilling. Instead, players are to revel in the subtle joy of trekking through the scenic landscapes, delivering packages to the grateful denizens of post-apocalypse America, and rebuilding a nation, one shelter at a time. This analysis considers Kojima's use of violence in Death Stranding as a conflicted meditation on video game violence, providing a lens for understanding our cultural sensibilities toward violence.

In "Are You Sure the Only You Is You? Domestic Violence and Critiquing the Other in the Spectral Remains of *P.T.*" (Chapter 4), Sara Skott and Karl-Fredrik Skott Bengtson plumb the depths of one of the most horrifying games produced to date, *P.T.* Short for "playable teaser," *P.T.* was released as a promotion for *Silent Hills,* a reimagining of the *Silent Hill* franchise. Unfortunately, development of *Silent Hills* was abruptly canceled by Konami and *P.T.* was pulled from the PlayStation Store. *P.T.* and *Silent Hills* were overseen by Hideo Kojima, the auteur behind the fan-beloved *Metal Gear* series, who abruptly left Konami following the cancelation of *Silent Hills*. Yet, despite these circumstances (or perhaps in part *because* of them), *P.T.* endures as one of the most celebrated horror games of all time. Skott and Skott Bengtson analyze the game's treatment of domestic violence, a central motif driving the game's horrific narrative and imagery. In particular, the authors argue that *P.T.* represents domestic abusers not as unusual or aberrant but, instead, familiar and intimate—that "the monstrous may exist in all of us." They then explore the haunting implications of such representations in popular culture and society at large.

Turning to other supernatural matters, Chad Posick examines the classic and deeply influential game *Diablo II* (Chapter 5). Here, Posick describes how the game demonstrates old-yet-persistent views toward crime, ones which consider rule-breaking as a matter of evil inextricably connected to spiritual forces. While many of us like to think that we, as a society, have moved on from such archaic ways of thinking, Posick demonstrates that such narratives endure in one form or another, and that analyzing such narratives can shed light on prevailing attitudes toward punishment and crime. When the reader arrives at this chapter, we encourage them—in the words of Deckard Cain—to "stay awhile and listen."

Chapter 6 involves an analysis of the *Red Dead Redemption* series, consisting of two immensely popular third-person open-world games that take place in the American Wild West. Developed by Rockstar Games, the *Red Dead Redemption* games are held by many to be the high-water mark of open-world story-telling. Shon M. Reed, Logan P. Kennedy, and Breanna Boppre use these games as a vehicle to explore three of the five prevailing philosophies of punishment (deterrence, incapacitation, and retribution) and the differential effect of these philosophies on characters within the games. In particular, the authors note that coercive and violence methods of punishment seem to cause more problems than they solve—that violence begets violence. The authors then consider how the events of the games might have been different were institutional conditions different—that perhaps things would be better if restorative or rehabilitative approaches were used in the administration of justice.

No consideration of popular culture and crime would be complete without some examination of one of the most popular intellectual properties in the world, *Star Wars*. In Chapter 7, Colin Atkinson explores representations of crime and justice in *LEGO Star Wars: The Skywalker Saga*. While it would be easy to dismiss what is marketed as a children's game, Atkinson asks us to consider how the transformation of serious subject matter—like murder and violence—into silly and whimsical gags can have a profound impact on how that subject matter is interpreted and internalized. In other words, when games, like *LEGO Star Wars: The Skywalker Saga* makes light of someone having a hand chopped off or selectively omits or alters a death scene, it also sanitizes such content. In terms of crime and justice, the implication is that the game may inadvertently strip out much of the gravity and significance of these issues for its audience—to "make light of darkness" as he explains.

A genre of games which has received relatively little attention, despite its long-standing and enduring appeal within the medium, is the role-playing game (RPG). In Chapter 8, Edward L.W. Green examines one of the most popular, engrossing, and thematically rich RPGs to come out in recent memory, *Disco Elysium*. The player assumes the role of Harry Du Bois, a detective who begins the game with alcohol-induced amnesia during the middle of a murder investigation. The player must then navigate the political and structural tensions of the game's world to solve the murder and, ultimately, determine the kind of arbiter of justice Harry will become. Green considers how policing dynamics manifest within the game mechanics and setting of *Disco Elysium*. He then considers three types of moral dilemmas the player must navigate as a police detective and how these dilemmas parallel the same kinds of dilemmas that routinely face real-world police officers.

Christina Fawcett and Steven Kohm, in Chapter 9, take on the immensely popular games *Marvel's Spider-Man* and *Marvel's Spider-Man: Miles Morales*—open-world games which feature everyone's favorite neighborhood web-slingers, Peter Parker and Miles Morales. In particular, Fawcett and Kohm consider the thematic and narrative tensions explored in the games surrounding race and ethnicity. Through Parker, Spider-Man has always been embodied by a white man. Though Parker remains Spider-Man in many runs of the comic books and in the Marvel Cinematic Universe, Morales—a young Afro-Latino boy—has donned the spider-mantle in an offshoot of the Spider-Man franchise which runs parallel to the Parker variant. In addition to his popularity in comic books, Morales was the feature character in two of the most popular Spider-Man movies of all time—*Spider-Man: Into the Spider-Verse* and *Spider-Man: Across the Spider-Verse*—with a third movie on the way. As such, it is unsurprising that Morales would be front and center in contemporary Spider-Man video games. Yet, Morales status as individual from two historically-marginalized racial and ethnic groups allows for creators—including those involved in his video games—to explore topics and perspectives unavailable to the Parker version of Spider-Man. To begin, Fawcett and Kohm explore more generally how these games represent issues such as vigilante justice, community responsibility, technologically-mediated policing, and the corporatization and militarization of security. They then consider how Morales's status as a Afro-Latino affects his interaction within the game world and his role within the justice apparatus.

Finally, in Chapter 10, James Popham, Andrea Corradi, Michael Ouellet, Sarthak Pal, Chris McDiarmid, Jocelyn Booton, and Michelle Goodridge combine their powers in a robust and systematic ethnographic content analysis of the indie game *Beat Cop*. While it may lack the budget or audience of more mainstream "AAA" releases, the authors demonstrate that *Beat Cop* is a useful vehicle for understanding popular representations and understandings of police work. In particular, the authors note that the game reveals a highly cynical view of police work and the role of police in society, not unlike movies like *Dirty Harry* or *Training Day*. They demonstrate how such cynicism manifests not just in the story but also in the gameplay mechanics, forcing the player to make difficult decisions, balance competing demands, and ultimately determine the kind of officer they are going to be in a system which seemingly incentivizes corner-cutting and corruption.

These chapters provide merely a glimpse into the kinds of robust insights awaiting criminology students and academics alike within the realm of video games. Our hope is that our book, in addition to other notable works in this burgeoning area, encourages folks to take play seriously. Given that a defining characteristic of games—video or otherwise—is interactivity, we think it fitting that we end this chapter with a question, one readers can hopefully answer upon finishing the book: *What will you do next?*

References

Adachi, P.J.C., & Willoughby, T. (2011). The effect of violent video games on aggression: Is it more than just the violence? *Aggression and Violent Behavior, 16*(1), 55–62.

Anderson, C.A., Shibuya, A., Ihori, N., Swing, E.L., Bushman, B.J., Sakamoto, A., Rothstein, H.R., & Saleem, M. (2010). Violent video game effects on aggression, empathy, and prosocial behavior in Eastern and Western countries: A meta-analytic review. *Psychological Bulletin, 136*(2), 151–173.

Atkinson, R., & Rodgers, T. (2016). Pleasure zones and murder boxes: Online pornography and violent video games as cultural zones of exception. *British Journal of Criminology, 56*, 1291–1307.

Barak, G. (1994). *Media, process, and the social construction of crime: Studies in newsmaking criminology.* Garland Publishing.

Barker, C. (2009). Foreword: A little light in the darkness. In B. Perron (ed.) *Horror video games: Essays on the fusion of fear and play* (pp. 1–2). McFarland & Company.

Denham, J., & Spokes, M. (2019). Thinking outside the "murder box": Virtual violence and pro-social action in video games. *British Journal of Criminology, 59*, 737–755.

Entertainment Software Association. (2022). *Essential facts about the video game industry.* Retrieved September 1, 2023 from https://www.theesa.com/wp-content/uploads/2022/06/2022-Essential-Facts-About-the-Video-Game-Industry.pdf

Exelmans, L., Custers, K., & Van den Bulck, J. (2015). Violent video games and delinquent behavior in adolescents: A risk factor perspective. *Aggressive Behavior, 41*, 267–279.

Fawcett, C., & Kohm, S. (2020). Carceral violence at the intersection of madness and crime in *Batman: Arkham Asylum* and *Batman: Arkham City. Crime Media Culture, 16*(2), 265–285.

Ferguson, C.J. (2015). Do Angry Birds make for angry children? A meta-analysis of video game influences on children's and adolescents' aggression, mental health, prosocial behavior, and academic performance. *Perspectives on Psychological Science, 10*(5), 646–666.

Ferrell, J. (2013). Cultural criminology and the politics of meaning. *Critical Criminology, 21*(3), 257–271.

Ferrell, J., Hayward, K., & Young, J. (2015). *Cultural criminology: An invitation* (2nd ed.). Sage.

Goldsmith, A., & Brewer, R. (2015). Digital drift and the criminal interaction order. *Theoretical Criminology, 19*(1), 112–130.

Green, A.M. (2022). Far Cry 5, American right-wing terrorism, and doomsday prepper culture. *Games and Culture, 17*(7–8), 1015–1035.

Grubb, J.A., & Posick, C. (2021). *Crime TV: Streaming criminology in popular culture*. NYU Press.

Hall, S. (2012). *Theorizing crime and deviance: A new perspective*. Sage.

Ilan, J. (2019). Cultural criminology: The time is now. *Critical Criminology, 27*, 5–20.

Kappeler, V.E., & Potter, G.W. (2006). *Constructing crime: Perspectives on making news and social problems*. Waveland Press.

Kelly, C., Lynes, A., & Hoffin, K. (2020). *Video games, crime and next-gen deviance: Reorienting the debate*. Emerald Publishing Limited.

Linnemann, T. (2022). *Horror of police*. University of Minnesota Press.

Linnemann, T., Wall, T., & Green, E.W.L. (2014). The walking dead and killing state: Zombification and the normalization of police violence. *Theoretical Criminology, 18*(4), 506–527.

McGregor, R. (2021). *A criminology of narrative fiction*. Bristol University Press.

Phillips, N.D., & Strobl, S. (2013). *Comic book crime: Truth, justice, and the American way*. NYU Press.

Picart, C.J.S. (2021). Introduction. In C.J.S. Picart (Ed.), *Monsters, law, crime: Explorations in Gothic criminology* (pp. 1–16). Rowman & Littlefield.

Picart, C.J., & Greek, C. (2003). The compulsion of real/reel serial killers and vampires: Toward a gothic criminology. *Journal of Criminal Justice and Popular Culture, 10*, 39–68.

PricewaterhouseCoopers (PwC) (2023). *Perspectives from the global entertainment & media outlook 2023–2027*. Retrieved September 1, 2023 from https://www.pwc.com/gx/en/industries/tmt/media/outlook/insights-and-perspectives.html

Rafter, N. (2007). Crime, film and criminology: Recent sex-crime movies. *Theoretical Criminology, 11*(3), 403–420.

Rafter, N.H., & Brown, M. (2011). *Criminology goes to the movies: Crime theory and popular culture*. NYU Press.

Reiss, A.J. (1951). Delinquency as the failure of personal and social controls. *American Sociological Review, 16*, 196–207.

Skott, S., & Skott Bengtson, K. (2022). "You've met with a terrible fate, haven't you?": A hauntological analysis of carceral violence in *Majora's Mask. Games and Culture, 17*(4), 593–613.

Steinmetz, K.F. (2018). Carceral horror: Punishment and control in *Silent Hill. Crime Media Culture, 14*(2), 265–287.

Steinmetz, K.F., & Henderson, H. (2012). Hip-hop and procedural justice: Hip-hop artists' perceptions of criminal justice. *Race & Justice, 2*(3), 155–178.

Steinmetz, K.F., & Petkovsek, M.A. (2023). Perilous policing: An analysis of the *Resident Evil* series. *Critical Criminology, 31*(1), 161–180.

Steele, M.J. (2023). Chippin' in: An analysis of the criminological concepts within cyberpunk 2077. *Games and Culture*. Advance online publication. https://journals.sagepub.com/doi/abs/10.1177/15554120231161042#con

Treadwell, J. (2020). 'Gaming the system?' The merits, myths and realities in understanding Prison Architect: Security, rehabilitation and violence as represented in the world's bestselling carceral video game. In C. Kelly, A. Lynes, & K. Hoffin (Eds.), *Video games crime and next-gen deviance* (pp. 175–199). Emerald Publishing Limited.

Veitch, S.A., & Steinmetz, K.F. (2018). The defamed deranged of Gotham: The social construction of mental illness as criminality in Batman comics. In S.E. Brown & O. Sefiha (Eds.) *Routledge handbook on deviance* (pp. 420–431). Routledge.

2

CHAINS IN *BIOSHOCK*

The Illusion of Freedom and Free Will

Melissa A. Petkovsek

The pursuit of identifying the origins of criminal and antisocial behavior will often cross into a discussion of agency. The Classical School of criminology abandoned the widely held belief that antisocial behavior was the result of demonic possession or temptation from the devil and instead embraced the concept that individuals possessed free will (Beccaria, 1764). Moving agency from supernatural forces to the individual was a watershed moment for the study of crime. Suddenly, it was possible to examine the factors surrounding the individual to understand *why* they committed a crime, and more importantly, crime prevention efforts were now within reach. Today, major criminological theories like rational choice theory, perceptual deterrence theory, and routine activities theory assume free will and choice underpin behavior, as do many court systems and criminal justice policies worldwide.

Free will is frequently juxtaposed to determinism—the view that, at its most extreme, humans lack agency and their decisions are fundamentally caused by internal or external forces. One of the most vilified (perhaps unfairly) forms of determinism is biological determinism. Though Lombroso's (2006) "criminal man" may have been a falsehood the pseudo-science of phrenology has been debunked for some time, current research in psychology, neuroscience, and genetics tell us that there are in fact some static, individualized factors that play a role in defining our behavior (Schwartz et al., 2019; van Hazebroek et al., 2019). The resurgence of academic interest in biological correlates of antisocial behavior have been argued to pull focus from societal risk factors for crime, as well as perpetuate the belief that antisocial behavior is predetermined (Wright et al., 2008).[1]

Like criminological theorizing, fiction has long explored the tensions between agency and determinism. Novels and films whether humans are masters

DOI: 10.4324/9781003346869-2

of their own destiny or subject to the control of internal or external forces (e.g., *The Matrix*, Wachowski & Wachowski, 1999), or imagine that individuals will descend into a state of barbarity when social controls are lifted, destroyed, or otherwise absent (e.g., *Lord of the Flies* (Golding, 1954)). Conversely, many famous fictional stories have considered the implications of authoritarian regimes and the suppression of agency (e.g., *The Handmaid's Tale* (Atwood, 1986)). It may be surprising that video games also take seriously the subject of agency. While some might scoff at the notion, one game in particular is renowned for its investigation of this complex philosophical debate—*BioShock* (Packer, 2010).

BioShock is set in an Objectivist utopia, cleverly exploring how individuals would act in a society free from regulation. As such, the game lays a foundation for a robust exploration of Randian Objectivism (Rand, 1964; 2005; Peikoff, 1993; Perry, 2012), biosocial criminology, and how both address human agency and the development of criminal (and often violent) behavior. The power struggle catechized by Randian societal structure combined with unregulated genetic manipulation in *BioShock* create the perfect backdrop for discussing the limits of freedom and free will, their intersection, and the extent of agency within nature and nurture. In fact, the immersive nature of video games brings players into an alternate reality in a much more convincing way than is possible with a book or even a movie. As Packer (2010) explains, "reading a novel about the virtues of Objectivism lacks the visceral effect of seeing crazed Objectivists charging across your screen trying to kill you" (p. 210). Players are forced to participate in the plot, and to make decisions within the universe which directly impact the outcome of the game (Jennings, 2019; Ruch, 2010; Tulloch, 2010).

This chapter will first consider *BioShock*'s contribution to the gaming community, and establish the continued importance of *BioShock* as cultural touchstone. The foundations of the plot in Objectivism and genetic determinism are discussed as the cause of *BioShock*'s lasting impact, particularly in the manner the plot challenges players to think about the origins of agency and choice. Finally, these themes are discussed as an example of the enduring struggle to define the origins of criminality and the resistance to biological explanations of behavior. So, I ask, would you kindly consider how a video game can warn us about the dangers of too much freedom, and the limits to free will?

Narrative Creates Legacy in BioShock

BioShock was released in 2007 by developer company 2k Boston & 2k Australia (also known as Irrational Games), and, to this day, remains highly regarded by video game critics and players alike.[2] During its release year, *BioShock* earned the British Academy of Film and Television Arts (BAFTA) award for Best Game in addition to over 50 Game of the Year awards (IMDb, n.d.). Over 3 million copies were sold within two years of release (Ivan, 2009) and the franchise has sold over 41 million copies since (VGChartz, 2020).[3] The original *BioShock* game continues to appear on lists of the greatest video games ever made (IGN Staff, 2023; Young, 2023). At the time of release, the game was lauded for the quality of design, immersive environment, and gameplay mechanics, and has been cited as a game that not only set a new standard for video games, but also one that helped define video games as an art form (Schiesel, 2007, Smithsonian American Art Museum, 2011; Suderman, 2016). What sets *BioShock* apart from other horror-based, first-person shooters is not how well the developers created the scenery, the weapons, or the blood-spatter effects. Instead, it is the narrative that keeps players engaged; specifically, how *BioShock* attends to the concept of freedom and free will.

Video games as a method of interactive storytelling are what define them as a legitimate category of art form. Few other forms of media engage their audience as thoroughly or for as long as a video game.[4] Video games require players to act in order to move the plot forward, and player choice became a mechanic to engage players in the narrative on a deeper and more personal level (Jennings, 2019). Morality was often attached to choice: do you wish to act selfishly, or altruistically? *BioShock* is unique in that it subverts the concept of player choice, and indeed, the contests the concept of free will altogether (Chan, 2022; Jennings, 2019). In a now-classic, terrifying twist, *BioShock* seems to ask gamers if when playing video games "What separates a man from a slave?" (2K Boston & 2K Australia, 2007).

Welcome to Rapture

The brassy pep of the Andrews Sisters singing Bei Mir Bist du Schon *crackles through a jukebox and echoes through the dark, gloomy hall. Tall, wide windows allow you to see a school of fish swim by, and behind them, the flickering lights of another of the city's buildings. A pipe above you is leaking and standing water has damaged the gorgeous hardwood floors, but the greater concern is the pipe will burst and fail to keep the ocean from surging inward. The walls are scorched with electricity and fire, the furniture is in disarray, and decaying corpses are strewn about. A fallen neon sign stubbornly proclaims "Happy New Year: 1959," and for a moment, you can see the art deco designs in their prime. You wipe the sweat from your brow, stand, and heft your grenade launcher over your shoulder. The launcher isn't very intimidating—the stabilizer is fastened on with a piece of a belt, and the grenade is composed of some chemicals you found and stuffed into a soup can. Suddenly, a low, rumbling groan cuts through the music, heavy stomps, and a thin, high-pitched voice calls: "When their lights go out, Mr. B and I come*

*to visit. Hurry, Mr. B! I can see the angels dancing in the sky." You duck
around a corner, leaning out just enough to watch a monstrosity in a diving
suit trundle into the room, escorting a barefoot little girl in a filthy dress. She
sings nonsense songs as she stabs a corpse with her long syringe, and her eyes
glow a haunting yellow as she slurps down her harvest. She's full of fresh
ADAM, and although you're tired, you need the power swirling in that tiny
host, so you advance. Her protector sees you creep forward, howling as he
activates his huge drill, and the metallic grind mingles with the girl's screams
as you ready your aim.*

This scene is one of only many that take place within the failed Randian utopia of Rapture, a city hidden deep in the Atlantic Ocean, built in 1946 by vi-
sionary Andrew Ryan to escape the regulations set by government and religion
on scientific discovery, industry, and artistic expression.[5] For Ryan, Rapture is
Utopia. Most of Rapture represents what we know about art deco style. The
supernatural abilities available to players are attributed to discoveries rooted in
science possible in the real world, albeit restricted due to ethics. The scientific
freedom offered in Rapture, and Ryan's purposeful recruitment of the best and
brightest minds to the city have led to the discovery of ADAM, a biochemi-
cal discovered in a fictional deep-sea slug that can rewrite genetic material by
supporting the growth of undifferentiated stem cells in the body. Geneticist Dr.
Brigid Tenenbaum discovered ADAM's potential and was involved in developing it into "plasmids" for commercial use. The average Rapture citizen could
eventually purchase plasmids designed to alter their genetic code for a specific
purpose, such as to be able to create fire, an electric bolt, or a windstorm from
their fingertips. Using plasmids requires EVE, the game's version of mana (the
conventional resource used for the casting of various magics in fantasy games),
to regenerate plasmid-driven powers.

BioShock's plot is driven by four main characters: (1) the player-character
Jack, the sole survivor of a plane crash in the middle of the ocean, mysteri-
ously outside the entrance to the city, (2) Atlas, who helps you navigate and
survive Rapture as he communicates with you via radio, (3) Ryan, Rapture's founder and dictator, and (4) Frank Fontaine, a grifter and nihilist
who leads a revolt against Ryan. Jack enters Rapture just after its downfall.
The widespread use of plasmids has sown disorder and disarray. Plasmid
use results in a host of grotesque side effects, and addiction to "splicing"
plasmids into their genetic code has turned a portion of the population into
violent psychotics, hell-bent on gathering more ADAM. Operating under
laissez-faire capitalism, the free market is overwhelmed by the demand for
ADAM. The answer to this need is a monstrous recycling system which requires young girls to be psychologically and genetically conditioned to harvest ADAM from corpses. These "Little Sisters" roam the city, generating
fear in citizens due to their haunting appearance, fear which is magnified
by their hulking protectors, "Big Daddies." A combination of the effects

of ADAM and growing tension with Ryan's stringent grip on his utopia resulted in an uprising led by Frank Fontaine (Remo, 2007). The Little Sisters, ADAM, and the citizens themselves all became pawns in a power struggle between Ryan and Fontaine, both driven to obtain as much power and control over Rapture as possible.[6]

The game's long-lasting acclaim is rooted in the plot—the "what if" depiction of a possible outcome of an unconventional political structure in isolation from the rest of the world (King, 2023). Ken Levine, *BioShock*'s creative director (Cox, 2011; Remo, 2007), was inspired to use Ayn Rand's philosophy of Objectivism to create "a fair look at humanity," to test how Objectivism would play out among imperfect characters that he felt better represented the breadth and limitations of human behavior, compared to the characters in Rand's novels. The character of Andrew Ryan was created as a representation of Ayn Rand herself, as well as a more realistic version of her famous hero from her novel *Atlas Shrugged* (Rand, 2005), John Galt. *BioShock* represents a test of Objectivism in which players must confront what horrors they will accept as the cost of freedom.

Ayn Rand and Andrew Ryan

It is impossible to discuss *BioShock* without first exploring its roots in Ayn Rand's philosophy of Objectivism. Rand set the foundations for Objectivism in her novels *The Fountainhead* (1996) and *Atlas Shrugged* (2005)[7] and expanded on the philosophy in later essays, non-fiction books, and presentations. *Atlas Shrugged* is the direct inspiration for the city of Rapture, which can be described as a "gulch," a term coined by Rand to describe "Galt's Gulch" in the novel, a sequestered and self-sustaining economic and social community. A thorough review of Rand's philosophy, including application, critique, and limitations is not possible here, but instead this section will summarize aspects of Objectivism pertinent to understanding the rise and fall of Rapture, with specific attention to the relationship between societal freedom and the development of crime and antisocial behavior among the populace.

Objectivism is built on three axioms: existence, consciousness (that one can perceive what exists), and identity (that everything has characteristics unique unto itself, its existence, that others are conscious of) (Peikoff, 1993). These axioms underlie the main tenets of Objectivism, which address the manner in which one obtains knowledge through the use of logic, and the purpose of morality, social systems, and art.[8] A great deal has been written to untangle the methods by which individuals identify reality, pursue knowledge, and employ logic—and, the correct manner in which logic should be employed—but *BioShock* does not reflect this aspect of Objectivism, certainly not as directly as others.

BioShock focuses on what Rand termed "the virtue of selfishness," or that the correct moral guide for one's life is in pursuit of selfish happiness while completely abstaining from altruism (Bernstein, 2008; Rand, 1964). Rand puts such value on selfishness because she believes that when people strive to live a self-sacrificing life, they in turn relinquish the individual values and abilities which may have allowed them to become the best versions of themselves, better able to make worthwhile contributions to society. Instead, she argues, altruism and self-sacrificing nobility can result in a life void of personal significance, full of caustic resentment (Bernstein, 2008). In other words, to be selfish is to be committed and loyal, morally, to one's self and personal values. To fail to be selfish is to be "self-less": letting society and others determine your values and worth, and therefore, lack the ability to control one's own life and purpose. In *BioShock*, Ryan is the primary example of Objectivist selfishness, frequently stating "A man chooses—A slave obeys." This phrase is meant to underscore that only in pursuit of self-interest is a person truly distinct, engaging in moral humanity, unlike those who submit to the will of others.

Society must therefore serve to support an individual's moral right to selfishness. Rand argues that the government should only serve to provide avenues of protection for those who initiate force outside of Objectivist ideals (Rand, 1964). These include only the police, the armed forces, and the courts. All three should only be employed when others act out or initiate the use of force; as Rand (1964) describes:

> . . . no man may obtain any values from others without the owners' consent—and, as a corollary, that a man's rights may not be left at the mercy of the unilateral decision, the arbitrary choice, the irrationality, the *whim* of another man.
>
> *(p. 106)*

Government should concentrate efforts to serve the interests of the people in these areas, and stay out of providing public services or regulating any products in the economy. Rand advocated for laissez-faire capitalism, a completely unregulated economic system which promotes competition in the market and complete freedom for producers to determine value and quality of services or goods (Peikoff, 1993; Rand, 1964). Under the tenets of Objectivism, a fully capitalistic, unregulated market is the only choice for an economic system which supports freedom and individual rights (Rand, 1964). Therefore, laissez-faire capitalism is moral.

Ryan created Rapture to avoid "the parasites": those that regulate and take advantage of the revenue produced by skills of others, which included government and organized religion. To completely avoid the influence of globalization, Rapture had to be self-sufficient and isolated. Citizenship was only granted to select individuals after a thorough vetting process, to ensure they would comply with Rapture's Objectivist regulations (or, lack thereof). Ryan especially promoted his ideal of "the Great Chain" of industry, in that each individual is a link in the chain of the market, free to act in their own self-interest to "pull upward" on the chain, and contribute to the evolution of the market without limit. As a result, Rapture is completely privatized, and provides no social or public services. First responder services such as police and fire are subscription-based. Even access to oxygen existed in a competitive, free market. Ryan believed that his ideals of the Great Chain and free market would produce unparalleled entrepreneurship and achievement in the arts and science—and he was correct. Total societal freedom created rich soil for incredible accomplishments in Rapture in only a decade. Indeed, the city boasted advancements in technology, science, medicine, and the arts beyond the thresholds of the rest of the world at that time, many of which would not have been possible without the freedom to pursue one's interests without the constraints and bureaucracy inherent to government and religious organizations on the surface.

Unfortunately, Ryan was so committed to certain tenets of his philosophy for Rapture that he regulated access to products from the outside world—most notably, beef and religious materials. Ryan would only allow Rapture's societal freedom to extend so far. He also refused to regulate access to or the quality of plasmids or ADAM, even when aware of the destruction they could cause, and the need to create Little Sisters to recycle ADAM from dead Splicers arose. Combined, Ryan's misuse of regulation unequivocally set in motion the downfall of Rapture, opening up an opportunity for Fontaine to create a black market for desired goods, and for plasmid users to become addicted to ADAM, seeking it out by any means necessary.

Although Rand articulates that one individual's pursuit of selfishness should not interrupt the boundaries of another's without their consent, she acknowledges that crime will occur from time to time (Peikoff, 1993; Rand, 1964). However, there is little consideration in her philosophy for how some may react to society without regulation. Many key characters infringe on the rights of others, as part of their active pursuit of selfishness—and they feel free and right to do so.[9] Objectivism, and Ryan, failed to integrate several components of the human condition. Rand (1964) strongly advocates for *rational egoism*, or that an action is only rational if it promotes one's self-interest, therein completely eschewing any act of altruism as illogical. Further, she states that "there are no conflicts of interests among rational men even in the issue of love" (p. 51). Rand's characters and descriptions of the "rational man" have been criticized for being too dichotomous—either perfectly heroic or perfectly evil (Packer, 2010). That said, *BioShock* demonstrates that among fully-realized characters, a rational, selfish pursuit can clash with the rational, selfish pursuit of another. Both Ryan and Fontaine seek to advance themselves in society, and both engage in ethically dubious behavior in pursuit of their desires. In establishing Rapture, Ryan also seemed to assume two contradictory notions: first, that the elite invited to the city would not balk at having to take on the most mundane of roles in society, and second, that establishing a society built completely on a highly competitive economic system would behave respectfully while trying to claw their way up his "Great Chain" of industry. Rand spoke of "opportunities" for progress, but the experiment of Rapture shows us that these are more likely opportunities to exploit others for wealth, greed, or power (Peikoff, 1993; Rand, 1964). Fontaine said it best, when discussing how he systematically took advantage of the disadvantaged:

> These sad saps. They come to Rapture thinking they're gonna be captains of industry, but they all forget that somebody's gotta scrub the toilets. What an angle they gave me . . . I hand these mugs a cot and a bowl of soup, and they give me their lives. Who needs an army when I got *Fontaine's Home for the Poor*?

Additionally, Objectivism holds that a system based on rational egoism will emphasize individual's personal brilliance, permitting advancements in science, industry, and art which in turn will benefit all of society (Peikoff, 1993; Rand, 1964). *BioShock* demonstrates that not all progress is ethical or desirable. In fact, most of the major "boss battles" in the game are against characters which are part of "Rapture's best and brightest,"[10] who each represent a different iteration of flaws within Objectivism.

The holes in Ryan's and Rand's philosophy point to the development of criminal behavior, which can be chiefly explained through the struggle for power. Rapture is brimming with violence and corruption, the origins of which are rooted in the freedom of agency intrinsic to Rapture's social order. The freedom valued in Rapture meant that citizens were free to take advantage of one another. The hyper-competitive environment created a sharp class disparity due to the lack of regulation on prices or access to even the most basic of needs, encouraging mundane criminal behavior (such as thievery and participation in the black market) among the lower class. The class system in Rapture underpins a crucial flaw in Rand's philosophy: societal freedom does not predicate equal opportunity to pursue self-interest. For example, Rapture was built by brilliant architects and construction crews, handpicked by Ryan. When Rapture was complete, the need for their contribution became obsolete, these workers and their families found themselves destitute. These builders and other citizens in similar situations are vulnerable to exploitation, victimization, and choosing criminal behavior themselves, to change their circumstances (Packer, 2010). In sum, Objectivist ideals failed Rapture due to the highly stratified social strata, driven in part by Ryan and Fontaine's split monopoly over industry. No degree of personal struggle or merit could overcome a completely free and privatized market.

Traditionally, the study of deviant behavior was a purely sociological one, focusing on factors such as disorganized communities, social class, and parenting strategies, and few criminological theories acknowledged the impact of individual differences or development (e.g., Moffitt, 1993), a point-of-view that includes Rand's take on the source of crime. Examination of Rapture's populace would reveal that many diverge from the expected behavior the societal structure, and questions arise that cannot be answered through sociological factors alone. Why do some of Raptures denizens avoid plasmid use? How would Rand explain addiction to ADAM, or Splicer violence? Individual differences in intelligence, brain structure and function, or even genes can provide answers. A biosocial perspective endeavors to explain behavior while considering all factors from all disciplines—essentially, to explore variables associated with nurture and nature equally.

Biosocial Criminology: Nature and Nurture

Importing ideas from biosocial criminology may help us make sense of antisocial behavior and violence in Rapture. This perspective employs interdisciplinary research to support the assumption that both sociological and biological factors are necessary to explain behavior (Moffitt, 2005; Raine, 2008). The plainest explanation of biosocial criminology is that it assumes that our nature informs our nurture and vice versa, and the connections between factors of nature and factors of nurture can be causal, correlated, interactive, rebounding, and more. It is both a highly complex and yet extremely simple perspective on behavior—complex in that untangling the connections between factors and establishing patterns over the life-course of populations is difficult and takes decades of data-gathering to accomplish, and simple in that this perspective argues that variables from all disciplines may inform how criminal behavior emerges, develops, and desists (Moffitt, 1993, 2005). Biosocial criminology assumes that genes underlie our brain structure and connectivity, and thus our personality, decision-making capabilities, and propensity for various behaviors, including crime (Rhee & Waldman, 2002; Schwartz et al., 2019). The genetic foundation for behavior via the brain explains the intergenerational transmission of antisocial behavior, and accounts for career criminals and resistance to rehabilitation just as well as it explains the rare individuals who abstain from antisocial behavior entirely. Sociological factors such as exposure to violence and abuse in childhood, economic deprivation, and delinquent peers are also considered to be impactful when understanding criminal behavior. Further, biosocial criminology understands that life events, such as physical brain trauma, psychologically traumatic experiences, and substance use may impact an individual *biologically*, creating an interaction between environmental and biological variables which may increase or even decrease a person's propensity for engaging in criminal behavior. One such example exists in the gene-environment interplay between physical injury and permanent changes in behavior. Research demonstrates that the rate of traumatic brain injury (TBI) is much higher in the incarcerated population compared to the general population (Farrer & Hedges, 2011), and supports the supposition TBI is linked to aggressive behavior and consequently, incarceration for violent crime. Further, inmates with TBI who were released from prison were found to recidivate sooner compared to inmates without TBI (Ray & Richardson, 2017). The interactive effects may also operate in reverse, such that an individual's biology increases (or decreases) the likelihood of encountering risky criminological environments. For example, an individual who is intrinsically aggressive is more likely to find themselves in environments which are accepting of aggression, be that a boxing ring or a gang (Scarr & McCartney, 1983).

Subtle differences in the genome have a discernable and sometimes significant impact on the development of behavior. Research has established that discrete gene differences directly and indirectly predict behavioral differences. One of the most notable genes related to antisocial behavior is monoamine oxidase-A (MAOA), a polymorphic gene which has five naturally occurring and heritable types (Sabol et al., 1998). The gene differentially impacts the level of MAOA enzyme in the brain depending on the version of the gene an individual carries. MAOA enzyme serves to regulate other neurological processes in the brain by breaking down or "recycling" unneeded neurotransmitters, such as dopamine or serotonin (Bortolato & Shih, 2011). Individuals who possess genes which produce low levels of MAOA enzyme have been found to be directly related to increased aggression and even violent criminal behavior (Stetler et al., 2014). Those with the low-producing variant of the MAOA gene are also at increased risk compared to those carrying high-producing variants for development of antisocial behavior and even violence if they experience abuse during childhood (Caspi et al., 2002), a relationship referred to as a "gene-environment interaction" (Scarr & McCartney, 1983). The robust connection between the MAOA gene and serious and violent antisocial behavior is only one such example of genes which are associated with various criminal behaviors; for instance, several dopaminergic genes are implicated in susceptibility to addiction (Gorwood et al., 2012). However, just as certain genotypes can put individuals at a higher risk for exhibiting adverse behaviors, others can act as protective factors or increase the likelihood of prosocial behavior (Conway & Slavich, 2017). Variations of the oxyoctin and serotonin genes have been implicated in increased empathy and cooperation. Connections between any genes and behavior are far more complex and intricate than depicted here, and a biosocial perspective of crime is only just experiencing acceptance in the discipline. Yet, both antisocial and prosocial behavior in *BioShock* can be explained using principles and findings from the biosocial perspective on behavior.

There are few video games which can so aptly represent biosocial perspectives on antisocial behavior. *BioShock*'s narrative is centered on the dangers of extremes within genetics and society, and so it is very "bio social." Crime in Rapture can be attributed primarily to two origins: calculated decisions to trespass into the sphere of another, and unhinged Splicer violence. Much of the antisocial behavior in Rapture before the city's downfall can be categorized as larceny, scheming, identity theft, and abuses of power, but not necessarily violent behavior. It is unclear how defined the "laws" are in Rapture, as many criminal acts seem to go unpunished, particularly if the offender holds a powerful role in society. Splicer violence seems to be accepted as a norm as well, the cost of traversing Rapture's streets. A great deal of all antisocial behavior can be traced back to Dr. Tenenbaum's discovery of the ADAM-producing sea slugs, and the resulting gene-altering potions which created Rapture's main industry, necessitated the development of Little Sisters and Big Daddies, and gave rise to the addicted mob of Splicers, harnessed by Fontaine to unleash riots across the city on New Year's Eve. None of these would have been possible due to manipulations in society or genetics alone—both Rapture's unregulated society and the application of gene-altering plasmids were necessary.

Biosocial research holds that experience in certain environments can cause changes in biology, which cause changes in behavior. The environment can be physical, such as a blow to the head can cause TBI, but chemical substances can also cause changes in brain chemistry and connectivity. The Splicers represent a supernatural form of addiction, fundamentally the same as those addicted to cocaine, amphetamines, or even alcohol, substances which are known to disrupt neurotransmission in such a manner that can predispose violent behavior (Boles & Miotto, 2003). Alcohol may be the best mirror of plasmid use in Rapture, as it is a legal substance and use is encouraged socially and in advertisements. Continued use of alcohol can cause irreversible atrophy and reduced brain volume in key areas, including the frontal cortex, the brain region responsible for impulse control, understanding consequences, and other high-level executive functions (Zahr et al., 2011). Plasmid use over time has led to addiction, likely permanent brain damage, and resulted in violent behavior—motivated by a compulsive need to gain access to the dwindling ADAM resource, and simply as a result of changes in brain function.

Perhaps more intriguing are the rare moments we experience prosocial behavior in Rapture. Named female characters in *BioShock* are all less violent than the named male characters. While this follows research across time, place, and context in the real world (Staniloiu & Markowitsch, 2012), it is unknown if this representation is a conscious choice of the developers, or simply a depiction of the schema inhabiting the subconscious of most: that we expect men to be more violent than women. Women in the game are depicted just as self-serving as the men (e.g., Julie Langford making a buck off privatizing her gardens in Arcadia, and Dr. Tenenbaum's single-minded concentration on scientific discovery), but with the exception of female Splicers, never violent. In fact, both female members of Ryan's "Best and Brightest" Council experience a change-of-heart and assist you during the game, expounding on regret for their contribution to Rapture's collapse. The Little Sisters also lack violence, despite their morbid purpose in Rapture.[11] It is interesting to note that an audio log from Dr. Tenenbaum notes that the process that transforms children into Little Sisters has been impossible in boys, perhaps alluding to the genetic differences between males and females which also underlie differences in behavior. Likewise, their protectors, the Big Daddies, are always men: the sex more predisposed to violence.

Determinism and Choice

Although BioShock was designed to be a test of Rand's Objectivism, the game also tests our comfort with biosocial assumptions of human agency. Intrinsically, we know addicts do not behave rationally, and we know men are more likely to be violent than women. The game goes further, using an intrinsic fear of determinism to create a sense of horror and expose vulnerabilities in the human condition. Determinism has been and remains a main critique of biosocial criminology, in that some academics believe this perspective dooms some to biological inferiority. Indeed, research in neuroscience testing the brain's ability to react almost in advance of our consciousness has given rise to dispute about the existence of "free will" (Schurger et al., 2021; Zwart, 2014). Determinism, whether it rises from genetics or the restraints of society, generates fear—that we cannot make ourselves safer, that the damned cannot be rehabilitated, that the sick cannot be cured. BioShock uses themes of determinism to generate horror, notably through scientific manipulation and social conditioning of Jack, the protagonist.

The Twist

BioShock is well-known for its twist, a plot point which runs up on the player almost too quickly to comprehend and subverts their expectations. In the video game community, BioShock's twist defined a new standard for what players expected from plot development in story-based games. The intensity of the twist and the conversations initiated by the now-iconic moment cannot be understated. It even gave us a highly quotable phrase to throw around cheekily to others, a form of "in the know" gamer-code: "Would you kindly . . ."

This is it. You've been working to get to Ryan the entire game. It's been a harrowing task to get here; even as you enter his private quarters, Ryan initiates a self-destruct sequence on Rapture itself. Klaxons wailing, you frantically search for a way to reach him, finally crawling through a heating duct to progress forward. You turn and see a gigantic board, pictures of Rapture's key players, all well-known to you by now, and notes connected with red string, with the words "Would You Kindly" haphazardly scrawled across all of it in red paint. What does this mean? No time to think about it now, you have to kill Ryan and stop the city's self-destruct mechanism. Atlas, your only friend, comes through over the radio and urges you to continue, to avenge his family, brutally murdered by Splicers at Ryan's command. There are audio logs recorded by Dr. Suchong . . . you listen with half an ear as he commands a child to kill a puppy, focused on finding Ryan instead.

You approach Andrew Ryan for the first time during the game. You've heard his voice through the radio, taunting you, insulting you in the most posh and degrading ways, but this is the first time you see him. His appearance is oddly normal—he wears a suit and is practicing his short game at golf. You'd expect the authoritarian overlord of Rapture to have taken some advantage of the ADAM he fought to control. The game enters a cutscene, and you lose control of Jack; the strangeness of a lack of control is notable. He's talking to you, referencing flashbacks you've had, challenging you to answer "Was a man sent to kill? Or a slave?"

As you concentrate on his message, you realize . . . you have been part of the fabric of Rapture for far longer than your memory would have you believe. Ryan uses your programmed phrase to force you to kill him with his own golf club, and as soon as you do, player control of the game returns. Atlas's voice burns through the radio, telling you to kindly override the destruction of Rapture . . . your mind is reeling from what you've learned as you turn the key. Atlas's unpretentious Irish accent devolves with a cackle into a heavy Bronx burr as he reveals himself as Frank Fontaine, using you as his tool this entire time.

The ultimate constraint on our freedom: being made a slave. Through an immoral science, you've been mentally conditioned into unerring obedience, unknowing if even your thoughts or desires are your own, or those planted by someone else. Jack's conditioning represents a lack of free will that underlies academic concerns with biosocial criminology, that the dark side of "nature and nurture" can be used to override an individual's agency. The twist in *BioShock* is also subtly meta, breaking a fourth wall that all gamers must acknowledge: regardless of how many "choices" are available to the player, decisions are prefabricated code that limits or permits every push of a button (Chan, 2022; Tulloch, 2010; Ruch, 2010). Can the same be said of ourselves, that we are slaves to our genetic code, unable to choose differently than we are programmed by our biology? Said differently, all gamers are Jack, slaves without freedom, subject to the will of the game developers (Sims, 2016). There is an allegory here to an age-old debate about fate or the will of a divine higher power, surely.

Conclusion

BioShock as a Randian metaphor has been analyzed by many others, more thoroughly than accomplished in this chapter, but the game also has much to say about the development of antisocial behavior as well. Both conversations surrounding capitalism and criminality come back to the foundational debate of the origin of freedom and agency, and who or what ultimately controls behavior. The deeper conversation surrounding the twist is whether or not we are truly free, or if we are slaves to a predetermined course of action. The history of a criminological understanding of individual behavior has vacillated between two extremes: are we slaves to our genes, or to the systems of society? The answer is, thankfully, somewhere in the middle. While we cannot ignore irrefutable evidence surrounding heritability of risk factors and environmental impacts on our ability to make rational decisions, there is equal proof we are not slaves to destiny.

In *BioShock*, Jack is able to overcome his conditioning and defeat Fontaine. In the same way, humans are resilient to even the most devastating of circumstances, and genetic risk for antisocial behavior does not denote causality. Integrating biological perspectives into understanding the human condition should inspire opportunities, not horror. Further, the Randian implications of the game show how a social order founded on freedom and self-interest lead to circumstances of predation and oppression. It is this social context which is shown to have criminogenic consequences for others. Not only does this environment encourage larcenous and exploitative behaviors by Rapture's various actors, but it has significant biological impacts on its citizens, most overtly demonstrated through the impact of ADAM. While the game suggests that there exists variation between individuals in their susceptibility to the deleterious effects of ADAM, it is also clear that these people may not have become violent Splicers were it not for the noxious environment produced under Rapture. Biology and society collide to show that monsters are not born but, rather, are made.

Which brings us back to the subject of criminology. Historically, many criminologists have rejected consideration of biological risk factors, perhaps due to the threat posed to the assumption of free will (Paternoster, 2017; van den Berghe, 1990; Wright et al., 2008). For many, the idea that all our actions and thoughts are somehow predetermined and that we are slaves to a fate we cannot know is a horrifying prospect to many. These fears are not unwarranted, as history has shown efforts to "improve humanity" through systematic eradication of certain biological traits in the population (Gibson & Rafter, 2006). Undeniably, links exist between Lombroso's phrenology, the eugenics movement, fascism, and genocide (though, some critics point out that purely sociological philosophies have been similarly blighted by problematic political movements and ethical atrocities) (Pinker, 2002).

Yet, it is difficult to argue that everyone is equally free-willed under all circumstances. Even Rand seems to support individual differences, but points to systems which oppress freedom rather than biological origins to explain why not all are capable of the same heights of achievement. Research on individual differences in brain function quickly poke holes in the assumption of equal access to free will. For instance, neuroscience tells us that the brain regions responsible for higher-level reasoning do not complete development until our mid-twenties (Moffitt, 2005), which underlies our differential expectations and systems for juvenile offenders. Addiction and mental disorders also imply variation in human agency. For example, it is difficult to imagine that a Splicer ravaged by ADAM addiction is able to engage in this process when debating whether or not to attack whomever he encounters in Rapture.[12] Whether or not these limits are naturally occurring due to genetics or maldevelopment, or the result of physical injury, psychological trauma, or substance abuse, the impact on behavior cannot be ignored.

Despite concerns, the biosocial perspective continued its slow creep into the field of criminology, and in actuality, biology is not as deterministic as was once believed (Schurger et al., 2021; Zwart, 2014). The addition of biological factors has only underscored the importance of the environment and experience (in other words, social factors) (Raine, 2008). Repeatedly, tests combining genetic and social factors to explain variance in antisocial behavior demonstrate that *both* are required to develop a complete analysis. Studies using behavioral genetic methodologies frequently conclude that overall, 50% of the variance in the population of antisocial behavior can be attributed to genetic differences, while the other 50% is attributed to environmental differences (Moffitt, 2005; Raine, 2008). Notably, this finding is an aggregate of many behavioral outcomes, and studies show that the division increases slightly in favor of genetic origins when the behavior examined is more serious and violent. However, less serious outcomes show favor toward environmental origins, further supporting that inclusion of all possible risk factors is necessary to view a complete picture of behavior. Research does not support determinism. The fear of discovery of a "criminal gene" has not been realized, and risk factors (both nurture and nature) are only that—factors of *risk*.

BioShock demonstrates a clear tension between free will and determinism. Rather than make a definitive statement on the matter, the game seems to declare that both assumptions are flawed. There is not such a thing as pure, unfettered free will and, if there were, it would mean we are ultimately unbounded to each other and self-serving. At the same time, we are not entirely pawns of our environments, internal conditioning, or biology—we can rise above. This is also the message of contemporary biosocial criminology. Both biology and environment matter. People make choices but we are not all equally capable of making those choices freely.

Notes

1 The resurgence is most prevalent in the United States; in fact, other European countries have included examinations of criminal and antisocial behavior as a category in psychological and medical study for some time (Lombroso, 2006).

2 It is of note that this paper only examines the original *BioShock* game, although two other games have been created in the franchise: *BioShock* 2 and *BioShock* Infinite. Although these games exist in the same universe, they have separate plots and focus on different philosophies and societal issues.

3 Due to the age of the game, it is difficult to untangle the exact sales of the original *BioShock* (2007) game from others in the franchise, or when the series is sold as a collection.

4 For example, the average length of a feature film is about 75 to 210 minutes (Academy of Motion Picture Arts and Sciences, 2023; Screen Actors Guild Awards, 2022), but *BioShock* takes an average of 12 hours to complete, with a thorough playthrough averaging closer to 22 hours (How Long to Beat, n.d.). Television shows can easily engage audiences well past 12 to 22 hours' worth of episodes, but still only engage at the level of *viewer*, not *player*.

5 Science, industry, and art are the three pillars of Rapture, and mirror important tenets of Ayn Rand's Objectivism.

6 It is worth noting that Frank Fontaine conned his way into Rapture, assuming the identity of the real Frank Fontaine of Fontaine Fisheries. Access to Rapture was invitation-only, after a thorough vetting process by Ryan. Accepting citizenship meant a one-way trip to Rapture, leaving the rest of the world behind forever. It could be argued that Ryan's inability to regulate the admission of this particular citizen upset the perfectly curated membership in Rapture, upsetting the Objectivist ideals.

7 Originally published in 1943 and 1957 respectively.

8 It is worth noting that this sentence summarizes whole texts on Objectivism, and this author is aware of the injustice of attempting to summarize a complex philosophy in such a condensed manner.

9 It is fair to note ADAM and plasmid use for each of these characters is unknown, and it is possible that they were suffering from the effects of ADAM addiction which may have altered their mental state somewhat. However, the game describes the decent into psychosis for several characters (e.g., cosmetic surgeon Dr. Steinman and artist Sander Cohen), which depicts their behavior as controlled and pointed toward self-serving tests of the limits of morality. These characters communicate their excitement at the freedom to pursue these avenues.

10 Named by the game developer Kevin Levine, this group is the closest entity to a ruling council or governmental group in Rapture. Unofficially formed, the members are Andrew Ryan, Frank Fontaine, Brigid Tenenbaum, Yi Suchong, Sander

Cohen, J.S. Steinman, Gil Alexander, and Sofia Lamb. Gil Alexander and Sofia Lamb do not appear in the narrative until *BioShock* 2.
11 Approaching them means an onerous battle, due to the Big Daddies that protect them.
12 Criminological theories which assume rationality as a foundation of human nature continue to attempt to address the issue of limitations and stipulations for determining "rational thought" at the expense of utility of the theory. *BioShock* is an example of this issue, in that there are numerous reasons a person may decide on a course of action (see Sander Cohen's desire to create grotesque living statues), but few would argue the choices are indeed "rational" (Paternoster, 2017; Steinmetz & Pratt, 2024).

References

2K Boston & 2K Australia. (2007). *BioShock*. 2K Games.

Academy of Motion Picture Arts and Sciences. (2023, January 9). *Rules and eligibility*. Oscars.org | Academy of Motion Picture Arts and Sciences. http://dx.doi.org/10.1093/ww/9780199540884.013.8938

Atwood, M. (1986). *The handmaid's tale*. Houghton Mifflin Harcourt.

Beccaria, C. (1764). *On crimes and punishments* (H. Paolucci, 1963, Trans.). Pearson Education Limited.

Bernstein, A. (2008). *Objectivism in one lesson: An introduction to the philosophy of Ayn Rand*. University Press of America.

Boles, S.M., & Miotto, K. (2003). Substance abuse and violence: A review of the literature. *Aggression and Violent Behavior*, 8(2), 155–174.

Bortolato, M., & Shih, J.C. (2011). Behavioral outcomes of monamine oxidase deficiency: Preclinical and clinical evidence. *International Review of Neurobiology*, 100, 13–42.

Caspi, A., McClay, J., Moffitt, T.E., Mill, J., Martin, J., Craig, I.W., Taylor, A., & Poulton, R. (2002). Role of genotype in the cycle of violence in maltreated children. *Science*, 297(5582), 851–854.

Chan, K.H. (2022, February 17). *Revisiting BioShock's "Would you kindly" twist, 15 years later*. TheGamer. https://www.thegamer.com/revisiting-*BioShock*-would-you-kindly-twist-15-years-later/

Conway, C.C., & Slavich, G.M. (2017). Behavior genetics of prosocial behavior. In P. Gilbert (Ed.), *Compassion: Concepts, research and applications* (pp. 151–170). Routledge/Taylor & Francis Group.

Cox, H. (2011, September 8). *Video games from a critical distance—an evaluation of BioShock's criticism of Ayn Rand's philosophy of Objectivism*. Game Developer. https://www.gamedeveloper.com/disciplines/video-games-from-a-critical-distance---an-evaluation-of-*BioShock*-s-criticism-of-ayn-rand-s-philosophy-of-objectivism

Farrer, T.J., & Hedges, D.W. (2011). Prevalence of traumatic brain injury in incarcerated groups compared to the general population: A meta-analysis. *Progress in Neuro-Psychopharmacology and Biological Psychiatry*, 35(2), 390–394.

Gibson, M., & Rafter, N. (2006). *Editors' introduction to Cesare Lombroso's criminal man*. Duke University Press.

Golding, W. (1954). *Lord of the flies*. Faber and Faber.

Gorwood, P., Le Strat, Y., Ramoz, N., Dubertret, C., Moalic, J.M., & Simonneau, M. (2012). Genetics of dopamine receptors and drug addiction. *Human Genetics*, 131, 803–822.

How Long to Beat. (n.d.). *How long is BioShock?* HowLongToBeat.com | Game Lengths, Backlogs and more!. Retrieved February 9, 2023 from https://howlongtobeat.com/game/1065

IGN Staff. (2023, March 4). *The top 100 video games of all time.* IGN. Retrieved March 15, 2023 from https://www.ign.com/articles/the-best-100-video-games-of-all-time

IMDb. (n.d.). *BioShock (Video game 2007, Awards).* IMDb.com. Retrieved November 29, 2022 from https://m.imdb.com/title/tt1094581/awards/?ref_=tt_awd

Ivan, T. (2009, June 18). *Take-two targets five million BioShock 2 sales | Edge magazine.* Wayback Machine. https://web.archive.org/web/20101003165615/www.next-gen.biz/news/take-two-targets-five-million-*BioShock*-2-sales

Jennings, S.C. (2019). A meta-synthesis of agency in game studies. Trends, troubles, trajectories. *GAME: Games as Art, Media, Entertainment,* 1(8), 85–106.

King, J. (2023, February 27). *Video games need to stop living in the shadow of BioShock.* TheGamer. Retrieved March 10, 2023 from https://www.thegamer.com/*BioShock*-atomic-heart-influence-legacy-ken-levine/

Lombroso, C. (2006). *Criminal man.* Duke University Press.

Moffitt, T.E. (1993). Adolescence-limited and life-course persistent antisocial behavior: A developmental taxonomy. *Psychological Review,* 100(4), 674–701.

Moffitt, T.E. (2005). The new look of behavioral genetics in developmental psychopathology: Gene–environment interplay in antisocial behaviors. *Psychological Bulletin,* 131, 533–554.

Packer, J. (2010). The battle for Galt's Gulch: *BioShock* as critique of Objectivism. *Journal of Gaming & Virtual Worlds,* 2(3), 209–224.

Paternoster, R. (2017). Happenings, acts, and actions: Articulating the meaning and implications of human agency for criminology. *Journal of Developmental and Life-Course Criminology,* 3(4), 350–372.

Peikoff, L. (1993). *Objectivism: The philosophy of Ayn Rand.* Penguin.

Perry, D.C. (2012). *The influence of literature and myth in videogames.* IGN. com, 18. Retrieved April 15, 2023 from https://www.ign.com/articles/2006/05/18/the-influence-of-literature-and-myth-in-videogames

Pinker, S. (2002). *The blank slate: The modern denial of human nature.* Viking.

Raine, A. (2008). From genes to brain to antisocial behavior. *Current Directions in Psychological Science,* 17(5), 323–328.

Rand, A. (1964). *The of selfishness.* Penguin.

Rand, A. (1996). *The fountainhead.* Penguin.

Rand, A. (2005). *Atlas shrugged.* Penguin.

Ray, B., & Richardson, N.J. (2017). Traumatic brain injury and recidivism among returning inmates. *Criminal Justice and Behavior,* 44(3), 472–486.

Remo, C. (2007, August 30). *Ken Levine on BioShock: The spoiler interview.* Shacknews. https://www.shacknews.com/article/48728/ken-levine-on-*BioShock*-the

Rhee, S., & Waldman, I. (2002). Genetic and environmental influences on antisocial behavior: A meta-analysis of twin and adoption studies. *Psychological Bulletin,* 128, 490–529.

Ruch, A. (2010). Interpretations of freedom and control in *BioShock. Journal of Gaming and Virtual Worlds,* 2(1), 84–91.

Sabol, S., Hu, S., & Hamer, D. (1998). A functional polymorphism in the monoamine oxidase A gene promoter. *Human Genetics,* 103, 273–279.

Scarr, S., & McCartney, K. (1983). How people make their own environments: A theory of genotype → environment effects. *Child Development,* 54(2), 424–435.

Schiesel, S. (2007, September 8). *Genetics gone haywire and predatory children in an undersea metropolis.* The New York Times—Breaking News, US News, World News and Videos. https://www.nytimes.com/2007/09/08/arts/television/08shoc.html

Schurger, A., Pak, J., & Roskies, A.L. (2021). What is the readiness potential? *Trends in Cognitive Sciences,* 25(7), 558–570.

Schwartz, J.A., Walsh, A., & Beaver, K.M. (2019). The biosocial perspective: A brief overview and potential contributions to criminological theory. In M. Krohn,

N. Hendrix, G. Penly Hall, & A. Lizotte (Eds.), *Handbook on crime and deviance* (pp. 89–111). Springer.

Screen Actors Guild Awards. (2022). *Eligibility criteria.* https://www.sagawards.org/awards/rules-eligibility/eligibility-criteria

Sims, D. (2016, September 27). *How BioShock mocked video-game morality.* The Atlantic. https://www.theatlantic.com/entertainment/archive/2016/09/BioShock-remastered/501809/

Smithsonian American Art Museum. (2011). *The art of video games: Traveling exhibition.* https://americanart.si.edu/exhibitions/games.

Staniloiu, A., & Markowitsch, H. (2012). Gender differences in violence and aggression—a neurobiological perspective. *Procedia-social and Behavioral Sciences, 33,* 1032–1036.

Stetler, D.A., Davis, C., Leavitt, K., Schriger, I., Benson, K., Bhakta, S., Wang, L.C., Oben, C., Watters, M., Haghnegahdar, T., & Bortolato, M. (2014). Association of low-activity MAOA allelic variants with violent crime in incarcerated offenders. *Journal of Psychiatric Research, 58,* 69–75.

Steinmetz, K.F., & Pratt, T.C. (2024). Revisiting the tautology problem in rational choice theory: What it is and how to move forward theoretically and empirically. *European Journal of Criminology,* 1–20. https://doi.org/10.1177/14773708241226537.

Suderman, P. (2016, October 3). *BioShock proved that video games could be art.* Vox. https://www.vox.com/culture/2016/10/3/13112826/BioShock-video-games-art-choice

Tulloch, R. (2010). A man chooses, a slave obeys: Agency, interactivity and freedom in video gaming. *Journal of Gaming & Virtual Worlds, 2*(1), 27–38.

Van den Berghe, P.L. (1990). Why most sociologists don't (and won't) think evolutionarily. *Sociological Forum, 5,* 173–185.

Van Hazebroek, B.C., Wermink, H., van Domburgh, L., de Keijser, J.W., Hoeve, M., & Popma, A. (2019). Biosocial studies of antisocial behavior: A systematic review of interactions between peri/prenatal complications, psychophysiological parameters, and social risk factors. *Aggression and Violent Behavior, 47,* 169–188.

VGChartz. (2020, February 8). *Game Search: BioShock.* Retrieved March 24, 2023 from https://www.vgchartz.com/gamedb/games.php?name=BioShock

Wachowski, L., & Wachowski, L. (1999). *The Matrix.* Warner Bros.

Wright, J. P., Beaver, K.M., DeLisi, M., Vaughn, M. G., Boisvert, D., & Vaske, J. (2008). Lombroso's legacy: The miseducation of criminologists. *Journal of Criminal Justice Education, 19*(3), 325–338.

Young, G. (2023, January 27). *The best 100 games of all time, ranked.* si.com. https://videogames.si.com/guides/best-games

Zahr, N.M., Kaufman, K.L., & Harper, C.G. (2011). Clinical and pathological features of alcohol-related brain damage. *Nature Reviews Neurology, 7*(5), 284–294.

Zwart, H. (2014). Genetic determinism. In H. ten Have (Ed.), *Encyclopedia of global bioethics* (pp. 1–10). Springer. https://doi.org/10.1007/978-3-319-05544-2_208-1

3

THE APPREHENSIVE VIOLENCE OF *DEATH STRANDING*

Meditations on Ropes and Sticks[1]

Kevin F. Steinmetz

I step out from the smooth concrete campus of Lake Knot City onto rocky and barren terrain that stretches for miles. The cold baritone of Die-Hardman (John Blake McClane) crackles over my cuff-link, a wrist-born communication device:

> You're passing through MULE territory. Move fast and quiet, 'cause if they see you—if they catch you . . . To think that their parents were porters like you who risked life and limb to try and keep our country together. And now their broken children carry on the work without any understanding of what it once meant. It's a ritual to them, the delivery. An insatiable addiction. And they'll be coming for you to get their next fix.[2]

I'm certainly not equipped for protracted combat at this point. In addition to rope, I've packed a couple of "maser guns"—taser-like weapons in rifle form. Given the cumbersome load on my back, prudence dictates I avoid conflict. I have two options: circumnavigate their territory, avoiding the sensors placed around the periphery, or sneak through, a faster but significantly more dangerous approach.

I opt for the long way around. Mountains line the horizon and the sky is clear. I don't mind taking my time. My boots beat a steady, rhythmic, almost hypnotic cadence on the rocky terrain. In the distance, the MULEs patrol their territory. There will be times when I must confront them, but it isn't today. For now, I revel in the subtle joy of package delivery.

This is *Death Stranding*, the brainchild of Hideo Kojima, the auteur known for deeply thoughtful, artfully designed, and often weird games like *Metal Gear Solid*, *Snatcher*, and *P.T.* (see Skott and Skott Bengtsson, in this volume).

DOI: 10.4324/9781003346869-3

Upon reflection, this moment—typical of my experience with the game—was unusual in the context of contemporary mainstream gaming. While *Death Stranding* is very much a "AAA" release—it sold over 10 million copies as of November 8, 2022 and had a massive development budget—the game is not typical among mainstream, high-budget games (Kojima Productions, 2022).[3] In a game which allows for frenetic combat, that I would not only find the idea of violent encounters unappealing, but the idea of pacifism enjoyable was a novel experience. It runs counter to the philosophy of many AAA games which frequently center violence in both gameplay and narrative including popular franchises like *Call of Duty, Assassin's Creed, Grand Theft Auto,* and *Halo,* to name only a few. While the jury is still out on whether video games cause violence or other forms of aggression (e.g., Ferguson, 2007; Prescott et al., 2018), there is little denying that violence sells. Seven of the top ten best-selling games in the United States in 2022 prominently feature either realistic or cartoonish violence (Batchelor, 2022).[4] Though many exceptions exist, much of contemporary gaming is mired in mayhem and mutilation.

Death Stranding, however, interrogates the role of violence in gaming. It continues what I call Kojima's longstanding *ambiguous aversion* toward violence. While certainly an option available to the player—and there are times when the player is forced into defending themselves—*Death Stranding* is designed in such a way that it discourages violence and, instead, encourages the player to enjoy activities many consider to be mundane—traversing terrain and moving cargo.

This chapter argues that, in *Death Stranding,* Kojima invites the player to question their attitudes toward violence in video games. It de-normalizes gaming violence and makes its gravity plain, both in terms of the physical toll of violence and its social costs. Violence, in other words, erodes or severs the connections that keep us—humans—joined together in social networks of mutual interdependence. *Death Stranding* thus advances a kind of "popular criminology" about simulated brutality (Rafter, 2007). To begin, this chapter first describes *Death Stranding* (as much as one can possibly describe such a game). It then considers the background of the game's creator, Hideo Kojima, and how that background may have informed his approach to the game's creation and design. Next, the chapter details examples that demonstrate the game's conflicted view toward violence. This analysis concludes with the implications of Kojima's ambiguous aversion.

What is *Death Stranding*?

Kojima games are steeped in contrast. They are often gritty, dark, and dramatic yet also playful, silly, and mirthful. The result is a style Chen (2020) has fittingly termed "Kojima Weirdness." His careful attention to detail and his wild creativity are well established as well. Admittedly, he has courted controversy—most notably with his depiction of women in his games, which have sometimes relied upon sexist and misogynist tropes (Chen, 2020). *Death Stranding*, however, is perhaps his most mature, artful, and—frankly—*bizarre* game to date. First released in 2019, with an expanded "Director's Cut" published in 2021, *Death Stranding* is difficult to describe as the game is characterized by creative world-building, complex narratives, and novel mechanics. At its core, however, it is a game about package delivery and building connections (Green, 2022).

Societies across the world were reduced to rubble when the worlds of the living and the dead became entangled—the eponymous "Death Stranding" event. The world of the dead is "The Beach," a purgatorial coast where folks can pass into the afterlife. Unless incinerated, the dead "necrotize" and become "Beached Things" or "BTs," ghosts stranded in the land of the living. When BTs contact the living, "voidouts" or massive explosions occur. As BTs are often invisible to the naked eye, individuals use "bridge babies" or "BBs" to detect their presence. In the world of *Death Stranding,* when a mother dies before giving birth, she becomes a "stillmother." Her unborn child—the BB—is removed from her womb and placed inside of a special pod. Because of their circumstances, BBs act as a conduit between the worlds of the living and dead and, as a result, can sense BTs and are thus used as bio-technical BT sensing devices. The Death Stranding also brought with it "timefall" or rain that rapidly ages anything it touches. With the dual threat of BTs and timefall, humanity fled underground into shelters.

The player adopts the role of Sam Porter Bridges (Norman Reedus), a "porter" who delivers cargo between shelters. In this dystopian future, porters are the lifeblood of humanity—the only remaining connection between these isolated shelters, carrying cargo, news, and hope. The remnants of the United States government—rebranded the United Cities of America (UCA)—endeavored to reconnect the shelters that dot the landscape through a new kind of telecommunications network, a task delegated to the Bridges organization. "Bridges I" was their first expedition across the country to lay the groundwork for reconnection. Upon reaching the West Coast, the Bridges I team was wiped out and their leader, Sam's sister Amelie (Lindsey Wagner), was supposedly taken hostage. Sam is coerced into becoming the sole member of the Bridges II mission. Using a device called a "Q-pid," a necklace resembling an ancient Inca quipu adorned with six rectangular objects, Sam connects shelters to the "Chiral Network"—a communications infrastructure that takes advantage of the temporal properties of The Beach to transfer massive quantities of data instantaneously.

Admittedly, this description only scratches the surface. It would take volumes to adequately describe the breadth and depth of *Death Stranding*. It doesn't touch upon DOOMs, an affliction gives some individuals special abilities, seemingly through a relationship to The Beach. Nor does it include descriptions of "extinction events," "chiralgrams," "cryptobiotes," or a multitude of other creations packed into the game. It should, however, give the reader a sufficient foundation for the discussion to come. With groundwork laid, this analysis pivots to the man behind the game—Hideo Kojima.

Hideo Kojima, Anti-Violence, and Loneliness

Kojima's employment at Konami began in 1986. Here, he was offered the opportunity to direct his own game, a property called *Metal Gear,* released in 1987 (Brusseaux et al., 2018). He would go on to develop several additional entries in the series as well as a bevy of other noteworthy games—either in some lead or supporting role—including *Snatcher, Policenauts, Boktai: The Sun is in Your Hand,* and *P.T.* Yet, the *Metal Gear* series is the one he is most famous for and, perhaps, the best starting point to consider his perspective on violence.

Originally envisioned as militaristic game based on shooting, Kojima elected to make the first *Metal Gear* game about stealth—avoiding combat. One reason was because the MSX2 console could not process more than a few enemies on screen at a time thus making large battle scenes infeasible (Brusseaux et al., 2018). This decision may have also been influenced by his parents' experiences World War II. In an interview with *The Guardian,* Kojima recounted that,

> My parents both lived through the second world war . . . They suffered. My mum would tell me about how she would have to step over dead bodies in the street, and eat pieces of tatami mat when there was no food.
>
> *(Parkin, 2022)*

His father also reinforced the horrific nature of war by showing him Holocaust documentaries. As a result, Kojima was uninterested in the carnage of war and, instead, expressed interest in "the context behind the on-screen conflict" (Parkin, 2022).

In this way, Kojima's games are marked by a contradiction. They present intense anti-war and violence messaging while also embracing violence as a tool for both storytelling and gameplay. This is what I mean by Kojima's *ambiguous aversion*—it is clear he is against violence in principle but the boundaries on when violence is acceptable and the kinds of violence permitted in his games are nebulous (Brusseaux et al., 2018, p. 219).[5] Characters in the stories, especially the antagonists, may engage in horrific acts of war. Players are frequently given the option to resolve situations with lethal *or* non-lethal force. There are moments when lethal force is *required* from the player, such as during many boss battles. There may be other scenarios where the player is rebuked by the game (and, indirectly, by Kojima) for engaging in violence (Burch & Burch, 2015, p. 61).[6] Violence may be treated with a comedic flair in some scenarios while grim in others. It is as if Kojima is saying to the player, "look, violence is bad, and we should agree that its bad, but we can have some fun with it—it is a game, after all."

Perhaps no scene demonstrates this ambiguous aversion than the boss battle with The Sorrow in *Metal Gear Solid 3*. At the beginning of the fight, The Sorrow remarks to Naked Snake (the game's protagonist) that,

> Battle brings death. Death brings sorrow. The living may not hear them. Their voices may fall upon deaf ears. But make no mistake . . . the dead are not silent. Now you will know the sorrow of those whose lives you have ended.

The player then pursues The Sorrow through a waterlogged ditch, confronted by the ghosts of every enemy the player has killed throughout the game. The more enemies killed, the more protracted the boss fight. Consistent with Kojima's staunch anti-war politics, it is a grim scene where the player is rebuked for killing virtual enemies. Yet, at the same time, the game allows the player to shoot enemies in the genitals or buttocks throughout with comedic effect. Any enemies killed in this fashion will appear during the encounter with The Sorrow clutching their groins, undermining what is otherwise a grim spectacle. The anti-war messaging is obvious. But also, *pee-pee shots are funny*.

There exist many entirely non-violent games (e.g., *Tetris, Animal Crossing, Mario Golf, etc.*). Yet, many Kojima games are arguably better ambassadors for non-violence because they specifically invoke the tension between gaming violence and player agency—noting that, with exceptions, violence is often a choice among options made by the player, one that may have consequences (Brusseaux et al., 2018; Burch & Burch, 2015). His games are often overt about the perils and pitfalls of violence. Even the levity with which violence is sometimes treated highlights its absurdity. Further, such humor is often a veiled jab at the violent tropes that permeate mainstream gaming. His games put violence and its folly front-and-center.

In addition to being anti-war and -violence, Kojima is a man self-admittedly wracked by loneliness and isolation—themes deeply embedded in *Death Stranding* (Green, 2022). He grew up as a latchkey kid and his father died when he was young. As a result, he has lamented in interviews to having felt lonely much of his life. *Death Stranding* was developed during a particularly lonely period. Kojima left Konami in 2015 after spending nearly three decades at the company. The circumstances of the departure are not entirely clear, but we do know that the split was not amicable and likely stemmed from Konami moving away from the development of "AAA" game titles toward mobile games as well as a significant reduction in creative autonomy among its developers, including Kojima (Sarkar, 2015). Konami scrubbed Kojima from much of their marketing materials and their websites. When Kojima officially left, he signed a deal with Sony Computer Entertainment and reformed Kojima Productions as an independent studio (ibid.). During this period, he reportedly felt both adrift and alone (Chen, 2020).

Though Kojima maintains, at the time of writing, a relatively prolific social media presence, he seems deeply pessimistic about the nature of contemporary connections, mediated as they often are through technologies like social media (once again, clearly a man of contradiction). These connections, according to him, are fragmentary and conflict-ridden. As he explains, "we're in an era of individualism . . . everyone is fractured. Even on the internet. It's all connected, all around the world, but everyone is fighting each other" (Gault, 2019). Despite the proliferation of mediated connections, he argues that we have become profoundly lonely. Instead of just connecting in a superficial sense, he wants us to be "thinking about others" (ibid.). *Death Stranding* was also developed in the mid-2010s, a time of intense social division. In fact, Kojima and his collaborator Kenji Yano reference the 2016 president campaign and election of Donald Trump and Brexit as influential events providing significance for the game's themes (505 Games, 2021; BBC Newsbeat, 2019).

Death Stranding brings together these two themes—Kojima's ambiguous aversion to violence and his concerns regarding connection. The game begins with a quote from the Japanese author Kobo Abe's short story entitled "Nawa" or "The Rope":

> The "Rope," along with the "Stick," are two of mankind's oldest tools. The stick to keep the bad away, the rope used to bring the good toward us. They were our first friends, of our own invention. Wherever there were people, there were the rope and the stick.

This quote occurs at the end of the story, one about an elderly man who watches a group of children abuse a puppy and (spoiler) two girls who kill their neglectful father—both acts of cruelty or revenge accomplished with rope. Interestingly, the description of the rope provided in the aforementioned quote is inconsistent with its use in the story.[7] Perhaps this is done for literary purposes as Abe embraced surreal depictions of human awful. Regardless, the use of the rope in the story seems, at least to this author, to be used for anything but "bringing the good toward us."

Kojima's use of Abe's metaphor clings more closely to a literal translation. He frames the "stick" as a tool of violence whereas the "rope" is a connection:

> There's a Japanese author I am a huge fan of called Kobo Abe. He has a short novel called "Rope" in which he makes a definition, a statement: the first tool mankind made was a stick. It was made to keep away bad things. It's a weapon. The next tool created by mankind was rope. The rope is not to keep away bad things. On the contrary, it's a tool used to keep good things close to you, to tie good things close to you. Sticks and ropes are some of the tools most used by mankind even these days. In most games you see that are online multiplayer or co-op—or even single player—the communication is through sticks. In this game you will be able to use what will be the equivalent of sticks. But I also want people to use what will be the equivalent of ropes.
>
> *(Kojima, as quoted in Digital Spy, 2016)*

In this manner, *Death Stranding* establishes itself from the outset as a rumination on both violence and connection. While the two are undoubtedly intertwined, this analysis will focus on the role of violence while discussing isolation and social connection when relevant. For a more complete examination of the theme of connections in *Death Stranding*, I refer the reader to Amy M. Green's (2022) *Longing, Ruin, and Connection in Hideo Kojima's Death Stranding*.

Death Stranding and the Ambiguous Aversion to Violence

This section explores specific examples highlighting *Death Stranding's* ambiguous aversion to violence. To be clear, detailing every such example would be a *massive* undertaking necessitating its own book. For this reason, selectivity is required. To avoid missing contrary evidence, I have thoroughly engaged with the game by playing and "one-hundred percenting" the game twice (once with the original version and again with the Director's Cut) amounting to approximately 200 hours of playtime.[8] I also read the two-part novelization written by Hitori Nojima (the penname of Kenji Yano, a scriptwriter for the game), watched, listened to, or read multiple interviews with Kojima, and considered other available literature on the game.

To begin, the gameplay of *Death Stranding* is designed in such a way as to discourage violence, though it is always an option available to the player. And when violence is necessary, players often have the option between lethal or non-lethal methods. They can use bolo guns (which wrap enemies with a bolo to immobilize them), mazer guns (which use electricity to incapacitate), stun bombs (another electricity-based tool), and other non-lethal means.

Most of the lethal weapons in the game have non-lethal variants such as the non-lethal assault rifle or the riot shotgun.

Admittedly, lethal force does offer to player some advantages. Namely, human enemies go down faster and stay down. If, for example, the player runs into a MULE camp with an assault rifle, they can make relatively short work of the enemies. These enemies won't get back up and when the player returns to the location later—they will be gone. Killing human enemies, however, introduces complications. If the player kills someone, the body may necrotize and become a BT unless disposed of in an incinerator (of which there are only two, making incineration inconvenient). A body left near a populated area, like a MULE camp, may result in others dying and, subsequently, many BTs appearing. Further, necrotizing bodies may voidout, creating a "game over" state forcing the player to reload the game from an earlier point. Thus, the game gives the player non-lethal options and integrates consequences for the use of lethal force. Any advantages afforded by lethal force are short-term and short-sighted.

None of this is to even mention *Death Stranding*'s burdensome locomotion. Some detractors refer to the game as a "walking simulator," a term derisively used for games with limited action content that emphasize environmental exploration and narrative discovery.[9] Given the spirit of this pejorative, it is inappropriate to call *Death Stranding* a mere walking simulator. The player is doing plenty of walking, for sure. But the gameplay is designed so that players must manage their loads and consider the topography of the terrain lest they slide, tumble, or fall, jeopardizing their cargo. The act of traversal requires thought and planning on the part of the player in a way that, I think, no other game up to this point has managed. In this context, combat runs additional risks. During such encounters, the player not only has to, you know, *fight* but must also consider the extra constraints imposed by the landscape and their cargo, which may make them slow and imbalanced. This runs counter to the philosophy of many combat-oriented games which are often designed around ease-of-movement for the player. Instead, movement in *Death Stranding* is often ponderous at best or downright cumbersome at worst. A player can choose to drop their cargo before entering combat, but situations in which this is a reasonable course of action are limited. When a player comes across an opportunity for battle, they may be tempted until they realize they consider all the ins-and-outs involved. It's as if the game is saying "you can fight but don't think this is going to be simple or consequence-free. It will be an *ordeal.*"

As a completionist, I engaged in combat against human adversaries quite a bit. There are items hidden inside of MULE and terrorist camps. The Director's Cut introduces an optional facility linked to missions reminiscent of *Metal Gear*, allowing players to stealth through or take on enemies directly. I did these scenarios because I wanted to do everything the game had to offer.

It made the experience more difficult, however. It would have been far easier to avoid combat—only engaging enemies when required to progress. Like *Metal Gear*, *Death Stranding* tries to respect player agency by frequently giving the player options to consider, but it puts its thumbs on the scales to make it clear that violence is burdensome and consequential—encouraging the player to consider whether violence is worthwhile.

Though many violent encounters are optional, there are multiple events in the game which *necessitate* player violence. Battles with Beached Things (BTs) are one example. In these encounters, the gravity of violence is mitigated by the fact that these beings are already dead or at least belong in the realm of the dead. One is not so much "killing" as they are sending them on their way. Yet, it is true that some of these events *require* the player to fight to progress or avoid repatriation (resurrect with varying consequences). As the situation is explained in the novelization, "destroying a BT meant severing whatever lingering attachment the wandering dead had to this world and sending them back to where they belonged" (Nojima, 2021a, pp. 182–183). In fact, given that some of the BTs are summoned by one of the game's antagonists, Higgs, a "terrorist" bent on bringing about an "extinction event," eradicating BTs is framed as an act of mercy for beings coerced into existence:

> Sam had to steer the dead back to where they belonged. If this BT had been summoned by Higgs, then it wasn't here through any fault of its own. If Higgs was going to exploit their bitterness and delusions, then Sam would have to be the one to purify them. Sam felt almost righteous as he grabbed the grenade.
>
> *(ibid., p. 183)*

Thus, in these cases, violence is justified as a matter of self-defense, for certain, but also because it restores the natural state of things. The dead do not belong in the realm of the living and must be repelled—by force if necessary.

The eradication of the dead is therefore a restoration of order whereas the killing of the living is a fundamental threat to order. The death of a human not only means that humanity's population is one step closer to extinction, but that the potential of a voidout may kill others. The consequences stemming from any single human death are so powerful that casualties can be felt across the social fabric as well as the physical landscape, leaving behind massive craters. Force must be applied in some situations, for sure, but the ramifications of needless or reckless killing are dire.

There are three urgent and necessary combat scenarios that occur in the game when Sam encounters Clifford Unger (Mads Mikkelsen), a dead ex-Special Forces member hunting for his son, one of the early victims of the BB program. In each of these events, Sam is transported to beaches which the character Deadman (Guillermo del Toro/Jessi Corti) suggests are "special" beaches "for soldiers who died in battle. A maelstrom of their bitterness and regret" (Nojima, 2021b, p. 39). These beaches are warped versions of World War I, World War II, and Vietnam War battlefields. The ghosts of the warring dead replay their deaths in a loop across landscapes of blood and gore. The soundscape is nightmarish. It is a place for people who died "at the hands of weapons designed to kill en masse" (Nojima, 2021b, p. 40). To escape this domain, the player is required to find weapons, combat undead soldiers, and dispatch Cliff. The player is thus required to fight, but this is not the run-and-gun action of *Doom*, *Borderlands 2*, or *Halo*. It is clunky and frenetic. It is also, at least for me, somewhat unenjoyable. Rather than being the immediately satisfying visceral experience that many shooters offer, the combat in *Death Stranding*, as previously indicated, often feels agonizing. Combined with the horrific tension of the setting, I found myself longing for peaceful vistas and cargo delivery.

Cliff and his henchmen (hench-skeletons?) are BTs, albeit unordinary ones. Violence against these ghosts is seemingly justified in *Death Stranding* because Cliff is single-minded and driven. He cannot be reasoned with, nor can he be deterred:

> Sam tried to ask why, but he couldn't. Before he had the chance, the man started to shake his head. Sam's gut was already telling him that he would never be able to converse with this man. Something had inhibited his thinking. Sam may have been overconfident in the fact, but if the man was refusing to be understood, what else could it have been? That idea itself made Sam feel unbearably sad.
>
> *(Nojima, 2021a, p. 284)*

Like with other BTs, a second death is an act of mercy. Yet, because Cliff is clearly more human-like than most BTs encountered in the game, Sam is conflicted. It isn't as evident in the game itself, but the novelization makes this clear,

> If Sam finished him off now, then he would be able to return to his own world. But his confidence was shaken. This man wasn't dead like a BT . . . Defeating him wouldn't send him back anywhere. This man was after a different kind of funeral.

Outside of the black ooze seeping from his eyes and the—*sigh*—the umbilical cords tethering him to his skeletal soldiers, Cliff is the most human-like undead being in the game. Yet it is also understood that he is not entirely human either. Perhaps in this scenario, violence is justified because reason and discourse—elements necessary for connection—are out of the picture. Cliff is a single-minded entity. Yet, it is not the same unflinching violence that might be visited upon a BT encountered elsewhere in the game. Sam is conflicted in these encounters.

Higgs Monaghan (Troy Baker), one of the chief antagonists of the game, is another useful character to consider when examining *Death Stranding*'s ambiguous aversion to violence.[10] He possesses supernatural powers that allow him to control BTs, teleport, and engage in other extraordinary feats. His name is a nod toward the Higgs-Boson particle, which he calls "the particle of God that permeates all existence." He was once a typical porter, dedicating himself to helping others through the delivery of packages, and joined with Fragile Express, one of the largest private porter enterprises. Yet, he turns away from the mission of human survival toward human extinction. He becomes the leader of the Homo Demens, a "terrorist" organization (the game explicitly uses the term "terrorist").[11] While his motivation and origins are murky in the game, the novelization makes it clear that Higgs himself is a product of violence, having been raised by a severely abusive uncle in almost absolute isolation from the rest of the world, a not-so-subtle gesture toward the "cycle of violence" (Widom, 1989). Further, his powers were gained by exposure to necrotizing bodies—providing him with an incentive to kill others, according to the novels (Nojima, 2021b, p. 204).

Higgs is Sam's foil. Sam seems content to deliver packages and create connections. Higgs delivers destruction. He concedes as much during his final confrontation with Sam: "Just a good old-fashioned boss fight. *Stick versus rope. Gun versus strand.* One more ending before the end . . . One last game over [emphasis added]" (Nojima, 2021b, p. 188). We can probe this contradictory relationship further through each character's relationship to Fragile (Léa Seydoux), the leader of Fragile Express—the largest porter network outside the UCA.

While he originally worked alongside Fragile to expand her enterprise, Higgs eventually turns on the organization. He exploits the network to deliver munitions to terrorist groups and tricks Fragile into delivering a nuclear bomb to Middle Knot City, eradicating it.[12] As Fragile attempts to stop him from sending another nuclear device into South Knot City, he captures her, strips her down to a white tank top and underwear, adorns her with a gas mask, and gives her a choice: either run through the timefall to throw the device in the "tar" to save the city at the cost of rapidly aging her body or teleport away to save herself, leaving the citizens of the city to their grisly fate.[13] She chooses self-sacrifice. While the city was saved, the reputation of Fragile Express is tarnished as it is widely believed that she was complicit with this act of terrorism. Through Fragile, Higgs slaughters, sows distrust, and severs connections.

Sam, on the other hand, collaborates with Fragile throughout the game. She uses the last bit of credibility she maintains among the "preppers" (individuals living in shelters unaffiliated with the UCA) to help Sam expand the chiral network. Reciprocally, the good deeds of Sam not only elevate the legitimacy of the UCA, but also help restore the reputation in Fragile Express. Higgs tore Fragile down through violence, Sam helped her build herself back up through connection.[14]

Then there is the matter of Die-Hardman's revolver, a prop that is likely the most on-the-nose symbol of the tension between violence and connection in *Death Stranding* (warning: significant spoilers ahead as well as descriptions of infanticide). Later in the game, it is revealed that Sam is Cliff's son. Sam was once a BB stored at a government compound. Cliff visited his baby Sam frequently, operating under the impression that his son would eventually be released into his care. He was unaware that Sam was destined to be a part of the BB program—to be treated as equipment. During one visit, Die-Hardman, who served in the military under Cliff, revealed the truth and gave Cliff an opportunity to take baby Sam and escape the facility. The escape attempt failed. Die-Hardman was forced by President Bridget Strand (Lindsay Wagner) to shoot Cliff with his revolver. In the altercation, he shot the BB (Sam) as well. Amelie, who lives on The Beach, found Sam and returned him to the land of the living where he was raised by Bridget. Unfortunately, this resurrection or "repatriation" ushered in the Death Stranding and allowed BTs to cross over to the land of the living.

After his confrontation with Higgs and a protracted interaction with Amelie, Sam is stranded on The Beach with Die-Hardman's revolver. He tries to kill himself with the gun to escape. It does not fire. The revolver, according to Amelie, "has another purpose." His friends—Deadman, Fragile, Die-Hardman, and Heartman—search far and wide to save Sam from this purgatory and eventually find him, pulling him back into the land of the living. It was the revolver that made the rescue possible:

> "In the end, this is what led us to you." Deadman reached inside his jacket and pulled out the revolver. "Just when we were about to give up, Die-Hardman reminded us about the revolver. So, we tried to follow it, and it led us to a far corner of your own Beach . . ." Sam once again found himself face to face with the gun that killed him and Cliff. The gun that started everything.
>
> *(Nojima, 2021b, p. 339)*

Thus, the gun became, in the words of Deadman, "not a weapon, but a lifeline. A stick that became a rope?" (Nojkima, 2021b, p. 340). As a stick, the revolver severed the connection between father and son and set in motion the events that would threaten all humanity with extinction. As a rope, however, it allows Sam's friends to find him—the great connector who helps humanity survive, at least for a little while longer.

Significance of the Ambiguous Aversion

Death Stranding is thus a game which comments on connection—and how easily these connections can be broken or corrupted (Green, 2022). Violence, in particular, is framed as the antithesis of connection. Yet, the fact remains that *violence is often an option* in the game. Despite the various gameplay and narrative elements present in *Death Stranding* which discourage violence or, at the very least, problematize it, the player is allowed to use force in many sections of the game. Like the *Metal Gear* series, *Death Stranding* is mired in Kojima's ambiguous aversion to violence. There are clear anti-violence messages but violence is also a significant source of dramatic tension and spectacle. It is no secret that Kojima loves cinema, a medium where violence is often a mechanism for elevating the stakes of a story—encouraging the audience to feel anxiety or tension over the fate of the protagonist, to have a reason to root against the villain, et cetera. Also, as previously mentioned, Kojima is interested in telling the stories behind conflict—which necessitates that conflict be present. One cannot comment on violence without referring to it, after all. Finally, as previously mentioned, providing violence as an option also respects player agency. Video games are an *interactive* media. Allowing violence gives players the opportunity to experience the consequences of violence as a result *of their own choices*—they are not just spectators but active participants in the navigation of the tension between violence and connection. Sure, the player can use their agency to ignore or undermine the message built into the game by Kojima, but the game will respond, administering its own consequences. Players who take their choices seriously, on the other hand, gain a deeper appreciation for the gravity of the struggle presented by *Death Stranding*. Further, as explained earlier in this chapter, it is precisely Kojima's approach to violence—permissive yet reproachful, serious yet absurd—that makes his games novel ambassadors for anti-war and -violence messaging. His idiosyncratic approach makes it difficult for players to avoid an intellectual confrontation with the role of violence in the game and their complicity in it.

Death Stranding also invites the player to consider the trope-ish treatment of violence throughout contemporary gaming. My own experience in this regard was not unlike Jeff Ferrell's (2003) with roadside shrines—memorials to the casualties of automotive wrecks. He notes that Americans maintain a willful ignorance of or blasé attitude toward the carnage of car culture, which kill tens of thousands of people per annum and injures many more. At the same time, the United States maintains a bizarre commitment to the war on drugs, a campaign that fundamentally changed the American criminal legal system and contributed to mass incarceration. He muses that:

> In their loving commemoration of so many lives lost, the shrines challenge us to confront the circumstances of this ongoing collective tragedy. They push us to look past the lies—past the ideological alchemy of war-on-drugs advertising campaigns, the slick unreality of television police chases, the commodified self-aggrandizement of corporate car commercials—and to notice instead the absurd imbalance of contemporary arrangements. Encoding the life-and-death consequences of such arrangements in the texture of human landscape, they help us understand that today, and every day, the greatest danger to human life comes not from the traffic in marijuana and methamphetamine, but from the steady flow of high-speed automotive traffic, the rolling big rig truck parade, and the cops in hot pursuit.
>
> *(Ferrell, 2003, p. 196)*

Just as Ferrell scratches his head at our collective indifference automotive calamity, *Death Stranding* encouraged within me a similar confusion regarding our collective acceptance of widespread wanton video game violence.

This is not a matter of pearl clutching—I have played (and enjoyed!) many hyperviolent games. My decades of gaming amount to a pixelated genocide. And, of course, people throughout the years have lamented the role of violence in video games. Yet, among gamers, violence is often accepted as a given. Further, as video games become more deeply embedded in societies across the world, claims that video game violence are harmful seem to be taken less seriously.

Death Stranding, however, produced in me an "attitude of strangeness" toward gaming violence. What used to seem like apex gaming engagement now seems like a cheap trick—as if relying upon video game violence was a crutch used by developers to capture and hook players. This is likely an unfair assessment. Creating good video game combat is an extraordinarily difficult endeavor. Yet, it is notable that we seem to crave digital barbarity and the visceral dominance of our adversaries. And that fighting and killing is normal and ordinary in gaming. My friend, Melissa Petkovsek, even noted that gamers sometimes differentiate "real" gamers from "casuals" based on one's engagement with skill-based simulated violence. A person who sticks to puzzle games may be considered less of a gamer by some than a person who plays competitive shooters, regardless of time committed to or skill accrued with the activity.

The normalization of video game violence is inseparable from gaming's militaristic history (Clark, 2017; de Jong & Schuilenburg, 2006; Ferrell, 2015, pp. 176–179). As Clark (2017) explains,

Video games, like so much of the technology we now use regularly, sprang from the military-industrial complex. The first video games were war games, commissioned and designed by the Department of Defense for the explicit purpose of simulating war with the Soviet Union. Many of the design aspects of video games still borrow from war games: the use of a "heads up display," the onslaught of enemy targets, the vast predilection for violence, and even the staggering amount of money the Pentagon spends financing the video game world—so much so, in fact, that the Pentagon considers video games one of their key recruitment tools.

Indeed, it seems that violence and militarism is fixed into the bedrock of contemporary gaming culture and business. In this sense, as *Death Stranding* de-normalizes violence, we may also consider it a rebuke of the militaristic history of gaming, an interpretation that would be consistent with Kojima's anti-war politics.

In addition to the militaristic history of gaming, *Death Stranding* is also embedded, as previously noted, in the politics of its time. In an interview with BBC Newsbeat (2019), Kojima connects *Death Stranding's* asynchronous multiplayer system to his concerns about online platforms which permit or even encourage "negative" interactions:

> The attacks and violence seen on online these days are out of control. So I designed this for people to take a step back and by connecting, relearn how to be kind to others. I don't think anyone in the world is opposed to that. . . . Trump is building a wall, and the UK is leaving the EU. In this game, we use bridges to connect things. But destroying those bridges can instantly turn them into walls. So bridges and walls are almost synonymous. That's one of the things I'd like the players to think about in the game.

Here, he is directly asking the player to contemplate the tension between building and destroying connections. It appears that Kojima wants players to ruminate on this tension in light of the present social context of social media, disinformation, propaganda, political discord, and a resurgence in far-right movements and rhetoric. In this way, *Death Stranding* is simultaneously one of the strangest games I have ever played and yet its themes are all too familiar and urgent.

Conclusion

Criminologists have long noted the relationship between violence and perceived threats to identity and social status (e.g., Anderson, 1999; Katz,

1988, pp. 25, 324; Matza, 1964; Sykes & Matza, 1957). Violence may seem legitimate and justifiable in moments of intense stress and emotion when our sense of self and standing are jeopardized (Agnew, 1992). Wars and other acts of national aggression may similarly stem from threats to collective identity and national narratives (Katz, 1988, p. 324). Depictions of violence in video games and other media are similarly grounded in narratives of justification. Slaughter the demons to protect humanity (e.g., *Doom*). Kill soldiers to liberate your people from oppression (e.g., *Far Cry 6, Freedom Fighters*). Murder rival gang members to secure your place in the market or ascend the ranks (e.g., *Grand Theft Auto*). In these scenarios, a failure to engage in violence is to *be* a failure of one kind or another (not to mention you'll quickly encounter a "game over" state or otherwise make no progress). Further, the narratives driving these games not only legitimate the infliction of harm, but also sterilize the violence from moral or ethical content in a manner fit for consumption (Ferrell, 2015, p. 170; Sykes & Matza, 1957).

Death Stranding problematizes this dynamic. It deliberately confronts the player with the consequences of violence (at least such acts committed against human targets). While certainly players can approach the game with a *laissez faire* attitude, the game itself invites conscious consideration of the decision to engage in violence and, if force is used, how those acts will be executed to mitigate consequences (e.g., use non-lethal weapons, stealth takedowns, etc.).

All of this is to say that, through *Death Stranding*, Kojima advances a kind of popular criminology (Rafter, 2007) that forces us to confront the absurdity and the consequences of violence. When we hurt others, we are not only inflicting bodily harm but eroding the invisible social ties that bind us all together. Violence, in this sense, is a threat to social order and well-being. We are only worse for it. Such reasoning is consistent with many criminological arguments which argue for the promotion, support, and preservation of social ties to reduce crime, victimization, and human suffering more generally while also noting the threat that violence poses collective cohesion (e.g., Anderson, 1999; Currie, 2020; Sampson et al., 1997; Shaw & McKay, 1942). At the same time, *Death Stranding* does not shy away from the fact that there may be times when violence is necessary. My interpretation is that *Death Stranding* encourages a deep consideration of the potential ramifications of these decisions; to not treat them lightly. Instead, we should consciously and earnestly commit ourselves to building connections and promoting positive interactions. Kojima wants us to learn this lesson and act accordingly. As he explained, "after spending dozens of hours in the game you will come back to reality in the end. When you do, I want you to use what you learned in the game. Connecting is one of those things" (Interview with BBC Newsbeat, 2019).

Notes

1 Special thanks to Melissa Petkovsek who was kind enough to review a draft of this chapter. Any and all mistakes herein are, of course, mine and mine alone.
2 Thanks to Redditor Snow_Guard who published the script for Death Stranding and made pulling quotes from the game much easier. The original Reddit post can be found at: https://www.reddit.com/r/DeathStranding/comments/ei6qrk/death_stranding_full_transcript_game_script/ (accessed November 22, 2022). The script is located at: https://game-scripts-wiki.blogspot.com/2019/12/death-stranding-full-transcript.html (accessed November 22, 2022).
3 It is currently unknown exactly how much it cost to make *Death Stranding*, at least publicly, but the consensus is that it must have been in the ballpark of a typical AAA title (Barder, 2021; Malgieri, 2020).
4 The top ten games of 2022, according to Gamesindustry.biz, were *Call of Duty: Modern Warfare 2, Elden Ring, Madden NFL 23, LEGO Star Wars: The Skywalker Saga, God of War: Ragnarok, Pokemon Legends: Arceus, Pokemon Scarlet & Violet, Horizon: Forbidden West, FIFA 23*, and *MLB: The Show*.
5 As Brusseaux et al. (2018, p. 219) note, "Kojima's constant refusal to condone war and its barbarous acts contrasts sharply with the objectives of the series' characters."
6 Burch and Burch (2015, p. 61) reference a scene in *Metal Gear Solid* where the antagonist, Liquid Snake, chastises Solid Snake (the protagonist) and, vicariously, the player about their use of lethal violence: "Why did you come here? Well, I'll tell you, then—you enjoy all the killing. That's why. . . . Are you denying it? Haven't you already killed most of my comrades? . . . I saw your face while you did it. It was filled with the joy of battle. . . . There's a killer inside you—you don't have to deny it."
7 I am deeply indebted to Tim Rogers (2019) for his translation of Nawa, which was published in *Medium*.
8 To "one-hundred percent" a game is slang for completing all the possible objectives available in the game, often through accomplishing all the "achievements" or "trophies" affiliated with the game, depending on the platform played. In my case, the platforms were the PlayStation 4 and PlayStation 5.
9 The game is tagged on the gaming platform Steam as a "walking simulator." This tag is assigned by Steam users, not the developers. I cannot find any evidence that Kojima Studios refers to *Death Stranding* as a walking simulator.
10 Given the byzantine nature of the story, it is difficult to say who, exactly, is *the* primary antagonist of *Death Stranding*. Higgs might be the most obvious villain, but he isn't necessarily the most important one, depending on one's interpretation, as that honor may be reserved for Cliff Unger or Amelie.
11 I don't believe the game ever explicitly translates "Homo Demens," but a quick Google Translate says it is Latin for "Crazy Men" or perhaps "Crazy People."
12 All of the major cities in *Death Stranding* are "knots," referring to the knots one would see in a quipu, a symbol used throughout the game. Another way to think about these "knots" is that they are treated much like nodes in a network.
13 The "tar" featured in *Death Stranding* is not tar in the traditional sense. It is a black ooze associated with BTs that has unusual properties.
14 Similarly, Green (2022, p. 62) uses Higgs and Sam to explore alternative relationships between the characters to masculinity: "Higgs . . . typifies behaviors associated with toxic masculinity, including his physical and verbal aggression and his abuse of women. This runs in stark contrast to Sam, who, while brave and physically capable, also proves capable of nurturing behavior and tenderness toward Lou [Sam's BB]."

References

505 Games [@505_Games]. Today's #DeathStrandingPC mini interview puts the spotlight on Kenji Yano (Writer) at @KojiPro2015_EN. Find out his favourite scene in DEATH STRANDING, favourite characters and more! Twitter. https://twitter.com/505_Games/status/1375477644448264192

Agnew, R. (1992). Foundation for a general strain theory of crime and delinquency. *Criminology, 30*(1), 47–88.

Anderson, E. (1999). *Code of the street: Decency, violence, and the moral life of the inner city.* W.W. Norton & Company.

Barder, O. (2021, August 8). If "Death Stranding" was such a massive success, why is Hideo Kojima striking a deal with Microsoft? *Forbes.com.* https://www.forbes.com/sites/olliebarder/2021/07/08/if-death-stranding-was-such-a-massive-success-why-is-hideo-kojima-striking-a-deal-with-microsoft/?sh=2b73ff611c96

Batchelor, J. (2022, December 20). Gamesindustry.biz presents . . . The year in numbers 2022. *Gamesindustry.biz.* https://www.gamesindustry.biz/gamesindustrybiz-presents-the-year-in-numbers-2022

BBC Newsbeat. (2019, November 4). *Death Stranding: Inside Kojima Productions* [video]. YouTube. https://www.youtube.com/watch?v=kjUpYlKs0nM

Brusseaux, D., Courcier, N., & El Kanafi, M. (2018). *Metal gear solid: Hideo Kojima's magnum opus.* Third Éditions.

Burch, A., & Burch, A. (2015). *Metal Gear Solid.* Boss Fight Books.

Chen, A. (2020, March 3). Hideo Kojima's strange, unforgettable video-game worlds. *New York Times.* https://www.nytimes.com/2020/03/03/magazine/hideo-kojima-death-stranding-video-game.html

Clark, N. (2017). A brief history of the "walking simulator," gaming's most detested genre. *Salon.com.* https://www.salon.com/2017/11/11/a-brief-history-of-the-walking-simulator-gamings-most-detested-genre/.

Currie, E. (2020). *A peculiar indifference: The neglected toll of violence on Black America.* Metropolitan Books.

De Jong, A., & Schuilenburg, M. (2006). *Mediapolis.* 010 Publishers.

Digital Spy. (2016, June 16). Hideo Kojima interview: Norman Reedus-starring Death Stranding is an action game like Metal Gear Solid, not a Silent Hills substitute. *Digital Spy.* https://www.digitalspy.com/videogames/ps4/a797994/hideo-kojima-interview-norman-reedus-starring-death-stranding-is-an-action-game-metal-gear-solid-not-a-silent-hills-substitute/

Ferguson, C.J. (2007). The good, the bad, and the ugly: A meta-analytic review of positive and negative effects of violent video games. *Psychiatric Quarterly, 78,* 309–316.

Ferrell, J. (2003). Speed kills. *Critical criminology, 11,* 185–198.

Ferrell, J. (2015). *Cultural criminology: An invitation* (2nd ed.). Sage.

Gault, M. (2019, November 8). "We're Not Thinking About Others." What Hideo Kojima Wants You to Learn From *Death Stranding. Time.com.* https://time.com/5722226/hideo-kojima-death-stranding/

Green, A.M. (2022). *Longing, ruin, and connection in Hideo Kojima's Death Stranding.* Routledge.

Katz, J. (1988). *Seductions of crime: Moral and sensual attractions in doing evil.* Basic Books.

Kojima Productions. (2022, November 8). *Death Stranding* connects 10 million porters worldwide. https://www.kojimaproductions.jp/en/DS10million-porters

Malgieri, F. (2020, May 30). Hideo Kojima: "*Death Stranding* wasn't a failure." *Gamereactor.eu.* https://www.gamereactor.eu/hideo-kojima-death-stranding-wasnt-a-failure/

Matza, D. (1964). *Delinquency and drift.* John Wiley & Sons, Inc.

Nojima, H. (2021a). *Death stranding: Volume one*. Titan Publishing Group.
Nojima, H. (2021b). *Death stranding: Volume two*. Titan Publishing Group.
Parkin, S. (2022, October 26). "I want to keep being the first": Hideo Kojima on seven years as an independent game developer. *The Guardian*. https://www.theguardian.com/games/2022/oct/26/i-want-to-keep-being-the-first-hideo-kojima-on-seven-years-as-an-independent-game-developer
Prescott, A.T., Sargent, J.D., & Hull, J.G. (2018). Metaanalysis of the relationship between violent video game play and physical aggression over time. *PNAS, 115*(40), 9882–9888.
Rafter, N. (2007). Crime, film and criminology: Recent sex-crime movies. *Theoretical Criminology, 11*(3), 403–420.
Rogers, T. (2019, November 1). "Nawa" ("The Rope") by Kobo Abe. *Medium*. https://medium.com/@108/nawa-the-rope-by-kobo-abe-19db9afa6dd3
Sarkar, S. (2015, December 16). Konami's bitter, yearlong breakup with Hideo Kojima, explained. *Polygon*. https://www.polygon.com/2015/12/16/10220356/hideo-kojima-konami-explainer-metal-gear-solid-silent-hills
Sampson, R.J., Raudenbush, S.W., & Earls, F. (1997). Neighborhoods and violent crime: A multilevel study of collective efficacy. *Science, 277*, 918–924.
Shaw, C.R., & McKay, H.D. (1942). *Juvenile delinquency and urban areas*. University of Chicago Press.
Sykes, G., & Matza, D. (1957) Techniques of neutralization: A theory of delinquency. *American Sociological Review 22*, 664–670.
Widom, C.P. (1989). The cycle of violence. *Science, 244*(4901), 160–166.

4

"ARE YOU SURE THE ONLY YOU IS YOU?"

Domestic Violence and Critiquing the Other in the Spectral Remains of *P.T.*

Sara Skott and Karl-Fredrik Skott Bengtson

In 2014, a game known as *P.T.* was released for PlayStation by Kojima Productions under the pseudonym "7780s Studio." Soon becoming a worldwide phenomenon, sparking enormous interest and discussion in the gaming community, it was quickly revealed that the game in fact was a playable teaser (hence *P.T.*) for an upcoming game in the *Silent Hill* series called *Silent Hills*, directed and designed by Hideo Kojima and famous horror film director Guillermo del Toro. Before the game could be finished, however, a break occurred between Kojima and Konami, the company that produced the game, which meant the installment was canceled. The game was subsequently removed from the PlayStation Store and, unusually, the possibility to re-install the game was eliminated, meaning that the game was essentially eradicated from existence.[1] Despite this, the influence of *P.T.* as a horror video game is immense. Not only is it regarded as one of the best horror games of all time, despite being a playable teaser (Purdom et al., 2018), but this "king of horror" (Nakamura, 2014) has also been described as "reimagining the horror genre" (Coskrey, 2014), evident in the massive influence *P.T.* has had on subsequent horror games, including *Layers of Fear, Visage*, and the critically-acclaimed *Resident Evil 7*.

As such, *P.T.* had substantial impact on popular culture, despite the fact that it is considerably shorter than most video games. However, very few studies have explored *P.T.* in relation to narratives surrounding crime and justice. As the influence and interest of this game remains strong even years later, evident for instance in the PC ports or remakes made by fans (Frank, 2018), this lack of scholarly attention is problematic. Not only does this lack of knowledge mean that the significance and effects of *P.T.*'s narrative remain unexplored, but this also means that the game's impact on popular culture

DOI: 10.4324/9781003346869-4

and the public imaginary of crime and justice is unknown. Drawing on the framework of popular criminology, this chapter will therefore critically examine the narratives of domestic violence in *P.T.*, interrogating the portrayal of perpetrators of such violence and how this relates to the public imaginary of domestic violence. As a framework that invites us to examine the representation of crime and punishment in its own right to uncover important public discourses surrounding criminality, popular criminology (Rafter, 2006, 2007) allows us to explore how a cultural text such as *P.T.* can affect the public imaginary of violence.

The spectral legacy of the game, suggested by the way the game seems to linger, despite having been removed, does not only haunt the gaming community, influencing the horror games subsequently produced, but its representation of horror and violence, of violence as lurking within the mundane, also haunts our understanding of horror. This also relates to the public imaginary around violence. In light of this, this chapter will also draw on ghost ethnography to contextualize the game in its absence and to understand how the lingering traces of this spectral game relates to the public imaginary of domestic violence. As such, this chapter lingers interstitially in the intersection of popular criminology, cultural criminology, and ghost ethnography, drawing on ideas of the meaning and relevance of narratives in games-as-texts and their effect on the public imaginary of crime and criminality.

We begin our analysis by first exploring how domestic violence is represented within the game, exploring how visual representations of domestic space relates to narratives of domestic abuse. This first part of our analysis will establish the centrality of domestic violence in the overall narrative of *P.T.* Second, we will explore how perpetrators of domestic violence are portrayed within the game; delineating how the game firmly roots domestic violence in the mundane, and thereby providing critique against the Othering of domestic violence perpetrators.

Before moving on to the results, however, the chapter will examine how video games in general, and the *Silent Hill* franchise in particular, have been interrogated in previous research, as well as providing the theoretical underpinnings for the analysis.

Video Games and *Silent Hill* in Previous Research

In recent years, scholars have begun to consider video games as more than just entertainment, but as cultural texts that hold, reflect, and transmit important meaning in relation to crime and culture (Rafter, 2007; Skott & Skott Bengtson, 2022; Steinmetz, 2018). Such work approaches gaming as a form of "popular criminology"—a "discourse parallel to academic criminology and of at least equal social and intellectual significance" (Rafter, 2007,

p. 404). Research utilizing this framework explores the reciprocal relationship between popular culture and crime, regarding popular cultural texts as meaningful conduits for publicly held understandings and explanations for crime and justice (Ferrell et al., 2015; Rafter, 2007). As such, popular criminology entails discourses about crime found in popular culture, including films, music, and video games, which both reflect societal ideas of criminality and justice as well as affect these ideas (Rafter, 2006, 2007). As Rafter (2007) argues, a popular discourse about crime needs to be recognized as well as analyzed if we are to fully understand the study of crime itself. This sort of analysis encourages the critical study of video games as cultural texts relevant for public policy as well as the public imaginary.

For instance, previous research that has explored the meaning of video games as cultural texts and their impact on the public imaginary surrounding crime has studied *Batman: Arkham Asylum* and *Batman: Arkham City* (Fawcett & Kohm, 2019). Exploring the representation of violence, crime, and madness in these two games, Fawcett and Kohm argued that while the games provide an elision of crime and madness, they also offer subversive and critical readings of this elision, allowing for critical reflections on contemporary criminal justice. Drawing on ideas of gothic and popular criminology as well as hauntology (Derrida, 1994), Skott and Skott Bengtson (2022) also explored themes of carcerality in the video game *The Legend of Zelda: Majora's Mask*, identifying themes of carceral violence within the text symptomatic of a haunting disillusionment with carceral justice.

One popular game series that has received much academic attention, is *Silent Hill*. For instance, Steinmetz (2018) explored carcerality as public imaginary in this game series, arguing that the games depict monstrous forms of retribution and punishment, which provokes critical questions about punitive ideologies and institutions of control. Other studies have explored the interconnected anxieties surrounding motherhood and childhood within the games, examining the construction of monstrous femininity and the monstrous child (Kirkland, 2008) and the uncanny as it is expressed by the appearance of the double, animism and involuntary repetition in *Silent Hill 2* (Green, 2021). Kirkland (2005, 2009) also explored the construction and representation of masculinity of the series' protagonists, arguing that the games tend to domesticate as well as feminize the male protagonists, grounding the games' narratives in the mundane and the ordinary. As such, while the games in the *Silent Hill* series have revolved around horror and the spine-chilling encounters with various psychological monsters, the series has always remained firmly rooted in the domestic; reveling in the horror of the mundane.

Despite the evident popularity of *P.T.*, which is part of the *Silent Hill* universe, very few studies have examined this game academically and even fewer have done so through a criminological framework. Exploring the interplay of representations of domestic violence and female body horror in *P.T.*, Chevalier (2021, p. 1) discovered that while the game critiqued domestic violence, it still "capitalize[d] upon the female victim, using her body as a source of shock-factor horror." Being part of a problematic horror media tradition, Chevalier (2021) argued that *P.T.* presented a narrative where real-world trauma is relegated to the realms of the fantastical and the monstrous. While Chevalier's study explores narratives of domestic violence in *P.T.*, it does not situate *P.T.* within the broader *Silent Hill* canon, nor does it explore how the narratives of domestic violence in *P.T.* relates to the publicly held understandings of this crime. As previous research has shown, the public imaginary of domestic violence both affects and is affected by narratives evident in popular culture (Skott et al., 2021). Such narratives of domestic violence, evident in various cultural mediums, usually portray offenders as unfamiliar, uncivilized, and extraordinary, harking back to ideas of "perfect offenders" and "perfect victims" (Christie, 1986; Rafter & Ystehede, 2010; Skott et al., 2021). Echoing the idea of Lombroso's atavistic other which "turned the criminal into a creature utterly different from normal man: a vampire, an atavism, a degenerate, closer to apes and savages and rodents than to law-abiding citizens" (Rafter & Ystehede 2010, p. 282), such narratives usually involve the pathologizing or vilification of offenders, where domestic violence perpetrators are constructed as either "mad" or as purely evil. These narratives work to distance domestic violence perpetrators from normal, ordinary men, effectively reinforcing the stereotype of dichotomized masculinities, where men are divided into "the respectable" and "the dangerous." As such, the perpetration of domestic violence is relegated to "abnormal," Othered men where the violent actions of ordinary men are obscured by discourses of violent monstrosity (Hatty, 2000).

P.T. is not the only game to comment on Othering and domestic violence in video games. For instance, the perpetrators of the medical and sexual violation of Alma in *F.E.A.R* (2005) were portrayed as corporate psychopaths, conducting the violence as part of medical experiments. Similarly, Jack Baker, who severely abuses his son Lucas in *Resident Evil 7* (2017), cutting off his hand with a knife, was portrayed as an evil fungi-infected serial killer. In another example, Alfred and Alexia Ashford, who both abused and imprisoned their father in *Resident Evil—Code: Veronica* (2000), were portrayed as inhumane psychopaths, who, in the case of Alexia, literally mutates into a monster later in the game. As such, the Othering of perpetrators of domestic violence appears to be a common theme in video games, where the offender is either pathologized or demonized in the games' narratives. Domestic violence is here understood to include different forms of violence that occur within the confines of the domestic, including intimate partner violence, violence between children and parents, and violence between siblings.

As *P.T.* is part of the *Silent Hill* universe, the following section will contextualize *P.T.* within the larger canon of *Silent Hill*.

P.T. and *Silent Hill*

The game series of *Silent Hill* is a horror media franchise developed and published by the Japanese company Konami, centered on a series of survival horror games that was heavily influenced by psychological horror. As a Japanese product created for both Japanese and Western audiences, the *Silent Hill* series has previously been considered reflective of both Japanese and Western cultural formations (Steinmetz, 2018). From 1999, eight main games have been released; *Silent Hill* (1999), *Silent Hill 2* (2001), *Silent Hill 3* (2003), *Silent Hill 4: The Room* (2004), *Silent Hill: Origins* (2007), *Silent Hill: Homecoming* (2008), *Silent Hill: Shattered Memories* (2009) and *Silent Hill: Downpour* (2012). Primarily the first four games received favorable reviews, with *Silent Hill 2* especially garnering widespread acclaim and being praised as one of the best horror games and one of the best games of all time (Meikleham, 2022). At the time of writing, new upcoming games in the franchise have been announced, including a remake of *Silent Hill 2*, and the ninth installment *Silent Hill: F* (Saunders, 2022).

As part of the *Silent Hill* universe, many of the characteristics and narratives prevalent in previous installments can also be found within *P.T.* As in most of the other *Silent Hill* games, the protagonist of *P.T.* is an average, everyday man, similar to *Silent Hill's* Harry Mason (a writer), *Silent Hill 2's* James Sunderland (a clerk), and *Silent Hill: Origin's* Travis Grady (a truck driver). Unlike in most other game series, where the protagonist is often depicted as a heroic archetype, the main characters of *Silent Hill* are intentionally chosen as regular, ordinary people (Perron, 2012).

Narratives of punishment and retribution are also very prevalent in the game series, and the titular town of Silent Hill, which serves as the narrative discourse for the entire franchise, is permeated by themes of punishment as well as guilt. Narratives of guilt can for instance be found in multiple installments, expressed both through the acceptance of guilt as well as through its deflection. In *Silent Hill 2*, James Sunderland, Angela Orosco, and Eddie Dombrowski initially try to deflect their own guilt over the transgressions they individually committed. Out of the three, James is the only one to fully admit to his guilt and is ironically the only one who has the option to leave Silent Hill alive, depending on which ending the player achieves. Meanwhile, Eddie is killed by James in an act of self-defense, while Angela is heavily implied to have committed suicide at the end of the game.

In *Silent Hill: Downpour*, the protagonist Murphy Pendleton, while in prison, murdered a child molester and killer, Patrick Napier, who murdered Pendleton's son. However, it's also revealed that he may have also murdered an innocent corrections officer, in return for his vengeful justice as part of a favor to cover up a corrupt man. Pendleton's guilt becomes a central theme throughout the game, evidenced for instance in the face reveal of the antagonistic creature called the Bogeyman, who wears both Napier's and Pendleton's features interchangeably.

Silent Hill 2 furthermore contains extremely tangible examples of inter-twining narratives of both guilt and punishment. James Sunderland is at-tracted to Silent Hill to find his wife Mary, despite having murdered her himself. Several corpses can be found littered across the town, all with hair and clothing with striking similarity to James, but the game never allows the player to see their faces. Pyramid Head, a monster that violently assaults the game's feminine, sexualized enemies, is a symbolic manifestation of Sunderland's desire for punishment, as explicitly stated within the game. It's an executioner created from his guilt over the truth that he murdered his own wife, faceless like the corpses.

The town itself can thus be regarded as a personal form of purgatory for its inhabitants, with either religious or psychological connotations, where the town punishes characters weighed down by guilt of previous crimes (Steinmetz, 2018). This punishment, which often includes retributive and even torturous elements, is individually tailored, meaning that the monsters and horrors experienced in Silent Hill differ depending on who enters it. For instance, Angela in *Silent Hill 2* is haunted by another monster, strongly suggestive of her traumatic past. As James defends her against a creature called Abstract Daddy, James perceives this monster as consisting of two humanoid figures, interlocked together on a bed frame, trapped underneath a sheet-like layer of skin. However, according to the art director and monster designer Masahiro Ito, Angela observes something different from James and the player, shaped by her own trauma and experiences (Ito, 2013, 2017, 2019a, 2019b). The monster design we witness in the game is clearly affected by James' perception, and consists of an amalgamation of James' guilt relat-ing to Mary as well as his ideas of what happened to Angela. Meanwhile, a child named Laura does not seem to perceive any of the creatures present in the town at all. A small girl, with no guilt or transgression, perceives nothing but fog, while others perceive monstrosities formed from their subconscious.

The psychological perception of creatures in *Silent Hill* is thus a mystery that is never truly resolved. In *Silent Hill 3*, there is a moment of doubt re-garding the true nature of the monsters the player has faced. The protagonist Heather is asked by Vincent, a member of the cult, whether "they look like monsters to you?," suggesting that the monsters she has been killing were in fact human, only distorted by Heather's own point of view. Although this is afterwards described as a twisted joke, the delivery of this moment induces uncertainty of what the true nature of these creatures are. This is one exam-ple in which the nature of Silent Hill gains a complex psychological dimen-sion that is defined by its uncertainty due to the fragmented perception the player experiences through the lens of the franchise's protagonists (Perron, 2012). Monsters and uncanny inconsistencies to reality that can be witnessed in Silent Hill throughout the game series can therefore be considered reflec-tions or projections of the main characters psyches; delusions reflecting the protagonists' twisted mentalities (Perron, 2012).

As such, in *P.T.* as well as in the rest of the *Silent Hill* franchise, it can both be argued that the aberrations perceived by the player are present as supernatural entities, and that they are merely products of mentally unstable, guilty, or drug-addled minds. Ultimately however, the purgatorial nature of Silent Hill, where the creatures, monsters, and experiences of the town changes depending on who enters it, renders this distinction irrelevant. Whether the experiences are real or figments of someone's mind is consequently beside the point as in both cases, they represent projections from the denizens' psyches.

Themes of domestic violence have also been very prevalent in previous *Silent Hill* installments. For instance, it is revealed in *Silent Hill 2* that James Sunderland had murdered his wife all along, even though most of the game is about finding out what really happened to her. In a similar vein, the protagonist Alex in *Silent Hill: Homecoming* is revealed to have accidentally killed his brother Joshua, even though he spends most of the game trying to find him. *Silent Hill 1, Silent Hill 3*, and *Silent Hill: Origins* all feature the character Alessa Gillespie who was tortured by her mother and the cult for occult purposes, instigating to the very origins of Silent Hill itself. There is furthermore a non-canonical ending in *Silent Hill: Downpour* that suggests that the protagonist Murphy in fact killed his own son and is set for execution. As such, domestic violence has been a prevalent theme in almost all of the *Silent Hill* games.

The following section will provide a brief description of the overall gameplay of *P.T.*

An Overview of *P.T.*

The game begins as the silent, faceless male protagonist wakes up on the floor of a concrete-lined room in front of a door. Upon walking through this door, the protagonist arrives at a hallway that continuously loops upon itself whenever he tries to leave through the only other open door. Dried up potted plants dot the hallway and old, dusty, and often broken or torn photographs and paintings line the walls. A digital clock is stuck ominously at 23:59. The protagonist will eventually be trapped in one singular loop unless he solves specific puzzles to progress. However, by solving these puzzles, the hallway and environment begin to deteriorate, becoming increasingly more hostile, emphasized by a female ghost haunting him. As the loops descend further into chaos, so are uncomfortable truths revealed. Only by confronting these truths and solving the puzzles is the protagonist allowed to properly leave the hallway and go outside, ending the game.

The Spectrality of *P.T.*

Before moving on to the methodology, we offer a brief reflection of the spectral nature of *P.T.* As previously mentioned, Konami's decision to delete and remove *P.T.* from all stores and consoles has left *P.T.* largely unavailable to study in its original form. Yet, the influence of the game still lingers, evident for instance by the many fan-based remakes and PC ports that have appeared, only to swiftly removed—or exorcized—from the platforms (Chapman, 2018; Frank, 2018). This haunting legacy of the game, being present while non-present, visible yet invisible, imbues the game with a certain spectral quality. As such, we are inspired by an approach which focuses on teasing out the spectral, namely ghost ethnography. As Armstrong (2010, p. 243) stated, "ghost" or "spectral" ethnography can be described as "a kind of ethnography of absence, an anthropology of people, and places and things that have been removed, deleted and abandoned to the flows of time and space." As such, it is a method focused on the excluded, the non-present and not-quite-there, aiming to "excavate absence" (Ferrell, 2022), as "an archaeology of the emptied present and of the vacant spaces of culture" (Armstrong, 2010, p. 243).

Drawing on the work of Armstrong (2010) and Ferrell (2016), we therefore attempt to explore *P.T.* despite its absence, studying the lingering traces left behind as "hollowed-out and spectrally resonant spaces of culture" (Armstrong, 2010, p. 243), in order to explore the effects still lingering of this ghostly remnant of a game. As such, we use ghost ethnography as a tool to understand the meaning of the game in the context of its absence and elimination. Considering it a "ghost text," "the subjective and nonhuman presences of culture" (Armstrong, 2010, p. 249), we study the spectral remnants of *P.T.* that linger to explore its impact on our culture and the public imaginary of violence.

Method

As the game was inaccessible to us in its original form, we instead chose to study uploaded videos of other people playing these games on YouTube, commonly known as playthroughs or Let's Plays, to analyze the game.[2] While this meant that we were not able to analyze a first-hand account of the game where we played through the game ourselves, the inaccessibility of the game left us with few options. Instead, playthroughs and Let's Plays of *P.T.* were watched, re-watched, and carefully analyzed using ethnographic content analysis (Altheide, 1987). As a highly reflexive and interactive method, ethnographic content analysis "documents and understands the communication of meaning, as well as verify theoretical relationships," and has been used in previous studies exploring video games (Skott & Skott Bengtson, 2022; Steinmetz, 2018). Using this approach, we analyzed the game's narratives, images, characters, plot devices, game mechanics, monsters and scenery, taking extensive notes and discussing our conclusions in depth as we watched the material. Our analysis was specifically focused on exploring narratives of domestic violence in *P.T.*, how perpetrators of such violence was portrayed and how these constructions related to the public imaginary of domestic violence. As one of the authors had also played the game before *Silent Hills* was canceled, their experiences and memories of the game was also included in the material.

Results

Removing the Veil: Representations of Domestic Violence

> The home is fundamentally predicated on aggression and fear rather than kindness and security.
>
> (Sorfa, 2006, p. 93)

Narratives of domestic violence is evident from the very beginning of *P.T.* The very space in which the entire game takes place can be considered the epitome of mundane, abused domestic space. We are walking through poorly lit hallways, cluttered with personal items and trash, including dusted family photographs, withering potted plants, empty beer cans, filled ashtrays, scuttling cockroaches, and numerous framed paintings covering the walls. The clear clues of familiarity as we enter the hallways firmly establish the environment not only as a domestic space, but as a neglected, possibly haunted, domestic space. The subject of domestic violence is subsequently introduced very quickly into the game's narrative. The radio transmissions of the very first loop of the hallway describes a familicide and two other domestic homicides happening in the area:

> [. . .] [W]e regret to report the murder of the wife and her two children by their husband and father. The father purchased the rifle used in the crime at his local gunstore two days earlier. This brutal killing took place while the family was gathered at home on a Sunday afternoon. The day of the crime, the father went to the trunk of his car, retrieved the rifle, and shot his wife as she was cleaning up the kitchen after lunch. When his ten-year-old son came to investigate the commotion, the father shot him, too. His six-year-old daughter had the good sense to hide in the bathroom, but reports suggest he lured her out by telling her it was just a game. The girl was found shot once in the chest from point-blank range. The mother, who he shot in the stomach, was pregnant at the time.
>
> *(P.T., 2014)*

As this gruesome description of acts of domestic violence is provided at the very beginning of the game, domestic violence is cemented as a central theme, grounding the game in a narrative of domestic violence. Before the protagonist even has had the chance to get his bearings, violence has irrupted into the everyday life the game evokes. While this violence is not immediate or even visible, it lingers, shaping the main narrative of the game.

The narrative of domestic violence is intensified as the game wears on. After a few more loops through the endless hallway, a big X and a message reading "Gouge it out!" appears on a woman in a framed wedding photograph. As the player engages with this picture, pressing X, the woman's eye is seemingly gouged out, a black-and-white sludge dripping from the hole in the picture. The pictured husband puts his thumb up in approval as this occurs. A few loops later, the protagonist is then encountered with a peep hole in the wall, allowing him to peek into the bathroom. While nothing is explicitly shown, this triggers the sounds of a woman being brutally stabbed to death, overlaid with the sounds of a new radio transmission, urging the listener that it's "time for action" and that "you know what to do! Now's the time! Do it!" (*P.T.*, 2014). As the protagonists then enters the bathroom, a voice, possibly emanating from the deformed fetus in the sink, can be overheard, making insinuating remarks about infidelity.

As these instances all occur in a domestic setting, perpetrated in the context of an intimate relationship, they are all clearly suggestive of domestic violence against women, which further cements domestic violence as the central narrative theme of *P.T.* This narrative is further emphasized by the haunting presence of the female ghost that appears in the hallway. This specter, usually referred to as Lisa, appears heavily pregnant in a once-white, soiled dress, stained with dirt and blood. One of her eyes appears to be gouged out, and the massive blood stain appears to be centered around her lower abdomen. As this ghostly image relates to other narrative clues in the game in various ways, the game's narrative is suggesting that Lisa, too, was a victim of domestic abuse. This is further supported by the fact that the ghost appears in relation to the bathroom, where the fetus in the sink is found as well as where the protagonist is encountered with the sounds of a woman being murdered.

This overarching narrative of domestic violence in *P.T.* is furthermore illustrated by the gradual perversion of the home. As the protagonist moves through the game, the mundane, domestic space in which the game begins becomes increasingly uncanny. As the boundaries of familiar and unfamiliar, self and other, interior and exterior elide, the uncanny embodies the home that has been turned unhomely (Fiddler, 2017). In fact, in the original German, the "unheimlich" directly translates to the "unhomely" or that which is "not from the home." The haunting presence of the ghost Lisa, hunting you through the hallways, along with appearances of cryptic messages, the disembodied sounds of crying children, strange radio messages, and blood, gradually turns the home unfamiliar. As such, *P.T.* distorts the domestic space, highlighting the home as a deeply unsafe place, a site of violence and fear that is inherently inescapable. No matter where you go, you always end up at the start of that hallway once more, unable to leave the house. This likens the domestic space in *P.T.* to a prison, which the game visually articulates further through the use of barred windows, and the constant, ever-present surveillance evident through the presence of pictured eyes later in the game, as well as by Lisa herself. Watching us from above, peeking over the banister of the upstairs staircase, itself a "site of clandestine surveillance and voyeurism" (Fiddler, 2017, p. 546), Lisa silently follows our every move. She also appears at random locations (e.g., outside the window, in the mirror reflection etc.), constantly watching, shadowing the protagonist. The sounds of another set of footsteps, following right behind you, furthermore becomes noticeable a bit further into the game, suggesting Lisa is constantly following right behind you.

The deeper we get into the game, the more pervasive the narrative of domestic abuse becomes, and the more perverted the domestic space appears. This would suggest that the increased distortion of the home reflects the horrifying cultural trauma of domestic violence, projecting the experience of domestic violence as inescapable, confining, and haunting.

Overall, these instances establish the centrality of domestic violence in the overall narrative of *P.T.* To examine how the game reflects as well as affects the public imaginary around this crime, we now turn to explore how *P.T.* portrays the perpetrators of domestic violence.

"There is a Monster Inside of Me": Perpetrators of Domestic Violence

> [Monsters] are paradoxical personifications of *otherness within sameness*.
> (Beal, 2002, p. 6, emphasis in original)

As *P.T.* firmly establishes domestic violence at its central theme, the game furthermore situates this violence in a mundane, ordinary context. The perpetrators of domestic violence described in *P.T.* are not extraordinary, evil, or insane; rather, these men are portrayed as ordinary family fathers. As the initial broadcast clearly explains:

> There was another family shot to death in the same state last month, and in December last year, a man used a rifle and meat cleaver to murder his entire family. In each case, the perpetrators were fathers. State police say the string of domestic homicides appears unrelated, though it could be part of a larger trend, such as employment, childcare, and other social issues facing the average family.
>
> *(P.T., 2014)*

As this central radio broadcast explains, the perpetrators of lethal domestic violence were seemingly ordinary fathers, part of "average" families. The explanations for the violence are situated in societal trends, such as issues with unemployment or other social issues, rather than within the individual mind of the offender.

This theme is later echoed in the scene with the fetus in the sink, where a disembodied voice, possibly the fetus itself, suggests that the motives behind the act of domestic homicide were jealousy, unemployment, and alcohol abuse:

> You got fired, so you drowned your sorrows in booze. She had to get a part-time job working a grocery store cash register. Only reason she could earn a wage at all is the manager liked how she looked in a skirt. You remember, right? Exactly ten months back.
>
> *(P.T., 2014)*

These examples highlight the ordinary and mundane character of the perpetrators of domestic abuse, situating this violence within an everyday context, rendering the offenders familiar and normal rather than unfamiliar and strange. Kojima himself has stated that the main character purposefully was cast as an ordinary person (Coskrey, 2014) and that a simple hallway was chosen as the setting rather than something like a ruin in order to evoke the everyday, regardless of the players' cultural background (Klepek, 2015).

The very last dialogue before the ending sequence, spoken by the same voice that encouraged action as you heard a woman being murdered, also reinforces this idea of average and seemingly "normal" offenders:

> Dad was such a drag. Every day he'd eat the same kind of food, dress the same, sit in front of the same kind of games . . . Yeah, he was just that kind of guy. But then one day, he goes and kills us all! He couldn't even be original about the way he did it.
>
> *(P.T., 2014)*

While this quote almost trivializes the acts of domestic homicide, it simultaneously underlines the ordinary nature of domestic violence and domestic violence offenders, firmly rooting this type of violence in the normal rather than the strange or extraordinary.

Similarly, the protagonist himself is portrayed as someone very ordinary, without any combat skills or even access to weapons. Armed with only a flashlight, dressed in everyday clothes, the protagonist, whose face isn't revealed until the final cutscene, is an everyday man, in typical *Silent Hill* fashion. While the game never explicitly states that the protagonist has committed domestic violence, there are several elements present within the game's narrative that allows for such a reading. For instance, while the repetitive, entrapping loop of the never-ending hallway can be understood as a reflection of the confining experience of domestic violence, this can also be read as being trapped in an ever-lasting cycle of punishment. Not being able to escape, with increasingly more disturbing visions of violent acts, the protagonist is forced to repeat the same stretch of hallway, again and again, reliving the traumatic events that occurred there in the past. The fact that the Lisa's vengeful ghost appears to be hunting the protagonist, watching him, killing him at certain points in the game also speaks to the protagonist's guilt.

While these events might not be directly related to the protagonist's own experiences, they are, in accordance with *Silent Hill* canon, the manifestations of someone's guilty mind. As the narratives of previous *Silent Hill* games would suggest that the experience of Silent Hill's purgatory can differ vastly between characters, it can be reasonably assumed that the haunting and violent experiences of *P.T.* in some way is a manifestation of the protagonist's own guilt. As such, all the horrifying events and experiences of domestic violence occurring within the game can be understood to be shaped by the guilt of a central character, most likely the protagonist. In light of this, the average, everyday character of the protagonist becomes even more important. If it is in fact the protagonist himself who has committed these violent acts against Lisa, which is a narrative that has been prevalent in previous *Silent Hill* installments, most notably in *Silent Hill 2*, the construction of this perpetrator is that of a normal, everyday man; not a monster. In fact, as the game progresses, a message appears above the door at the end of the hallway, reading "Forgive me, Lisa. There's a monster inside of me" (*P.T.*, 2014).

This message is not only indicative of the protagonist's guilt of having committed domestic violence, but it is also suggestive of a multifaceted, pluralistic understanding of the Other. Importantly, the text does not declare that the person writing it *is* a monster; merely that a monster exists *inside of them*. As such, this allows for the simultaneous existence of the Other, or the monstrous, within the Self, suggesting in fact that the monstrous Other was always and already *within* the protagonist's average, everyday mind. This does not only allow for a multifaceted understanding of offending behavior, but the game effectively also provides a critique for the entire Othering process.

This critique of the process of Othering becomes even more evident when we, at a later point in the game, are killed by Lisa and re-emerge in the concrete room where the game initially began. A blood-soaked paper bag appears on a table, and as the player engages with the paper bag, it begins to speak:

> I walked. I could do nothing but walk. And then, I saw me walking in front of myself. But it wasn't really me. Watch out. The gap in the door . . . it's a separate reality. The only me is me. Are you sure the only you is you?
>
> *(P.T., 2014)*

This statement, made by the unknown contents of the bag, provides a clear indication that the protagonist may not be who he seems; that there may be more than one aspect of his persona or personality, beyond good or evil. Much like a tell-tale heart, the bloodied bag is suggestive of the protagonist's guilt, divulging secrets in the basement, buried underneath the floorboards, but this statement also provides a critique against the process of Othering offenders, as the "you," in fact, is not the *only* "you." The protagonist, as well as all the other perpetrators of domestic violence that figures in the narrative of *P.T.*, are ordinary, everyday-men even though they committed extraordinary acts of violence. They are not evil, or insane, but average family fathers. As such, the game's narrative is rendering them *both* monstrous and mundane. The protagonist is the repressed that returns, and while the monster existed inside of him this entire time, this was not the only version of him; the only you is therefore *not* you, but simply a part of you. As such, *P.T.* serves to critique the process of Othering violent offenders by breaking down the myth of separation between Self and Other (England, 2006; Fiddler, 2013, p. 285), exposing that the Other, in fact, already dwells within; that we all have the potential of becoming violent offenders, with secret monsters hiding inside of us.

Discussion and Conclusion

Drawing on Rafter's (2007) framework of popular criminology as well as ghost ethnography, this chapter has aimed to critically examine narratives of domestic violence in the video game *P.T.*, interrogating the portrayal of perpetrators of such violence and how this relates to the public imaginary of domestic violence. By exploring the aesthetic accounts of domestic violence and domestic violence perpetrators within this spectral cultural text, we have argued that not only is domestic violence a central narrative to *P.T.*, but this game also offers a subversive critique against the process of Othering these offenders, demonstrating that the monstrous may always and already exist within the mundane.

As popular criminology, *P.T.* thus provides a critique against locating the causes of domestic violence within the twisted, disturbed psyche of abnormal, "mad" offenders, relegating the issue of domestic violence to a problem of abnormal, Othered men. Such discourses do not only displace the narratives of domestic violence, but they also feed into larger discourses of the medicalization of dangerousness and the pathologizing of offending behavior (see for instance Federman et al., 2009), underpinned by the belief that the perpetration of crime is a personal choice, unaffected by the effects of social structures. As such, narratives conflating mental illness and criminality risk reinforcing the biological etiology of crime, which in turn may lead to an emphasized Othering, if not a monstrification (see Skott et al., 2021) of offenders perpetrating domestic violence. While this could have long-lasting effects on punitive policies and the criminal justice system, advocating punitive populism and harsher punishment as the monstrous always needs to be annihilated (Skott et al., 2021; Valier, 2002), it also risks rendering violence committed by "normal" offenders invisible, as such "mundane" circumstances of violence do not fit within the imaginary of the monstrous.

An important limitation of this analysis is, however, its inherent subjectivity. While we argue that *P.T.* and the *Silent Hill* canon offers one of only a few prevalent examples where the Othering of domestic offenders is critiqued, this only constitutes one of many possible readings. Other scholars, using different theoretical frameworks might consequently conduct different readings of the text. As such, while Chevalier (2021) argues that *P.T.* displaces the cultural trauma of domestic violence to the realm of the fantastical and monstrous, our reading of the game is in fact the complete opposite. We would argue that by clearly contextualizing the domestic violence narratives in the mundane, *P.T.* in fact provides a critique against the displacement of domestic violence and the Othering of offenders of this crime, suggesting instead that the monstrous may exist in all of us.

In line with cultural criminological perspectives such as popular criminology, as well as the emerging field of Ghost Criminology (Fiddler et al., 2022), we can furthermore begin to explore the lingering effects such narratives may have on the public imaginary of violence, exploring how narratives prevalent in cultural texts such as *P.T.* may reflect and affect understandings of violence. As argued, the public imaginary of domestic violence both affects and is affected by popular culture narratives, evident in various cultural mediums, including video games (Skott et al., 2021). Such narratives of domestic violence tend to construct offenders as unfamiliar, uncivilized, and extraordinary, which not only echo the ideas of "perfect victims" and "atavistic offenders" (Christie, 1986; Rafter & Ystehede, 2010; Skott et al., 2021) but which also tend to divide men into "the respectable" and "the dangerous," relegating the perpetration of domestic violence to "abnormal," Othered men, obscuring the violent actions of ordinary men by discourses of violent monstrosity (Hatty, 2000). Such ideas and narratives have furthermore been exacerbated by the increased prevalence of punitive populism. Since *P.T.'s* release in 2014, punitive populism, alarmist rhetoric, and stricter punishment have been on the rise in most Western countries (Hermansson, 2018; Tham, 2018) as well as in Japan (Brewster, 2020). This punitive turn has been characterized by a declining confidence in rehabilitation as well a reduced belief in experts, a more favorable attitude towards punishment and an individualized discourse, framing the problem of crime as an individual or moral issue rather than a structural one (Estrada, 2004; Hermansson, 2018). As a Japanese-Western production, the narrative critiquing the Othering of domestic violence perpetrators prevalent in *P.T.* can be read as an opposing understanding of justice which challenges this punitive turn, as well as the dominant public imaginary of domestic violence, allowing for subversive understandings of violence.

However, as *P.T.* has been canceled and deleted; virtually exorcized from existence by its creators, this subversive reading of violence offered by the game has been removed along with it. This elimination of dissident perspectives on punitive populism can in itself be regarded a reflection of the punitive turn affecting Western as well as Japanese countries. Yet, the game spectrally lingers, evidenced by its persistent influence and fan-made remakes (Frank, 2018), bringing the game back to life. By drawing on ghost ethnography, the lingering effects of the narratives identified within this game has been exhumed, enabling us to tease out its spectral traces and to contextualize it in its absence. Excavating absence and exploring what is no longer there promotes a different kind of "seeing" (Armstrong, 2010; Ferrell, 2016), which serves to identify specters of the past still haunting us, exacerbating the temporal disjointedness affecting late modern life (Fiddler et al., 2022; Young, 2007). While no longer a playable game unless reanimated, this study has shown that *P.T.* remains starkly present in its absence, visible in its invisibility (Derrida, 1994). As such, *P.T.'s* narrative critiquing the Othering of domestic violence perpetrators still haunts punitive justice narratives, challenging the mainstream criminal justice discourses and carrying with it an injunction for change. By breaking down the boundaries between Other and Self; by demonstrating that we all have the potential to be both Self and Other and that the monstrous may in fact reside within all of us, *P.T.* simultaneously argues for a more nuanced understanding of the perpetration of domestic violence.

Such an understanding does not provoke punitive populism or demand harsher punishment for a particular, Othered group, but is rather suggestive of a more comprehensive, rehabilitative criminal justice. As previous video game scholars have argued (Fawcett & Kohm, 2019; Skott & Skott Bengtson, 2022), this subversive understanding of violence as popular criminology discourse becomes even more impactful due to the interactive and visceral experiences of gameplay, meaning that video games hold a very specific position in promoting critical dialogue on criminal justice issues. By exploring this critical potential in relation to narratives of domestic violence and the portrayal of domestic violence offenders, this chapter has demonstrated that video games such as *P.T.* not only can be considered relevant cultural texts which reflect real-life cultural anxieties, but that such games also hold the potential to critique and interrogate such anxieties, affecting the public imaginary around criminality as well as criminal justice issues.

Much like the Derridean specter, this game of the past consequently haunts our present in order to prompt a different future. And as we should attempt to "live with our ghosts" (Derrida, 1994), we must listen to this specter in order to hear its injunction. In these current times, when punitive populism, alarmist rhetoric, and stricter punishment are on the rise (Hermansson, 2018; Giritli Nygren et al., 2024), the subversive reading of the spectral remains of *P.T.* offers a critique against these criminal justice policies which, when exhumed and "given back their speech" (Derrida, 1994, p. 221) provides an injunction "in the other in oneself" (Derrida, 1994, p. 221) to which we need to listen.

Notes

1 There are some copies of the game still in circulation, particularly from people who kept it saved on their consoles.
2 For instance, one of the playthroughs we studied was SHN Survival Networks' playthrough: https://www.youtube.com/watch?v=bjDmGGtglEY

References

Altheide, D.L. (1987). Ethnographic content analysis. *Qualitative Sociology, 10*(1), 65–77. https://doi.org/10.1007/BF00988269

Armstrong, J. (2010). On the possibility of spectral ethnography. *Cultural Studies, Critical Methodologies, 10*(3), 243–250.

Beal, T.K. (2002). *Religion and its monsters*. Routledge.

Brewster, D. (2020). Crime control in Japan: Exceptional, convergent or what else? *British Journal of Criminology, 60*(6), 1547–1566.

Chapman, T. (2018). Konami shuts down fan-made Silent Hill P.T. Remake. *ScreenRant*. https://screenrant.com/silent-hills-p-t-remake-konami-removed/

Chevalier, K. (2021). *"Forgive Me, Lisa:" P.T., allegory, and the monstrous-feminine* [Unpublished Master's thesis]. University of Vermont. Retrieved February 27, 2024 from https://scholarworks.uvm.edu/hcoltheses/395

Christie, N. (1986). The ideal victim. In E.A. Fattah (Ed.), *From crime policy to victim policy* (pp. 17–30). Palgrave Macmillan.

Coskrey, J. (2014). Kojima's terrifying world of the unknown. *Japan Times*. https://web.archive.org/web/20150322074611/http://www.japantimes.co.jp/life/2014/09/26/digital/kojimas-terrifying-world-unknown/#.VZWcQvlVikr

Derrida, J. (1994). *Specters of Marx*. Routledge.

England, M. (2006). Breached bodies and home invasions: Horrific representations of the feminized body and home. *Gender, Place & Culture, 13*(4), 353–363.

Estrada, F. (2004). The transformation of the politics of crime in high crime societies. *European Journal of Criminology, 1*(4), 419–443.

Fawcett, C., & Kohm, S. (2019). Carceral violence at the intersection of madness and crime in Batman: Arkham Asylum and Batman: Arkham City. *Crime Media Culture, 16*(2), 265–285.

Federman, C., Holms, D., & Jacob, J.D. (2009). Deconstructing the psychopath: A critical discursive analysis. *Cultural Critique, 72*, 36–65.

Ferrell, J. (2016). Postscript: Under the slab. In M.H. Jacobsen & S. Walklate (Eds.), *Liquid criminology: Doing imaginative criminological research* (pp. 221–229). Routledge.

Ferrell, J. (2022). Ghost method. In M. Fiddler, T. Kindynis, & T. Linneman (Eds.), *Ghost criminology: The afterlife of crime and punishment* (pp. 67–87). New York University Press.

Ferrell, J., Hayward, K., & Young, J. (2015). *Cultural criminology* (2nd ed.). Sage.

Fiddler, M. (2013). Playing funny games in the last house on the left: The uncanny and the "home invasion" genre. *Crime, Media, Culture: An International Journal, 9*(3), 281–299. https://doi.org/10.1177/1741659013511833.

Fiddler, M. (2017). There's no place like home: Encountering crime and criminality in representations of the domestic. In M. Brown & E. Carrabine, (Eds.), *Routledge international handbook of visual criminology* (pp. 540–552). Routledge.

Fiddler, M., Kindynis, T., & Linnemann, T. (Eds.), (2022). *Ghost criminology*. New York University Press.

Frank, A. (2018). *P.T.* PC remake is playable, perfectly scary. *Polygon.* https://www.polygon.com/2018/7/2/17519118/pt-remake-windows-pc-free-download

Giritli Nygren, K., Nyhlén, N., & Skott, S. (2024). The spectropolitics of Swedish people's home: Tracing the "no longer" and the "not yet" in the Swedish 2022 election campaign [Manuscript submitted for publication]. Department of Humanities and Social Sciences: Mid Sweden University.

Green, J. A. (2021). "Aren't you Maria?" The uncanny and the Gothic in Silent Hill 2. *Gothic Studies, 23*(1), 1–20.

Hatty, S.E. (2000). *Masculinities, violence and culture*. Sage Publishing.

Hermansson, K. (2018). The role of symbolic politics in exceptional crime policy debate: A study of the 2014 Swedish general election. *Journal of Scandinavian Studies in Criminology and Crime Prevention, 19* (1), 22–40.

Ito, M. [@adsk4]. (2013, February 16). *"Abstract Daddy" means Angela's father (or brother) who is hanging over her body on a "bed."* [Tweet]. Twitter https://twitter.com/adsk4/status/302829911113084928

Ito, M. [@adsk4]. (2017, November 27). *The creatures of Silent Hill 2 have metaphor for James's guilt in order of appearance.* [Tweet]. Twitter https://twitter.com/adsk4/status/935208330728849408

Ito, M. [@adsk4]. (2019a, March 13). *Abstract Daddy which James was looking at was little different from Angela's one.* [Tweet]. Twitter https://twitter.com/adsk4/status/1105929282650427392

Ito, M. [@adsk4]. (2019b, February 18). *Only Angela knows what she sees, her Abstract Daddy.* [Tweet]. Twitter https://twitter.com/adsk4/status/1097577262612770816

Kirkland, E. (2005). Restless dreams in Silent Hill: Approaches to video game analysis. *Journal of Media Practice, 6*(3), 167–178.

Kirkland, E. (2008). Alessa unbound: The monstrous daughter of Silent Hill. In S. NiFhlainn (Ed.) *Dark reflections, monstrous reflections: Essays on the monster in culture* (pp. 73–78). Interdisciplinary Press.

Kirkland, E. (2009). Masculinity in video games: The gendered gameplay of Silent Hill. *Camera Obscura, 24*(2), 161–183.

Klepek, P. (2015). The 10 best horror video games. *Kotaku.* https://thebests.kotaku.com/the-10-best-horror-games-1685727700

Nakamura, T. (2014). Hideo Kojima and Shinju Mikami talk horror games. *Kotaku.* https://kotaku.com/hideo-kojima-and-shinji-mikami-talk-horror-games-1641562015

Meikleham, D. (2022). The 30 best video game stories ever. *GamesRadar.* https://www.gamesradar.com/the-best-videogame-stories-ever/

Perron, B. (2012). *Silent Hill: The terror engine*. University of Michigan Press.

Purdom, C., Hughes, W., Dowd, A.A., Barsanti, S., Breault, C., Budgor, A., Muncy, J., Gerardi, M., & Martin, G.D. (2018). The 35 greatest horror games of all time. *AV Club.* https://www.avclub.com/the-35-greatest-horror-games-of-all-time-1830082156

Rafter, N. (2006). *Shots in the mirror: Crime films and society* (2nd ed.). Oxford University Press.

Rafter, N. (2007). Crime, film and criminology. *Theoretical Criminology, 11*(3), 403–420. https://doi.org/10.1177/1362480607079584

Rafter, N., & Ystehede, P. (2010). Here be dragons: Lombroso, the Gothic and social control. In M. Deflem (Ed.), *Popular culture, crime and social control (Sociology of Crime, Law and Deviance, Vol. 14)* (pp. 263–284). Emerald Group.

Saunders, T. (2022). Silent Hill new games explained: Every project announced at showcase. *Radio Times.* https://www.radiotimes.com/technology/gaming/silent-hill-new-games/

Skott, S., Nyhlén, S., & Giritli Nygren, K. (2021). In the shadow of the monster: Gothic narratives of violence prevention. *Critical Criminology, 29*(2), 385–400.

Skott, S., & Skott Bengtson, K-F. (2022). "You've met with a terrible fate, haven't you?": A hauntological analysis of carceral violence in Majora's Mask. *Games and Culture, 17*(4), 593–613.

Sorfa, D. (2006). Uneasy domesticity in the films of Michael Haneke. *Studies in European Cinema, 3*(2), 93–104.

Steinmetz, K.F. (2018). Carceral horror: Punishment and control in silent hill. *Crime, Media, Culture: An International Journal, 14*(2), 265–287. https://doi.org/10.1177/ 1741659017699045

Tham, H. (2018). *Kriminalpolitik. Brott och straff i Sverige sedan 1965* [Criminal policy. Crime and punishment in Sweden since 1965]. Norstedts juridik.

Valier, C. (2002). Punishment, border crossings and the powers of horror. *Theoretical Criminology, 6* (3), 319–337.

Young, J. (2007). *The vertigo of late modernity.* Sage.

5

DEMONOLOGY, DARK FANTASY, AND THE DEVIL

Representations of Early Criminological Theory and Justice in *Diablo 2*

Chad Posick

In January of 1997, Blizzard Entertainment (*World of Warcraft, Starcraft, Overwatch*) released *Diablo,* a dungeon-crawling video game filled with angels, demons, and humans stuck in the middle of an epic battle between good and evil. The player starts in the town of Tristram where they learn that the world is in peril from demons led by one of the "prime evils": Diablo. The player (who can choose to be one of three "classes" including Warrior, Rogue, or Sorcerer) must make their way through 12 levels of dungeons culminating in a face-off with Diablo (a.k.a. The Lord of Terror) in Hell.

At the very beginning of the game, the player is introduced to a church taken over by evil reflecting what many individuals used to believe—and some still believe—is the cause of antisocial behavior. As the gameplayer enters the very first level, the character chimes somewhat famously, "the sanctity of this place has been fouled." That a church's sacred holiness is destroyed is a powerful introduction to the game and to the entire franchise as it sets the foundation for a grand standoff between good and evil with the world at stake.

Diablo ends with the player attempting to contain The Lord of Terror's soul within himself/herself and, instead, becomes possessed by Diablo. Thus, in *Diablo II* (released in June of 2000), the player must contend with the possessed warrior as well as Diablo's minions. Furthermore, Diablo has begun to set free his brothers, Mephisto and Baal (who make up the other two of the three prime evils). In this video game release, the player can experience the quests as a set of new characters including Amazon, Barbarians, Necromancer, Paladin, or Sorceress; all equipped to battle evil in fantastic fashion. Additionally, there are new expanded quests, new foes, as well as online

DOI: 10.4324/9781003346869-5

gameplay. Now over 20 years old, the game is still played by old and new gamers alike and enjoyed for its addictive quality of endless upgrading and questing for unique items (DarcFoolery, 2023).

Diablo II is an entertaining and fun experience that can be enjoyed by players of most ages (while violent, the main play is not gory and there is not much adult content). It also serves to illustrate important concepts in criminology and criminal justice. In this chapter, I discuss how *Diablo II* illustrates concepts around criminal behavioral theory, morality and sin, and punishment. The approach I take is mostly associated with demonological theories but includes other concepts related to antisocial behavior, criminal labeling, and criminal justice. I conclude with how media—particularly video games—plays an essential role in perceptions of criminal behavior and how society responds to wrongdoing by its members.

Why *Diablo II*?

The Entertainment Software Association (ESA) reports that there are currently over 3 billion video game players worldwide and 39% of these individuals regularly play action games which equates to 1.21 billion people (ESA, 2021). It is clear that there is a substantial number of people who play and may be influenced by video games. In fact, the most recent *Diablo* game as of this writing is *Diablo IV* which generated over US$665 million less than a week from its release. With that much attention, gamers are exposed to depictions of what society believed about crime and criminal behavior prior to the Enlightenment. While obviously fantastical, many individuals did believe that dark spirits roamed the earth much like in *Diablo* and that bad behavior was attributable to evil including possession. This provides an opportunity to illustrate early criminological thought to those who are familiar with the game.

The Diablo franchise includes the original *Diablo* game as well as (in order of release) *Diablo: Hellfire, Diablo II, Diablo II: Lord of Destruction, Diablo II: Resurrected, Diablo III, Diablo III: Reaper of Souls, Diablo III: Rise of the Necromancer, Diablo Immortal,* and *Diablo IV.* These games share many characteristics with slight differences between expansions such as additional or different weapons, characters, skills, and quests. Here, I will focus mainly on *Diablo II.* In this game, the storyline advances from the first game to include more focus on issues relevant to criminology and criminal justice without getting into the complex detail of later *Diablo* games which contain characters and quests outside the scope of the chapter. However, interested readers are encouraged to play and read about more recent games in the franchise as they progress the storyline and include more interesting topics including politics and cults.

The Story

Diablo II progresses through "acts" that are viewable through the player's "quest log." Acts are major segments of the game which each contain smaller segments called quests. When describing a topic in this chapter, I will use acts and quests to locate the topic within the game (e.g., Act 2, Quest 3). This is not always appropriate as some themes are found throughout major parts of the game. Concepts such as morality, evil, possession, and violence are ever present both within individual characters and places.

Diablo II is narrated by Marius who is the lone survivor after the Dark Wanderer (the player's character in the first *Diablo* game) loses control and releases hell upon Marius's village and tavern. The original version has four acts, and the expansion pack adds a fifth which is not a focus of my analysis. The story begins with Act I where the player is set in the Rogue Encampment. This Act is modeled after boreal forests in which the player must navigate through trees and plains. The main objective is to rescue the wise Deckard Cain from the original game and begin the search for the Dark Wanderer. It should be noted that Cain is a scholar and is very knowledgeable about evil and its place in the world. He is relied upon by the player and in-game characters alike much as a priest would be on such issues centuries ago. This gives the impression that Deckard is both wise and responsible, such as a religious figure in the Middle Ages who would be consulted on issues related to crime and justice.

In Act II, the player travels to Lut Gholein—modeled after the Middle East during the crusades—a time when evil appeared to be everywhere, and religious soldiers sought to bring their Christian religion to "cure" society. Here the player has a daunting challenge as they head into the tomb of a powerful mage, Tal-Rasha, who hosts a soulstone in his head where Baal exists. Soulstones are a key part of the Diablo story and are physical entities that can capture and contain evil beings such as the three prime evils.

Marius accidentally releases Baal from the soulstone and he joins the Dark Wanderer to search for their third brother Mephisto. Therefore, in Act III the player must make their way to the Temple of Kurast to confront Mephisto and the other brothers. The location of this Act is modeled after Central American jungles and the lost Mayan civilization. Here, the player must beat Mephisto and return him to the soulstone. Even when they do, Diablo escapes through a portal to hell. The adventurer must then travel to hell for the final act. In Act IV, which is located in the fiery inferno of hell, the player must defeat Diablo, return him to the soulstone, and destroy both soulstones that host Mephisto and Diablo.

The Analysis

Each Act of *Diablo II* offers illustrations of demonology or criminal justice "in action." I will discuss how the game brings forth these specific issues or concepts and what it offers the player in terms of understanding early theories of crime and justice. I'll also discuss why it is important to consider video games—such as the ones in the *Diablo* series—in analyses of crime and justice.

Before getting into how *Diablo II* illustrates the—often neglected—demonological perspectives on crime and crime control, it's worth noting that the player must set up their character before starting the game. While the character's appearance cannot be changed, the player can choose and name their "avatar." This itself is significant as gamers can begin to identify with their avatars and even change some of their beliefs and behaviors (Praetorius & Görlich, 2020). Therefore, not only does *Diablo II* give us a representation of various approaches on crime and criminal justice but might also shape thoughts and behaviors—however slightly (see Kolek et al., 2021).

Possession, Morality, Hate, and Fate: The Demonology of Diablo

The theme of possession (and "evil" broadly) is central to the *Diablo II* story. As mentioned, the previous hero in the first game is possessed by Diablo and goes on his or her path of destruction. Many of the foes in the games are also possessed, often by lesser demons. Before the Enlightenment period (also known as the Age of Reason) that started in 17th-century Europe and spread around most of the world, possession—and, by extension, evil—was seen as a legitimate theory of criminal behavior. In fact, it was a leading theory of crime in certain periods including through the Salem Witch Trials that took place from winter 1692 to summer 1693.

The Salem Witch Trials exemplify demonological theories as witches were literally thought to be doing the bidding of Satan and their acts were in direct services to him. The acts of witches were believed to be evil, and eradication of witches led to inhumane criminal justice responses including downing and burning at the stake. During this time, even the most educated and influential people bought in to the fact that witches existed to do evil at the Devil's behest (Schiff, 2015). And it didn't end there.

While witchcraft is no longer seen as a major cause of crime, one can still see the influence of the perspective in some cultures. In 2022, Papua, New Guinea saw a rise in what is referred to as sorcery-accusation-related violence (SARV). SARV generally consists of the public torture and killing of women accused of witchcraft. One instance involved a man named Jacob Luke who died of a likely heart attack or stroke in Lakolam Village in the Enga Provence. After his death, several women were accused of kaikai lewa—ripping out his heart and eating it to gain virility. After threats from Luke's tribe, one woman admitted to the practice. Along with eight other women, she was doused with gasoline and lit on fire. After surviving this horrific act, five of the women were then publicly tied naked to poles and sexually assaulted with hot irons. Research found that hundreds in the region had suffered similar fates and that, out of about 15,000 perpetrators, only 19 were incarcerated for their abhorrent crimes (Neubauer, 2022).

Anton Lutz, an activist who has rescued several women and children from these crimes stated in an interview with Al Jazeera (Neubauer, 2022):

> Many Christians are told that demons are real and that it is therefore plausible that there are evil people in the community who do Satan's bidding. I think it goes back to their theology, where they believe in incarnate spiritual evil, which makes it hard to take a stance against witch-hunting because they could be accused of defending witches.

As this quote illustrates, the idea that people on earth can do the bidding of an otherworldly entity can still be seen. It is also seen in *Diablo*. Witches appear regularly in earlier games and are a significant presence in later games (namely *Diablo IV*). In *Diablo II*, the player must battle and defeat Dark Familiars—a flying villain that tries to electrocute the player. Familiars are "friends" of witches and are often pet animals such as dogs and cats.

However, there are "good" witches, along with "bad" witches. For example, the first witch that the gameplayer meets (in the original *Diablo*) is Adria—a witch in town that assists the player. However, Adria was not always so good. In fact, she once was close with another witch, Maghda, who is a character in *Diablo III,* who joins Adria to start a cult that was built on the torture of others. Torture in the *Diablo* games and torture in society is a traditional form of social control. It is used to harshly punish those who break norms and to signal to others that non-conformity will be met with pain.

Many witches in *Diablo* are healers and practitioners of magic. Historically, "cunning folk" were folk healers and spell casters who helped people and warded off bad witches/spirits in the Middle Ages all the way up until the 20th century. The view of "good" witches is held today along with the views of bad witches exemplified in the SARV cases mentioned previously. In fact, a recent phenomenon found on the social media platform TikTok is what is referred to as "WitchTok." WitchTok is a group of proclaimed witches who share their ideas and insights with followers on the platform and the majority identify as light or good witches. The most popular of these individuals is Frankie Castanea who has almost 1.5 million followers and over 90 million likes on her witchcraft content—not a small sphere of influence (Jones, 2022).

The role of "evil" as a cause of crime and violence has certainly lessened across the globe. However, evil continues to be referred to as a cause of heinous crimes. After the mass shooting in an Aurora, Colorado movie theater in 2012, United States President Barack Obama gave a speech in Fort Myers, Florida where he stated, "Even as we learn how this happened and who's responsible, we may never understand what leads anyone to terrorize their fellow human beings like this. Such violence, such evil is senseless; it's beyond reason." He suggested prayer and reflection as a source of healing (NPR, 2012). Similarly, President Donald Trump referred to a school shooting in Florida as "a scene of terrible violence, hatred and evil," illustrating a leader once again referring to crime as evil (AP, 2018).

Demonological theories of crime locate antisocial behavior in otherworldly forces. Einstadter and Henry (2006) describe demonological theories through two periods: before and after Christianization. In the pre-Christian period, demonological theory was based on pagan ideals. pagans believed in many gods and that crime was an insult to those gods. Demons were the primary (if not sole) cause of crime as they do the bidding of the ultimate evil—Satan, The Devil, or chief demon. One can see this in *Diablo* as many of the game's monsters are demons who carry out the will of Diablo himself. Some even take similar names referring to Lucifer such as "Fallen One."

In demonological theories of criminal behavior, antisocial behavior can occur through a couple of mediums. First is through temptation. People can be tempted when they are weak-willed. Often, these individuals do not have a strong relationship with God and can be easily deceived and manipulated by evil forces. Because evil forces intend to inflict pain and terror in society, they can use the weak individual to carry out their criminal whims (Posick, 2018). Criminals in this way are viewed as heretics. Heretics have beliefs that are contrary to the church and its leaders. In later *Diablo* games, there are entire quests dedicated to obtaining a new character named The Heretic.

The second medium for evil to accomplish its goals is through possession. This perspective suggests that evil forces are able to "take over" a person's body and use it as if it is their own. Again, these are usually individuals who have weak faith. Individuals with strong faith can "ward off" spirits and fight against evil. Temptation and possession both engage in victim-blaming. The person who is tempted to commit crime and who becomes processed are responsible for their actions because it was their lack of faith that got them into trouble in the first place. The only salvation is through religion. Even today post-Enlightenment, there are those who believe that crime and antisocial behavior can be "cured" through religious counseling or Christian coaching (Einstadter & Henry, 2006). Other organizations, such as Prison Fellowship International, work to reform criminal justice and "cure" crime through religious conversion (Bernard et al., 2016).

It is not surprising that demonological perspectives were traditionally promoted by the church and religious individuals. One of the earliest and ardent supporters of this perspective was St. Augustine who, around

400 A.D., declared that evil was the cause of crime and that criminals were possessed by the Devil. In the early centuries A.D. and into the 1200s, most of the authority on crime and criminality came from the clergy. Morality, the key to being the strong-willed person described earlier who can fend off evil, was imparted by priests. Even today there is evidence that religious leaders continue to blame evil as the root cause of violence. In a 2014 speech given by Cardinal George Alencherry in Sarajevo, Bosnia, he declared that, "Violence is really coming from an evil inspiration, and this evil inspiration can come from any kind of phenomenon that happens in society" (quoted in Harris, 2014).

Wesleyan University philosopher Elise Springer cautions against referring to people—even those who commit acts of violence—as evil. In *Diablo,* as in the "real world," evil is something that corrupts the heart entirely. Evil people are driven not by societal forces but by individual corruption. Further, this corruption is irreversible and irredeemable. If criminals are evil, then there is no chance to rehabilitate these individuals. Paradoxically, if evil people are corrupted and driven by evil, then their morals are corrupted by otherworldly forces. This implies that it is impossible for them to be blameworthy and to take responsibility for their actions to benefit victims and society as a whole (Springer, 2022).

While demonological theories are now viewed by the vast majority of individuals as pseudoscientific, many still believe that immorality is a primary cause of criminal behavior that must be addressed through a strong relationship with God. Early demonological theories set the foundation for contemporary theories related to free-will and deterministic causes of crime. Religious perspectives suggest that people have free-will as granted by God and that antisocial behavior is the result of individual weakness. In *Diablo,* we see that many of the possessed were weak-willed and corrupted by evil. In fact, the name of one of the most popular villain groups is called The Corrupted.

The crux of the *Diablo* series is possession and rule by the three prime evils—Diablo, Mephisto, and Baal. In Act 1, Quest 3, the wise scholar of the franchise, Deckard Cain, explains the dark times ahead for the land of Tristram. To fill in the game player, Cain describes The Hero's descent into madness (basically this is the character one plays in the original *Diablo*). Importantly, he ascribes the decent to two major factors: (1) depression and (2) possession. The Hero became very depressed after his original quest and, perhaps because this made him vulnerable, he was possessed by Diablo. Throughout the game, mental and physical health, and possession are the major factors that account for sin and antisocial behavior. This is similar to the beliefs held in early centuries A.D. described previously which were sustained even into the Enlightenment period.

Not only was possession responsible for the fall of The Hero, but it's also responsible for one of the first quests in the game. In Act 1, Quest 2, the player must confront and beat a previously revered war captain who was corrupted and possessed by the "lesser" demon Andariel. This possessed captain, Blood Raven, represents what happens when someone is corrupted by evil. She (Blood Raven) was a previous hero who fought against Diablo until her possession by Andariel (one of the few female demons). This is not the only instance where gender is important in *Diablo II*. Charsi and Kashya (both female) in the Rogue Encampment are particularly interested in "strong warriors" when the player is a female character and are keen to point out how "many of our sisters" battled Diablo. There are feminist aspects that occur as the player makes their way through the game which was not found in the original *Diablo*. While beyond the scope of this chapter, a feminist bent to the game may reflect the storied history of demonological perspectives that overwhelmingly targeted women and girls suspected of witchcraft, possession, and evil. One need not look further than one of the most famous possession cases in popular culture to find 12-year-old Regan MacNeil of *The Exorcist* possessed by the demon Pazuzu. Even in the more recent movie, *The Whale*, the behavior of Ellie (played by Sadie Sink), is deemed to not stem from her troubled childhood but by evil.

A similar demonological theme that stands out in *Diablo II* is the concept of fate. Fate played a big part in determining behavior in pre-Enlightenment theories of crime. At the very end of Act II, Cain declares that heaven is directly interfering with human affairs because man cannot help himself. Dagnon, a magic shop owner in the town of Lut Gholein of Act II, suggests that what is happening is due to fate and there is little to be done. In this way, fate is set and unalterable.

Many people still believe in supernatural forces that dictate the fate of people in the natural world. A recent study by Wilt et al. (2023) found that the stronger the belief in supernatural forces (e.g., God(s), demons, ghosts) and impersonal forces (e.g., karma, fate, luck) the stronger the belief that they can have a tangible impact on the "real world." These effects can include bringing forth antisocial behavior and corrupting other people's wills. Research also indicates that belief in impersonal forces like karma and fate can impact attitudes toward justice. Individuals who believe that "bad" people will get what is coming to them because it is destiny or fate, or that their bad karma will come back to haunt them, are less likely to be vengeful and endorse harsh punishment (Goyal & Miller, 2023). Like Dagnon, those who steadily believe in fate think that little can be done to reverse what is already predestined and that supernatural forces will have the last say in human affairs.

Along with the sin that emerges from possession and evil, hatred is a common theme throughout the *Diablo* franchise. Mephisto—one of the prime evils—is the Lord of Hatred. In Act III, Quests 3 and 5, Ormus, a once wise mage who "now lives like a rat on a sinking vessel" (his own words), discusses the importance of hatred in criminality. In his view, the wickedness brought forth by supernatural forces has created a society of hatred. This hatred expressed is violence. For many, hatred can be seen in today's society and is a major psychological force that is responsible for the most heinous crimes (Gaylin, 2003). After all, how could one murder or torture someone who they do not hate?

Many believe that Ormus, walking around in loincloth and bare feet, is, himself, "insane" —a once very credible explanation for criminal and deviant behavior (Rafter et al., 2016). Moral insanity theories claim that those who commit violent crimes are uncontrollable and remorseless in their behavior (Rafter, 2004). While Ormus is not, to our knowledge, violent, he does appear to have mental health problems that may be related to his "homelessness." Decades worth of empirical research shows that poor mental health is positively associated with homelessness (Padgett, 2020). These tangential characters in *Diablo II* constantly remind players of the causes of crime and beliefs in justice.

Evil as a Label

In every Diablo game, the player must battle against a cadre of "bad guys." Most of these are various types of demons, undead, ghosts, and ghouls. Some of these villains have names that reflect religious devotion like Zealot, Guardian, Sexton, and Faithful. Others have names reflecting their evil such as Fallen One, Devilkin, Dark One, Burning Dead, and Hell Clan. Early labeling theories contend that the labels—or names—that people give one another can have profound impacts on how they see themselves. This is so much so that over time, a person can start to identify with their label. If someone is continually called evil, dark, or fallen, they can begin to view themselves that way and behave accordingly. Cooley (1902) described this as the "looking glass self." If you look in the mirror and only see the labels forced upon you, at some point, you'll become how society views you. While this may seem far-fetched in a game like *Diablo II*, it reinforces the concept of labels reflecting societal views of "others." And when people become "othered" it is much easier to see them as villains.

Another set of villains have names such as Deformed, Misshapen, and Grotesque. Early theories of criminal behavior contend that you can predict antisociality from physical features of a person's body. Those with physical deformities are particularly implicated as antisocial in these theories. These theories fit broadly in physiognomy. Demonological theory would suggest that evil people are corrupted on the inside and that can start to corrupt their physical bodies. Therefore, their bodies reflect their inner corruptness.

Punishment and Criminal Justice from a Demonological Perspective

Diablo II not only touches on criminological theory from a demonological perspective, but the criminal justice theory that emerges from these perspectives as well. One of the most profound and heartfelt comments by The Hero is when, as a Barbarian, he enters "The Jail" in Act 1, Quest 3. Upon seeing people locked away, The Hero declares that "no one deserves to be caged." When the player is an Amazon, she exclaims, "What nightmarish tortures took place here." The jail is filled with torture devices such as electric chairs and breaking racks. Blood covers the floor. These scenes remind us how far we have come and, possibly, make one think where we must go in the future. Possession is also seen as a form of being caged. Throughout Act IV, the player kills "trapped souls" to finally set them free. This concept is also reflected in the evil villain Enslaved. Freedom is seen as an ultimate goal in *Diablo II,* whether it be in this life or the next.

In *Discipline and Punish,* Michel Foucault (1975) argues that punishment that took place up until the 18th century was designed to be particularly harsh, gruesome, and open to the public. In other words, a spectacle (see also Bennett, 2021). This is exemplified throughout *Diablo II* but especially in Act 1. Criminals are punished harshly and publicly. Foucault describes this system of punishment as taking the sin out of the sinner—a direct impact on the physical body. The result is a reform of the soul.

Indeed, one of the contemporary interventions espoused by many religious individuals and groups is restorative justice. Instead of incarcerating or painfully punishing someone, repairing harm is principal. Restorative justice centers the victim and calls for the offender to take responsibility for their own actions and work to make the victim whole again. Research indicates that the restorative justice approach is successful in reducing recidivism and increasing satisfaction with the criminal justice system (Latimer et al., 2005). This approach is in direct opposition to the barbarity present in *Diablo* but serves to illustrate where we have been and hopefully where we are going in creating a fairer, more just and efficient, criminal justice system.

Diablo II character, Gris, discusses another criminal justice issue in Act II; vigilantism. At the point the player meets Gris, it is well known that Tristram is overtaken by evil. Most of this evil is related to possession from demons including Baal and Diablo. Like pre-Enlightenment thought, this was determined to be the explanation for bad behavior. It also suggests that the only response to evil behavior, aside from exorcism, is confinement (jail or dungeon). There is little law in Tristram and what exists is related to vigilantism. Lee Johnston (1996) argues that vigilantism has six necessary features: (i) it involves planning and premeditation by those engaging in it; (ii) its participants are private citizens whose engagement is voluntary; (iii) it is a form of "autonomous citizenship" and, as such, constitutes a social movement; (iv) it uses or threatens the use of force; (v) it arises when an established order is under threat from the transgression, the potential transgression, or the imputed transgression of institutionalized norms; (vi) it aims to control crime or other social infractions by offering assurances (or "guarantees") of security both to participants and to others.

Really all the social control that is witnessed in the games is that of vigilante justice. There are no formal systems of criminal justice such as militaries, police, or even centralized and coordinated local efforts. Instead, "bands" of like-minded worries team up (sometimes) to counter evil. This harkens back to the time before formal criminal justice efforts. This is critical to understand concepts of justice presented by those such as Thomas Hobbes in the mid-1600s, who argued for a social contract. These theorists understand that a world of vigilante justice is brutish and harsh. Instead of continually having to watch your back, lest some band of vigilantes seek revenge on you or seek to take advantage of you, a criminal justice system would take the place of the victim and impartially adjudicate the situation.

The open-world of Diablo and the ability to team up is seen largely in later games, but it is still present in *Diablo II*. The player wonders mostly by themselves to seek justice and conquer evil, but they are able to collaborate with others such as mercenaries who can help the gameplayer complete missions. Mercenaries are "hired guns." They take money to serve a person or army. They make a plan, volunteer for the mission, and carry out social control through violent means as Johnston (1996) describes. In true "life imitates art" fashion, this is true in the game as well as reality.

Conclusion

Video games in general should be studied to uncover associations with actual behavior and beliefs. They can also be used as pedagogical tools to engage students. The connection between media and crime/criminology is seen through the pioneering work of Nicole Rafter and Michelle Brown in *Crime goes to the Movies* which links criminological theories to classic movies as well as the work of Jonathan Grubb and Chad Posick in *Crime TV* which similarly links criminology and criminal justice theories and issues to streaming television shows. In this book, video games can serve the purpose of illustrating theory and practice. I argue that the *Diablo* series can serve a purpose in bringing to light early theories of crime and justice including demonological theories. Since these theories, and the social contexts in which the theories appear, are often gleaned over in textbooks and in most courses, the game can serve as an entertaining way to engage students with key concepts of evil, possession, and morality that dominated explanations of antisocial behavior for centuries.

So often possession and evil are seen as concepts that no longer apply to the criminological landscape but as many of the stories presented in this chapter highlight, may be alive and well in our societal discourse. When presidents, church leaders, and other high-profile figures point to evil in society as an element of antisocial behavior, it likely influences how others view crime and criminality. When communities across the globe still believe that witches and other evil entities have impact on the physical world, there is still a place to discuss demonological theories of crime and justice. In fact, because women and racial minorities are often the victims of accusation and violence stemming from demonological beliefs, it is imperative that we understand and respond to efforts to demonize one group over another.

Further, as *Diablo II* shows, the way we do criminal justice remains harsh. While society has largely done away with the chambers and dungeons presented in the games, the death penalty and long prison sentences are common especially in the United States. This is true even though public opinion shows support for rehabilitation and reintegration; certainly not something we witness in the *Diablo* series. The game is instructive yet again in producing images reflective of early criminological practice. Students and interested individuals have a lot to gain by coupling the game with study of early theories of antisocial behavior to fully understand the roots of criminology and criminal justice.

References

AP. Associated Press. (2018). Trump: School shooting "terrible violence, evil." https://www.oleantimesherald.com/trump-school-shooting-terrible-violence-evil/youtube_8d326df1-2416-5e3a-a918-113f677d758b.html

Bennett, J. (2021). "Let's make this show happen, people": *Black Mirror* and populist punitiveness. In J.A. Grubb & C. Posick (Eds.). *Crime TV: Streaming criminology in popular culture* (pp. 129–145). NYU Press.

Bernard, T.J., Snipes, J.B., & Gerould, A.L. (2016). *Vold's theoretical criminology*. Oxford University Press.

Cooley, C.H. (1902). *Human nature and the social order*. New York, NY: Scribners.

DarcFoolery. (2023). Why are Diablo games so addicting: Why do we like to play them and love them so much. https://vocal.media/gamers/why-are-diablo-games-so-addicting

Einstadter, W.J., & Henry, S. (2006). *Criminological theory: An analysis of its underlying assumptions*. Rowman & Littlefield.

ESA (Entertainment Software Association). (2021). *2021 essential facts about the video game industry*. https://www.theesa.com/wp-content/uploads/2021/08/2021—Essential-Facts-About-the-Video-Game-Industry-1.pdf

Foucault, M. (1975). *Discipline and punish: The birth of the prison*. Random House.

Gaylin, W. (2003). *Hatred: The psychological descent into violence*. Public Affairs.

Goyal, N., & Miller, J.G. (2023). Beliefs in inevitable justice curb revenge behaviours: Cultural perspectives on karma. *European Journal of Social Psychology, 53*(4), 732–745.

Grubb, J.A., & Posick, C. (Eds.). (2021). *Crime TV: Streaming criminology in popular culture*. NYU Press.

Harris, E. (2014). Violence stems from evil in society, cardinal observes. *Catholic News Agency*. Retrieved from https://www.catholicnewsagency.com/news/29891/violence-stems-from-evil-in-society-cardinal-observes

Johnston, L. (1996). What is vigilantism?. *The British Journal of Criminology, 36*(2), 220–236.

Jones, C. (2022, October 31). WitchTok: The witchcraft videos with billions of views. *BBC News*.

Kolek, L., Šisler, V., Martinková, P., & Brom, C. (2021). Can video games change attitudes towards history? Results from a laboratory experiment measuring short- and long-term effects. *Journal of Computer Assisted Learning, 37*(5), 1348–1369.

Latimer, J., Dowden, C., & Muise, D. (2005). The effectiveness of restorative justice practices: A meta-analysis. *The Prison Journal, 85*(2), 127–144.

Neubauer, I. (2022). Papua New Guinea fails to end "evil" of sorcery-related violence *Al Jazeera*. https://www.aljazeera.com/news/2022/8/16/papua-new-guinea-struggles-to-end-evil-of-sorcery-related-violence

NPR. National Public Radio. (2012). President Obama: "Such violence, such evil is senseless; it's beyond reason". https://www.wgbh.org/news/2012-07-20/president-obama-such-violence-such-evil-is-senseless-its-beyond-reason

Padgett, D.K. (2020). Homelessness, housing instability and mental health: Making the connections. *BJPsych Bulletin, 44*(5), 197–201.

Posick, C. (2018). *The development of criminological thought: Context, theory and policy*. Routledge.

Praetorius, A.S., & Görlich, D. (2020). How avatars influence user behavior: A review on the proteus effect in virtual environments and video games. In *Proceedings of the 15th International Conference on the Foundations of Digital Games* (pp. 1–9). FDG: Foundations of Digital Games.

Rafter, N. (2004). The unrepentant horse-slasher: Moral insanity and the origins of criminological thought. *Criminology, 42*(4), 979–1008.

Rafter, N., Posick, C., & Rocque, M. (2016). *The criminal brain: Understanding biological theories of crime*. New York University Press.

Schiff, S. (2015). *The witches: Salem, 1692*. Little, Brown.

Springer, E. (2022). Blaming "evil" for mass violence isn't as simple as it seems— a philosopher unpacks the paradox in using the word. *The Conversation*. https://theconversation.com/blaming-evil-for-mass-violence-isnt-as-simple-as-it-seems-a-philosopher-unpacks-the-paradox-in-using-the-word-184289

Wilt, J.A., Stauner, N., & Exline, J.J. (2023). Beliefs and experiences involving God, the devil, spirits, and fate: Social, motivational, and cognitive predictors. *The International Journal for the Psychology of Religion, 33*(1), 19–35.

6

"WE'RE THIEVES IN A WORLD THAT DON'T WANT US NO MORE"

The *Red Dead Redemption* Series as a Case Study of the Philosophies of Punishment

Shon M. Reed, Logan P. Kennedy and Breanna Boppre

The *Red Dead Redemption* series, created by Rockstar Games, consists of two games that transport players to the dying days of the American Wild West. The series was released over the seventh (e.g., Xbox 360, PS3) and eighth (e.g., Xbox One, PS4) generation of consoles as well as the PC and has been a smash hit having sold over 70 million copies cumulatively (Strickland, 2022). Additionally, players and critics alike praise the richness of the game world, where they can engage in a bevy of both legal and illegal activities like fishing, bounty hunting, horse thievery, and murder. Rockstar Games are known for their expansive game settings and novel gameplay systems, such as their wanted system that escalates law enforcement response against players based on their criminal activities.

Much like the wanted system in the series, the American criminal legal system often uses harsh punitive actions, such as incarceration or even death, under the justification that these measures will bring "justice" with retribution or prevent future crime through deterrence or incapacitation (Beccaria, 1983; Cullen & Jonson, 2016). These philosophies of punishment are greatly debated within American public discourse. Some believe in retributive justice, in which punishment is emphasized, while others believe that the system should rehabilitate those who commit crime or restore the harm caused by the crime (Cullen & Jonson, 2016). Regardless of the reader's position on justice, the *Red Dead Redemption* series showcases a world that exemplifies a lack of tolerance for those who commit crime. Players and their avatars often clash with law enforcement and vigilante mobs throughout the game. Such reactions in a simulated world provide opportunities for players to reflect on real-world legal practices.

DOI: 10.4324/9781003346869-6

This chapter provides readers with an overview of how deterrence, incapacitation, and retribution are portrayed through narrative and gameplay within the *Red Dead Redemption* series. We begin the chapter by describing the world of the *Red Dead Redemption* series broadly and how it attempts to portray the American West. We then outline the philosophies of punishment to prime readers with a greater understanding of the justice dynamics present in the series. Following this, we provide a summary of the *Red Dead Redemption* series' narrative to set the stage for our analysis that assesses the presence of the philosophies of punishment throughout the series. The chapter concludes with our discussion of how players can use the *Red Dead Redemption* series[1] as a springboard to consider the American criminal legal system today.

How the West was "Won": Setting the Stage for the *Red Dead Redemption* Series

The *Red Dead Redemption* series portrays the American West in the late 1890s through the early 1900s during the westward expansion of the United States. *Red Dead Redemption 2* (released in 2018), a prequel to the first *Red Dead Redemption* game (released in 2010), takes place in 1899 during the decline of the American frontier and the emergence of progressive reformation. *Red Dead Redemption 1* is set in 1911 and further shows the decline of the American West and the urbanization of the Western portions of the country. The series portrays various fictitious gangs modeled after outlaw factions such as Butch Cassidy's Wild Bunch and the Doolin-Dalton Gang (Donald & Reid, 2020). Members of these gangs serve as the primary protagonists and antagonists of the series.

Players feel tension between the outlaws who prefer to be free from governance (e.g., the Van der Linde Gang) and the settlers who seek more "civilized" approaches to crime control, through formalized law enforcement, jails, and public executions. Outlaw gangs often traversed the country in search of riches and to escape potential arrest and conviction. *Red Dead Redemption 2* also captures civil unrest and racial tensions during the Progressive Era as wealthy families began to gain power, monetary success, and land used for political and social capital at the expense of Indigenous and other marginalized people.

Although Rockstar Games claims authenticity in the *Red Dead Redemption* series (Rockstar Games, 2010), it ultimately represents historical fiction. Scholars question the accuracy and authenticity portrayed in the series as much of the content is dramatized depiction of the Western frontier (Donald & Reid, 2020). The games, as well as other forms of "cowboy media," have been criticized by some (Williams, 2016; Wright, 2021) as the developers rely on narratives of "progress" and "civilization" that extend harmful ideologies

shaped by white supremacy during the Western settlement and colonization of the Indigenous peoples. Further, the games largely perpetuate the idea
of "white saviors" attempting to assist Indigenous peoples in protecting
their land; a phenomenon that whitewashes and undermines the true efforts
and hardships of Indigenous people during colonization (Wright, 2021).
While the *Red Dead Redemption* series may not provide a 1-to-1 representation of the dying days of the Wild West, and certainly does include
problematic narratives of white supremacy, it provides players the opportunity to transport themselves in time to the days in which the American
criminal legal system, and the philosophies that guided it, developed across
the country.

The Five Philosophies of Punishment

There are five main philosophies of punishment: retribution, deterrence, incapacitation, rehabilitation, and restoration (Alarid & Reichel, 2017; Cullen & Jonson, 2016). These philosophies vary in their approaches to crime
prevention, the use of prisons or jails, the infliction of physical and psychological pain, and the role of reconciliation with those who were victimized.
Though the United States has shifted between punishment philosophies over
the centuries, it has consistently embraced punitive approaches to criminal
legal sanctioning relative to other Western industrialized democracies—even
today it maintains the highest incarceration rate in the world and continues
to employ the death penalty (Walmsley, 2014).

Retribution and deterrence can be traced back to early medieval and ancient times. Physical pain and death were used as tools to deter future crime
(i.e., deterrence) and to punish for crimes committed (i.e., retribution). Retribution is represented by the common term "an eye for an eye," whereby
the punishment must fit the crime and law breakers must feel the pain that
they have caused others/society. Under retribution, punishment is used for
the sake of punishment without other motives for public good. On the other
hand, deterrence seeks to use punishment to prevent crime, taking two forms:
specific and general. Specific deterrence seeks to deter the individual from
reoffending, while general deterrence attempts to deter others beyond the
perpetrator from committing crime (e.g., the general public). To achieve general deterrence, punishment is publicized to ensure the community sees the
consequences of crime to prevent further illegal acts.

Deterrence stems from the classical criminological theory that criminal
behavior is a rational decision someone makes. Beccaria (1983) and other
classical criminologists posit that people engage in a cost-benefit analysis
of whether to commit illegal acts (McCarthy & Chaudhary, 2014). Similarly, philosopher Jeremy Bentham's hedonistic calculus is often used to contend that people will engage in decisions to commit crime with the intention

of maximizing profits and minimizing harm (Steece & Hodwitz, 2022). The concept of deterrence aims to shift decision-making so that the negative consequences outweigh the potential benefits. Under classical criminology, effective deterrence occurs through swift, certain, and severe punishments (Tomlinson, 2016). People may commit illegal acts if the likelihood they will get caught and punished is low. However, a major issue with deterrence is its reliance on rationality, where environmental or psychological factors (e.g., poverty, mental illness) can influence the logical engagement of "rational" decision-making or cost-benefit-analyses (Cullen & Jonson, 2016).

In contrast, Jeremy Bentham proposed incapacitation as an alternative to physical punishment (Zimring & Hawkins, 1995). Underlying incapacitation is the notion that people who commit crime are dangerous and should be secluded from the community to ensure safety of its people. Jails were initially used in London as a form of detention while awaiting sentencing. While their intent may have initially been for holding, the purpose of jails shifted towards the use of punishment as deprivation from freedom. Prisons emerged in the early 1800s in the United States dedicated to housing and reforming people who committed crimes for longer periods of time, thus removing their ability to break the law and harm others. Though the original intent of prison was to incapacitate, they began to be used as punishment towards deterrence and retribution as well (Cullen & Jonson, 2016).

In contrast, rehabilitation reflects a medical model that seeks to understand and treat the underlying causes of illegal acts to reduce recidivism (i.e., reoffending; Alarid & Reichel, 2017). Rehabilitation provides individualized treatment to help those who broke the law conform to societal norms. It is believed that rehabilitation should occur in the community (e.g., probation) to provide support and treatment while maintaining social connections within the community. Although rehabilitation has been a philosophy of punishment in some places around the globe since the early 1900s, it was not adopted in America until around the 1930s and still has not been widely accepted across the country (Cullen & Jonson, 2016; McWilliams, 1986).

Lastly, restoration, or restorative justice, is the newest philosophy of punishment as it was not utilized until the 1970s in the United States (González, 2020). Restoration seeks to restore the harm caused by illegal acts. This often involves mediation with the crime victim, restitution to provide financial support for the damages caused, and peacemaking within the community. Restoration assumes that the person who committed the crime is remorseful, and that the person victimized can forgive them. The objective is that, once the process is complete, the individual who committed the crime is accepted back into the community and the victim is emotionally restored.

In sum, these five punishment philosophies shape law enforcement and other criminal legal responses to crime. As deterrence, retribution, and incapacitation are focused on punishment, whether through physical/ psychological harm or incarceration, these approaches often overlap and are used simultaneously due to their cohesive focus on punishment. Rehabilitation and restoration counter more punitive philosophies because they are focused on conflict management and harm reduction. As rehabilitation and restoration emerged after the *Red Dead Redemption* series time periods (late 1800s to early 1900s) and are therefore not reflected in the games, we focus on retribution, deterrence, and incapacitation within narrative and gameplay. For our analysis, we provide a summary of the *Red Dead Redemption* series' narrative and assess how these punishment philosophies were represented within the games.

The Narrative of the *Red Dead Redemption* Series

Red Dead Redemption 2 begins with the primary protagonist, Arthur Morgan, and the ill-fated Van der Linde Gang escaping to the mountains as they flee a failed riverboat heist in the town of Blackwater. Through dialog, players learn that the gang attempted to steal bank funds from a riverboat but were foiled by members of the Blackwater Police Department and the Pinkerton Detective Agency. Rather than seeking to apprehend the gang, a shootout occurred which led to the death of an innocent woman at the hands of Dutch Van der Linde (the Gang's leader) and several members of Dutch's Gang. During their time in the mountains, the gang commits a train heist where they steal railroad bonds from railroad tycoon Leviticus Cornwall.

With their newfound success, the Gang relocates to New Hanover (a fictionalized state representing parts of the American West and Midwestern regions). Shortly after their relocation, Arthur is approached by two members of the Pinkertons, Agents Milton and Ross, who are currently unaware of the gang's whereabouts. They offer Arthur freedom from prosecution in exchange for Dutch and any other members of his gang. Being loyal to Dutch, Arthur declines the opportunity.

Shortly after this encounter, the Van der Linde Gang migrates to Rhodes, a city in the fictional South. During this time, Dutch and other members of the gang decide to adopt pseudonyms and become deputies of the local sheriff's department as a means of investigating a historical rivalry between two wealthy families in the region. This deception ultimately takes a turn for the worse when the Gray family (of whom the local sheriff is a part of) realizes Dutch's deception and the gang's role in recent criminal activities. Rather than attempting to apprehend them, Sheriff Gray, his deputies, and other family members and employees of the Gray family ambush Arthur and several other gang members, killing one member, Sean Macguire, in the process.

The shootout in Rhodes draws attention to the Van der Linde Gang's location, as Agents Milton and Ross soon appear at the camp to threaten the party to surrender. The gang manages to threaten the agents enough to get them to leave, but this interaction eventually forces the group to relocate to an old plantation house outside of Saint Denis (a fictionalized version of New Orleans). Their next major interaction with law enforcement occurs during a failed robbery at a trolley station in Saint Denis. Upon finding that the station's safe was nearly empty, Arthur, Dutch, and Lenny (a young member of Dutch's crew) realize that they were set up by a local crime boss. The three attempt to flee using a passing trolley and the Saint Denis police immediately open fire, even though the trio used no lethal force, and no civilians were at risk of serious physical harm. This event has a wide-reaching impact on the rest of the series as, though not officially confirmed, Dutch suffers a head injury that causes his personality to become more erratic and temperamental.

The fourth chapter of the game closes on a robbery at a major bank in Saint Denis. Shortly after entering the vault, the gang realizes they are surrounded by Pinkerton agents and local police officers. During the standoff, Agent Milton stands in the street holding a gun to Hosea's head and tells Dutch that he has captured Abigail (another member of the Van der Linde Gang and recurring character in the *Red Dead Redemption* series). He warns Dutch that if he does not surrender, he will kill Hosea. Without warning or provocation, Milton shoots Hosea in the chest, instantly killing him. This enrages Dutch, leading to a widespread shootout. In the ensuing escape, Lenny, who was attempting to flee and was unarmed, is executed by two Pinkerton agents. Ultimately, Arthur, Dutch, Micah, Bill, and Javier become separated from the rest of the group and attempt to escape Saint Denis via a cargo ship heading out of the docks. The ship sinks shortly thereafter and the five of them end up waylaid in Guarma (a fictionalized version of Cuba). They assist in a coup and receive boat passage back to America where they reunite with the other members of the Van der Linde Gang who are sheltering in the bayou.

This reunion is short-lived as they are attacked by the Pinkertons and forced to escape to Annesburg, a fictional proxy for Southeastern America. Arthur learns that John was arrested during the Saint Denis bank robbery and is being held at Sisika Penitentiary while awaiting public execution. Arthur gives this information to Dutch, who seems to care more about funding their escape, rather than rescuing John. Arthur and Sadie Adler (a recent member of Dutch's Gang) successfully break John out of prison anyway, much to Dutch's dismay.

The final mission of the game includes a lengthy sequence with Arthur attempting to help innocent members of their group escape from Dutch and the incoming Pinkertons. During a standoff which pits Arthur and John against Dutch and his comrades, the Pinkertons swarm the camp until Arthur and John can hold them off. Arthur soon learns that Milton kidnapped Abigail and is holding her hostage to coax Arthur and the others to surrender. Arthur and Sadie stage a rescue for Abigail and Agent Milton ultimately gets killed by Abigail in an effort to defend Arthur. The main narrative of the game concludes with Arthur either being killed by Micah, a gang member who turned informant for the Pinkertons, or through succumbing to tuberculosis.

The epilogue for *Red Dead Redemption 2* sets the stage for the narrative of the first game. Immediately after Arthur's death, players take control of John as he seeks to reform himself through honest work. He attempts to avoid illegal acts by becoming a farmhand until he can save enough money to purchase his own plot of land to build a ranch. While John works hard on the farm, he must subsidize his income with bounty hunting with Sadie, who reappears late in the story. Ultimately, the violent actions of nearby gangs and the reappearance of Micah and Dutch draw John back into the life of crime as he commits murder as a means of rectifying wrongdoing against himself and his employers. The game concludes with a standoff between John, Dutch, and Micah, where Dutch escapes, Micah dies, and John recovers the lost Blackwater heist money.

Red Dead Redemption 1 begins four years after the conclusion of *Red Dead Redemption 2*'s epilogue. The story starts off with John being escorted to a train on its way to the Town of Armadillo by Agent Ross and his partner, Agent Fordham. Players soon learn that John's wife and son, Abigail and Jack, have been kidnapped by the Bureau of Investigation and are being held hostage until John can kill or capture two former members of the Van der Linde Gang, Bill Williamson and Javier Escuella.

John quickly tracks and confronts Bill outside of a fort and is shot in the stomach. John is saved by a local farmer, Bonnie McFarlane, and works for her as a means of recompense. During this, John becomes acquainted with some of Armadillo's locals, including US Marshal Leigh Jonson, con artist Nigel West Dickens, and a grave robber named Seth. While working here, Bill's gang attacks Bonnie's ranch, which prompts John to enlist the help of his new allies to infiltrate Bill's fort. They successfully attack the fort, eradicating Bill's gang in the process out of revenge for Bonnie, but soon learn that Bill has fled to Mexico to seek the help of Javier Escuela. With this information, John travels to Mexico to track Bill and Javier.

Shortly after arriving in Mexico, John is pulled into a revolution where both sides exploit him upon promising that they will help him pursue his ex-compatriots. Colonel Allende, the leader of the Mexican army, promises John that if he assists in shutting down the revolution, he will provide information on Javier and Bill's location. John acquiesces to this deal but quickly learns from the leader of the Mexican rebels, Reyes, of the atrocities Allende has committed against the Mexican people. John sides with Reyes and receives assistance in capturing Javier. Shortly after, John learns Allende has been hiding and protecting Bill in his compound. With this knowledge, John and the rebels lay siege to Allende's compound and kill him and Bill.

Believing his task to be accomplished, John returns to Blackwater to request that Agent Ross release his family. Upon his return, John is told that Dutch has been spotted in the area and is forming a new gang of disenfranchised, young Indigenous people. Ross tells John that if he kills Dutch, his debts to society will be repaid. John unsuccessfully attempts to capture Dutch and returns to Ross to request reinforcements. Ross calls upon the US Army, who assists in assaulting Dutch's camp. After a shootout, John corners Dutch on a cliff, where Dutch commits suicide to avoid capture. Seeing his debt as paid to the government, John reports Dutch's death and returns back to his ranch to reunite with Abigail and Jack.

For a time, John believes that he will finally be able to live a legitimate life. This dream is broken, though, as he is attacked by Ross and the US Army. John helps Abigail and Jack escape but stays behind to repel the onslaught. In his last stand, John is ultimately gunned down. Following this, Jack and Abigail return to the ranch to find John's body, where they bury him and Jack swears revenge.

After John's burial, players are flashed forward three years to an adult Jack, who pursues revenge against Agent Ross. He quickly learns that Ross has retired from the Bureau of Investigation and now lives on the Mexican border. After speaking with Ross' wife, Jack tracks him to a nearby river. Jack confronts and challenges him to a duel to avenge his father's honor, where he quickly kills him and the credits roll.

The narrative of the *Red Dead Redemption* series presents a complex story that can take players hundreds of hours to experience, depending on their playstyle. Throughout this story, players encounter a wide cast of characters who represent both outlaw and civilized cultures. Further, the story presents players with many complex dilemmas that can lead them to question the purpose of punishment in society. The following sections provide an analysis of the philosophies of punishment in the narrative and gameplay of the *Red Dead Redemption* series. The games showcase deterrence, incapacitation, and retribution as key themes while eschewing rehabilitation and restoration.

Philosophies of Punishment in Narrative

As mentioned previously, the philosophies of punishment often overlap in practice. For instance, in the American criminal legal system, extended prison sentences not only serve to incapacitate those that commit crime, but also attempt to provide specific (i.e., the individual) and general (i.e., the public) deterrence. It is important to note that scenes in the *Red Dead Redemption* games may be interpreted as multiple philosophies of punishment. Despite this, the legal system present in *Red Dead*'s narrative clearly indicates efforts to deter or incapacitate many of the protagonists and antagonists and seek retribution for their many crimes.

Evidence of the punishment philosophies occur early in *Red Dead Redemption 2* during Arthur's confrontation with Agents Milton and Ross, where Agent Milton espouses beliefs of retribution. Agent Milton states, "I enjoy society, flaws and all. You people venerate savagery, and you will die savagely. All of you" (Rockstar Games, 2018). A keystone to Milton's character is his belief in the colonization and urbanization of the American West. To Milton, society no longer has room for outlaws. He views their existence and continued lawlessness as a slight to society. His strong commitment to these values fuels his beliefs that Arthur and his comrades are harming society and that their punishment must fit their crimes. Agent Milton doubles down on these values during a later confrontation at the gang's camp outside of Rhodes, where he states,

> I don't know if you're aware, but this is a civilized land now. We didn't kill all them savages only to allow the likes of you to act like human dignity and decency was outmoded or not yet invented. This thing [the gang and their actions] it's done.
>
> *(Rockstar Games, 2018)*

In addition to the overt racism against Indigenous people, it is clear that Milton, as a representative of the government, believes that harsh punishment is the only thing that will protect society. Milton then tells the gang that if Dutch surrenders, where he will be executed by hanging, they will be free to leave. When Dutch asks him why he would spare other outlaws, he says, "I don't wanna kill all of these folk, Dutch, just you" (Rockstar Games, 2018). When threatened by the gang and told to leave, Milton warns, ". . . when I return I'll be with fifty men. All of you will die" (Rockstar Games, 2018). Milton's initial comments indicate that executing Dutch will reduce the gang's illegal behavior, which lends itself to two potential interpretations: (1) the incapacitation of Dutch and (2) general deterrence. Killing Dutch will inherently inhibit his ability to commit more crime and remove his criminal influence on others. Alternatively, executing Dutch may deter the other outlaws as they do not wish to be executed either.

During the failed bank robbery in Saint Denis, we again see Milton employ deterrence measures in an effort to shut down the robbery. At the time in which Milton holds Hosea hostage, Dutch and his crew have not killed anyone. Instead of attempting to offer a peaceful resolution to the situation, Milton shoots and kills Hosea, an unarmed man, as a show of force. While this inherently incapacitates Hosea, this action was intended to serve as a general deterrence measure against others.

As the story continues, Milton becomes more unhinged in his violent tendencies. During the bayou ambush, Milton announces himself at their camp and tells them to step outside to be arrested. Milton is then shown turning to one of his officers and saying, "Give them to the count of five, then give 'em everything [open fire]. Actually . . . let them have it" (Rockstar Games, 2018). He then signals an officer with a gatling gun to open fire on the camp even though there are women and children inside. After a brief escape to a different part of the camp, Arthur hears Milton yell,

> Now I will show strength and you may mistake it for brutality. There is no escape for any of you. I shall hunt you to the ends of the Earth and the end of time. I've killed your friends, and I've enjoyed killing them and now I'm gonna kill each and every one of you!
>
> *(Rockstar Games, 2018)*

Through this dialog, we can see that Milton's repeated failures to deter or incapacitate the gang have shifted his punitive efforts toward retribution. Milton sees Dutch and the group's repeated escapes as increased slights against himself, the Pinkertons, and society. As such, he believes that executing the members will lead to retributive justice for himself and society.

Although Milton serves as the main antagonist of *Red Dead Redemption 2* and is our primary lens into the criminal legal system's views of punishment, other actions within the game lend further evidence to these philosophies. Late in the game, the Van der Linde Gang's rival, Colm O'Driscoll, is set to be executed by hanging in Saint Denis. Colm's crimes include murder, rape, and robbery. At his execution, a legal official states, "For sometimes a man is so savage, the only way to deal with him justly is by savagery" (Rockstar Games, 2018). Again, this statement lends itself to multiple philosophies of punishment, namely retribution and incapacitation. It is noted in the dialog that Colm has escaped many imprisonment and execution attempts, meriting a more severe response. The legal official, as well as the general reactions by witnesses to his public execution, show excitement for stopping Colm's crime spree.

The main narrative of *Red Dead Redemption 1* is rife with deterrence, incapacitation, and retribution. John's role as a tool of the federal government was to incapacitate his former comrades and administer retribution for their past deeds. Ross, who seemed more mild-mannered than Milton in the prequel, has adopted some of his former partner's ideals. Using John as a pawn to kill his former friends serves as a cleaner measure of retribution and general deterrence as he notes around the halfway point of the game that the government's direct killing of the outlaws could serve to make them martyrs in the eyes of those who disagree with the urbanization of the West. John's killing of Bill, Javier, and Dutch, accomplishes Milton's goal of a safer society and acts as both deterrence for future crime and revenge against those who killed his former partner. In executing John at the end of the game, Ross fulfills this goal and gains retribution against the Van der Linde Gang.

Evidence of the support of these philosophies of punishment is not only present in governmental actions but that of the protagonists of the games and other non-playable characters (NPCs). At the end of *Red Dead Redemption 2*, Arthur clearly seeks retribution against Milton for kidnapping Abigail, even though Abigail ultimately kills Milton. Further, Jack's primary goal during the epilogue of *Red Dead Redemption 1* is to kill Ross for executing his father. Such behaviors show that, while they may not share the same beliefs of urbanization as the government, they share similar philosophies of justice. Likewise, during a side mission (*The Mercies of Knowledge*) where players can assist in developing the electric chair, players are tasked with capturing Wilson McDaniels, a wanted murderer. After capturing McDaniels and gathering the necessary supplies to build the chair, he is set to be publicly executed. The execution goes awry, and McDaniels dies a slow and painful death. We then see an exchange between two Saint Denis residents where one says, " . . . don't seem overly humane to me." And the other responds, "I think it's mighty fine" (Rockstar Games, 2018). It's clear that the more "civilized" residents of the *Red Dead* series are supportive of retributive punishment.

Through the story of the *Red Dead Redemption* series, the criminal legal system heavily relies on the punitive philosophies of punishment (i.e., deterrence, incapacitation, and retribution). Although the narratives of the *Red Dead Redemption* series offer a breadth of evidence regarding the theories of punishment, the emergent gameplay of the series and how the legal system responds to player actions offer further evidence of such philosophies. The following section showcases how the games' reactions to player behaviors allow the player to further experience the philosophies of punishment.

Philosophies of Punishment in Gameplay

The simulated world of the *Red Dead Redemption* series allows players to engage in a wide range of illegal acts ranging from relatively minor crimes, such as horse thievery, to more serious crimes, such as kidnapping, robbery, and murder. At times, the games encourage the player to engage in deviance. For instance, players can earn an achievement[2] in *Red Dead Redemption 1* for kidnapping a woman and leaving her on railroad tracks to await an oncoming train. While *Red Dead Redemption 2* notably toned down the acceptance or celebration of particularly violent behaviors, both games include a wanted system that reacts to players' actions within the games. These wanted systems serve to represent the ability to foster emergent gameplay, while providing players with some form of punishment for their misdeeds (Tapsell, 2021). Due to technical constraints of the time, the wanted system in *Red Dead Redemption 1* was much more basic than its sequel. As such, this section focuses on the wanted system present in *Red Dead Redemption 2*.

Within the game, players are largely left to themselves by law enforcement outside of some scripted scenarios between in-game missions (e.g., Blackwater is off-limits prior to the epilogue of *Red Dead Redemption 2*). For the wanted system to activate, players must commit a crime in front of an NPC (e.g., townsfolk, law enforcement). Following this, that person will attempt to report the crime to the nearest law enforcement official. Players can kill, bribe, or intimidate these witnesses to deter or otherwise prevent their reporting. In most instances, so long as players are not immediately hostile, they will have the option to surrender to police, where they are arrested and imprisoned. This results in a brief incarceration (i.e., incapacitation) and loss of the player's resources.

When players retaliate against law enforcement, their wanted rating will increase, and all nearby police will become hostile on sight. If the player manages to survive and continues fighting back, they will be met with increasing resistance from law enforcement. This escalation goes from local law enforcement and armed bounty hunters who will hunt the player to—at the highest rating—members of the United States Marshals who carry high-powered weapons and have higher damage resistance. This increase in "strength" of the legal representatives highlights an increased effort to deter or incapacitate players.

No matter the player's response to their wanted rating, they will accrue a bounty that increases with every illegal action they take. This bounty is maintained even after the player is killed and does not go away unless the player pays the bounty to clear their name. Bounties can make gameplay difficult for some players as they will be attacked on sight in certain areas, and players may not have the money to clear their names. The combination of violent response and heavy monetary sanctions is indicative of deterrence, as it may deter players from engaging in illicit acts until they can afford to pay off such bounties.

The wanted system in the *Red Dead Redemption* series offers players the opportunity to experience deterrence, incapacitation, and retribution firsthand. While this may serve as a minor inconvenience for most, it can be a frustrating element when their crime was accidental (e.g., getting on the wrong horse and being accused of horse thievery) or if they were attempting to accomplish a specific goal. Most who have played the games will note the wanted system's quick escalation of violence, which reflects retribution. Even if players engage in violence towards a rival gang member (an action that is often lauded throughout many of the games' missions), it is likely that police will intervene and immediately attack the player.

The wanted system engages players in considering swift, certain, and severe punishments. The certainty of getting caught may impact players' decisions to engage in crime. If they think they can outrun law enforcement, they may still engage in crime but know that continuing to do so likely increases their chances of being caught—thus increasing certainty. Players' punishment is also swift in gameplay as they do not undergo a trial or await sentencing. Instead, players are either killed by authorities or incarcerated, where they lose resources. It is up to players to determine the level of severity needed to deter their behavior. The threat of death or loss of resources may be enough for some, while others will attempt to keep fighting against ever-increasing punishment. In essence, the severity of the punishment must outweigh the rewards to deter players.

Like many of those who consider illegal acts in real life, the decision to engage in crime rests upon the benefits of the crime versus certain punishment (Stafford & Warr, 1993). Each player's cost-benefit analysis is individualized, and not every player will engage in the same level of crime. While we see violence occur between residents through emergent gameplay (indicative of these responses failing to perpetuate general deterrence), for some players the fear of inconvenience, a lack of ammunition, or funds to pay for their bounties might deter them from committing further crimes. Such responses indicate that the series' wanted system can perpetuate specific deterrence as players may learn that their illicit actions in the past do not bear repeating. Some players may choose to increase their wanted level as much as possible to test their resilience, but ultimately these approaches to gameplay will get in the way of narrative progress.

Of note, deterrent, incapacitative, and retributive justice are not only administered by the formal criminal legal system within the games but by informal agents of control as well. Local residents, who are not affiliated with the game's wanted system, will choose to attack the player if they commit crime in the absence of formal police. Such instances do not always lead to a wanted rating unless one of the witnesses tracks down law enforcement. Therefore, mob/vigilante justice can serve as a proxy for formal legal systems. Such instances are particularly common in the game's representations of the rural American South compared to the game's other regions. Stylistically, the developers may have deliberately chosen to make this phenomenon more common in this region of the game, as this approach was often seen as a viable alternative to formal legal responses during this time period in the South (Gregory, 2022; Hagen et al., 2013; Hill, 2009).

Both the narrative and gameplay of the *Red Dead Redemption* series offer players an excellent opportunity to experience and witness deterrence, incapacitation, and retribution in action. Regardless of whether players engage in criminal acts in their own emergent gameplay, they will inevitably face the consequences of either their or their avatars' actions. Such harsh punitive measures force players to confront their own decision-making. Even when they choose to retaliate against the oppressive legal system, they will eventually succumb to the system's pressure.

Discussion

One may think the *Red Dead Redemption* series is a simple "shoot 'em up" cowboy story, but Rockstar Games delivered players a dynamic narrative that captures the historical and philosophical foundations of the American criminal legal system. *Red Dead Redemption 2*'s story depicts a burgeoning formalized criminal legal system (e.g., Pinkertons, federal law enforcement agencies, local police) that seeks to promote a more "civilized" Western frontier. The narrative and gameplay in the series present three punitive punishment philosophies historically present in the early American West: deterrence, incapacitation, and retribution. Law enforcement antagonists in the games, such as Agent Milton and Agent Ross, seek to contain the protagonists and their comrades in an effort to reduce crime and violence (incapacitation and deterrence), but also through their own vengeance (retribution).

Engaging with these philosophies of punishment via gameplay may lead players to question the effectiveness of the criminal legal system. As seen throughout the series, law enforcement efforts often lead to increased violence and harm. Officers' own histories and frustration with the protagonists can cloud their responses and escalate violence, as is the case for Agent Milton. Further, the wanted system brings up questions about the effectiveness of deterrence in preventing crime. The swift, certain, and severe punishments in the game are difficult to enact in reality, as many await trial and sentencing for years while the majority of illegal acts are never discovered or reported (Cullen & Jonson, 2016). Scholars have voiced considerable opposition to punitive approaches, and some studies have shown that deterrence and incapacitation do not reduce crime (e.g., Cullen et al., 2011; Pratt et al., 2006). In addition, some question whether "justice" is achieved through retribution as the public wants the criminal legal system to do more than simply punish but also prevent future crime (Cullen & Jonson, 2016).

Red Dead Redemption's emphasis on deterrence, incapacitation, and retribution makes the pursuit of justice in reality appear cruel and morally contentious as they come with human collateral and even a body count. Due to strict sentencing laws, the United States is the world leader in incarceration, with about 5% of the world's population, but 20% of the world's prison population (Walmsley, 2014). Punitive policies resulting in overincarceration impact not only those incarcerated, but also their families and communities (Travis, 2005). The removal of a person from the community places distinct burdens on families, financially, socially, and emotionally (DeHart et al., 2018). Reentering society following incarceration with a felony record comes with further consequences, including barriers to housing, employment, education, and voting (National Inventory of Collateral Consequences of Conviction, 2023). Beyond incarceration, the death penalty also poses stark societal impacts. One in eight death sentences results in exoneration due to innocence or wrongful conviction (Equal Justice Initiative, 2023). Hence, the communal weight of these punitive approaches is even greater in the United States justice system today compared to the days of the Wild West.

Players might consider how life in the Wild West might have been more civilized if other philosophies of punishment were embraced. During the epilogue of *Red Dead Redemption 2,* John seeks a legitimate life by purchasing a plot of land for a ranch and building a home. That said, he is forced to obtain a bank loan under false pretenses and with the support of a fellow rancher. One might question how John's life may have turned out differently had he been able to legally obtain a bank loan and develop a legitimate ranching business with government support under rehabilitation or restoration. Further, John's actions in *Red Dead Redemption 1* on behalf of the federal government led to great harm for side characters, such as Bonnie McFarlane. Players might consider how the events of the game would play out differently had the legal system used restitution over the more punitive forms of punishment. Would capturing and forcing characters such as Bill, Javier, or even John to face the victims of their crimes lead to different outcomes and a reduction in future crimes? We may never know, but we certainly see John, and Arthur in *Red Dead Redemption 2*, reconcile their actions with those who abide by the law. Hence, the *Red Dead Redemption* series may open players' minds to consider other approaches to crime and criminal behavior that seek to restore harm and rehabilitate. In general, rehabilitation has far stronger empirical support than punitive approaches (Cullen & Gilbert, 2013). Restoration used in combination with rehabilitation shows potential to reduce recidivism while engaging the victim in the process (Cullen & Jonson, 2016).

Much as the justice system fails many of the characters within the *Red Dead Redemption* series, the American justice system fails much of the population. In line with the dialog surrounding the depiction of race in cowboy media, it is important to note the racial tension present throughout the games and how it relates to American justice. Critical scholars argue that state-sponsored punishment is used as social control of those who pose a racial threat (Liska, 1992). The *Red Dead Redemption* series portrays the oppression and displacement of Indigenous people as well as other marginalized people, particularly in the South. Such dynamics in the game allow players to consider the racist colonial roots of America that have led to the over-representation of Black, Indigenous, and Latiné people in arrests (Ward, 2022), use of force (DeAngelis, 2021), and incarceration (Sawyer, 2020). Such outcomes are present within the game as people of color are often killed by law enforcement without a fair trial. An inequitable criminal legal system can undermine efforts toward deterrence due to the increased certainty and severity of punishment among people of color compared to other groups.

Rockstar Games created one of the most, if not the most, detailed worlds in all popular media. Their *Red Dead Redemption* series transports players to a different time period in America and allows them to explore the world at their leisure. Mixed with emergent gameplay, players can experience a criminal legal system that is not so philosophically different from that of the real world. By engaging with the world of the *Red Dead Redemption* series, players can think more critically about whether the criminal legal system perpetuates more harm than good. If nothing else, players will be able to explore the dying days of the American Wild West and witness when America decided to take harsh steps against lawlessness and banditry. The *Red Dead Redemption* series is one that we encourage all gamers to experience if they are interested in dialog surrounding American responses to crime. In fact, we *insist* they do.

Notes

1 Of note, Rockstar Games first created the *Red Dead* universe in their 2004 release, *Red Dead Revolver*. This game was less well received, having sold less than 2 million copies, and had much less of an impact on the gaming landscape in comparison to the *Redemption* series. Further, the events of this game do not connect with the *Red Dead Redemption* series outside of minor callbacks and Easter eggs (Rockstar Games, n.d.). Additionally, the forthcoming analysis does not include any narrative from *Red Dead Online* as the missions included within that game mode are tangential to the overall narrative of the *Red Dead Redemption* series. Therefore, this analysis only focuses on the events and gameplay of single-player modes of *Red Dead Redemption 1* and *2*.
2 Achievements are digital awards provided on the Xbox console ecosystem for completing certain in-game tasks. They award a range of points that are represented on players' player cards to document game progress. Sony's PlayStation consoles offer similar awards (i.e., trophies) and some PC gaming services (such as Valve's Steam) also offer similar awards.

References

Alarid, L.F., & Reichel, P.L. (2017). *Corrections*. Pearson Allyn & Bacon.
Beccaria, C. (1983). *An essay on crimes and punishments*. Branden Books.
Cullen, F.T., & Gilbert, K.E. (2013). *Reaffirming rehabilitation*. Routledge.

Cullen, F.T., & Jonson, C.L. (2016). *Correctional theory: Context and consequences*. Sage.

Cullen, F.T., Jonson, C.L., & Nagin, D.S. (2011). Prisons do not reduce recidivism: The high cost of ignoring science. *The Prison Journal, 91*, 48S–65S.

DeAngelis, R.T. (2021). Systemic racism in police killings: New evidence from the mapping police violence database, 2013–2021. *Race and Justice*. https://doi. org/10.1177/21533687211047943

DeHart, D., Shapiro, C., & Clone, S. (2018). "The pill line is longer than the chow line": The impact of incarceration on prisoners and their families. *The Prison Journal, 98*(2), 188–212. https://doi.org/10.1177/0032885517753159

Donald, I., & Reid, A. (2020). The Wild West: Accuracy, authenticity and gameplay in Red Dead Redemption 2. *Media Education Journal, 66*, 15–23.

Equal Justice Initiative. (2023) *Death penalty*. https://eji.org/issues/death-penalty/

González, T. (2020). The state of restorative justice in American criminal law. *Wisconsin Law Review. 2020*(6), 1147–1197.

Gregory, A. (2022). Policing Jim Crow America: Enforcers' agency and structural transformations. *Law and History Review, 40*(1), 91–122. https://doi.org/10.1017/ S0738248021000456

Hagen, R., Makovi, K., & Bearman, P. (2013). The influence of political dynamics on Southern lynch mob formation and lethality. *Social Forces, 92*(2), 757–787. https://doi.org/10.1093/sf/sot093

Hill, A.L. (2009). *Lynching and spectacle: Witnessing racial violence in America, 1890–1940*. University of North Carolina Press.

Liska, A.E. (Ed.). (1992). *Social threat and social control*. SUNY Press.

McCarthy, B., & Chaudhary, A.R. (2014). Rational choice theory and crime. In *Encyclopedia of crime and criminal justice* (pp. 4307–4315). Springer.

McWilliams, W. (1986). The English probation system and the diagnostic ideal. *The Howard Journal of Criminal Justice, 25*(4), 241–260.

National Inventory of Collateral Consequences of Criminal Conviction. (2023). "Collateral Consequences." https://niccc.nationalreentryresourcecenter.org/resources/ sentencing-project-collateral-consequences#:~:text=The%20Sentencing%20Pro ject%20promotes%20effective,%2C%20economic%2C%20and%20gender%20 justice

Pratt, T.C., Cullen, F.T., Blevins, K.R., Daigle, L.E., & Madensen, T.D. (2006). The empirical status of deterrence theory: A meta-analysis. In F.T. Cullen, J.P. Wright, & K.R. Blevins (Eds.), *Taking stock: The status of criminological theory* (pp. 367–395). Transaction Publishers.

Rockstar Games. (2010). *The true West—History that helped inspire Red Dead Redemption. Bad guys gone good . . . and vice versa—Part one: Frank James*. Rockstargames.com. https://www.rockstargames.com/newswire/article/ak14o8839aoa1a/ the-true-west-history-that-helped-inspire-red-dead-redemption-ba.html

Rockstar Games. (2018). Red Dead Redemption 2. (PlayStation 4 Version) [Video Game]. Rockstar Games.

Rockstar Games. (n.d.). *Red Dead Revolver*. Rockstargames.com. https://www.rock stargames.com/games/reddeadrevolver

Sawyer, W. (2020, July 27). *Visualizing the racial disparities in mass incarceration*. Prison Policy Initiative. https://www.prisonpolicy.org/blog/2020/07/27/disparities/

Stafford, M.C., & Warr, M. (1993). A reconceptualization of general and specific deterrence. *Journal of Research in Crime and Delinquency, 30*(2), 123–135. https:// doi.org/10.1177/0022427893030002001

Steece, D., & Hodwitz, O. (2022). The Classical School and utilitarianism. In *The Origins of Criminological Theory* (pp. 72–91). Routledge.

Strickland, D. (2022). *Red Dead Redemption franchise sales break 70 million.* Tweaktown.com. https://www.tweaktown.com/news/89483/red-dead-redemption-franchise-sales-break-70-million/index.html

Tapsell, T. (2021). *Red Dead Redemption 2 bounty and wanted level—how to pay bounties and lose your wanted level explained.* Eurogamer.net. https://www.eurogamer.net/red-dead-redemption-2-bounty-wanted-how-to-pay-bounties-lose-wanted-level-4975

Tomlinson, K D. (2016). An examination of deterrence theory: Where do we stand. *Federal Probation, 80,* 33–38.

Travis, J. (2005). *But they all come back: Facing the challenges of prisoner reentry.* The Urban Institute.

Walmsley, R. (2014). *World prison population list* (11th ed.). King's College London, International Centre for Prison Studies. Retrieved from http://www.prisonstudies.org/sites/default/files/resources/downloads/world_prison_population_list_11th_edition_0.pdf

Ward, M. (2022). The legacy of slavery and contemporary racial disparities in arrest rates. *Sociology of Race and Ethnicity, 8*(4), 534–552.

Williams, L. (2016). *How Hollywood whitewashed the Old West.* Theatlantic.com. https://www.theatlantic.com/entertainment/archive/2016/10/how-the-west-was-lost/502850/

Wright, E. (2021). Rockstar Games, Red Dead Redemption, and narratives of "progress." *European Journal of American Studies, 16*(3), 1–19.

Zimring, F.E., & Hawkins, G. (1995). *Incapacitation: Penal confinement and the restraint of crime.* Oxford University Press.

7

MAKING LIGHT OF DARKNESS

Crime and Justice in *LEGO Star Wars: The Skywalker Saga*

Colin Atkinson

Released across multiple gaming platforms on April 5, 2022, *LEGO Star Wars: The Skywalker Saga* adapted—in LEGO form and with an irreverent comedic style—the characters, settings, and events from across all nine of the main franchise movies: from *Star Wars: Episode I—The Phantom Menace* (1999) to *Star Wars: Episode IX—The Rise of Skywalker* (2019). Additional downloadable content was subsequently released allowing players to access characters and content from other Star Wars media, including the 2016 theatrical release *Rogue One: A Star Wars Story*, the prequel story to the original *Star Wars* movie (1977), and the television series *The Mandalorian* (2019—).[1] This video game was an immediate global smash hit. The publisher, Warner Bros. Games, reported sales of 3.2 million copies globally in its first two weeks across all platforms (Williams, 2022). *LEGO Star Wars: The Skywalker Saga* would go on to become the fifth biggest selling video game of 2022 in the United States (Kaser, 2023). This popularity is undoubtedly rooted in the transgenerational appeal of the multiple products of both LEGO (Wolf, 2018) and Star Wars (Booy, 2021) as standalone franchises, and their powerful intersection in a video game format (Buerkle, 2014).

As individual franchises both LEGO and Star Wars have engaged with issues of crime and justice and represented a range of associated ideas, practices, and politics (see Lee, 2020; Black et al., 2016; Lueth, 2017; Atkinson, 2022, 2023; Wilczak, 2021). As a transmedia text at the intersection of these franchises *LEGO Star Wars: The Skywalker Saga* is uniquely positioned to re-interpret these issues for those familiar with the franchise and for new fans. This video game appeals to younger players in its aesthetic style and relatively uncomplicated gameplay, but is also attractive to those older

DOI: 10.4324/9781003346869-7

generations nostalgic to play through, perhaps as their favorite character, the scenes and settings of this galaxy far, far away.

This chapter considers *LEGO Star Wars: The Skywalker Saga* worthy of popular criminological inquiry (Rafter & Brown, 2011). In doing so it accepts the position that popular cultural texts, including those texts aimed at children (Kennedy, 2021), can communicate powerful narratives about crime and justice and their underpinning politics. Sensitized by the proclivity of the LEGO franchise to engage with social, cultural, and political issues through comedy (Goggin, 2017; Mattes, 2019; Hunting, 2019) this chapter explores the extent to which *LEGO Star Wars: The Skywalker Saga* uses humor in both narrative and gameplay to portray issues of crime and justice within the Star Wars universe, and the potential effects of these representations on a diverse demographic of players. The chapter focuses upon three case-study sites, utilizing critical discourse analysis to explore how the politics of crime and justice are communicated across the game.

The chapter begins with a short contextualization of *LEGO Star Wars: The Skywalker Saga* in the lineage of Star Wars video games, tracing the development of the LEGO Star Wars series. It then progresses to detail the methodology used, which was inspired by, but moves beyond, Giddings and Kennedy's reflective account of "not being very good at the 2005 video game *LEGO Star Wars*" (Giddings & Kennedy, 2008). In particular, the arguments developed in this chapter are informed by the analysis of audiovisual data from a total of 117 dedicated video game play sessions of *LEGO Star Wars: The Skywalker Saga* on the Nintendo Switch; the purpose of which is to surface the gameplay structures, aesthetics, and narratives that prompt, shape, and sometimes limit, encounters with crime and justice in play. Beginning with an exploration of the capital of the galaxy during the Skywalker saga, the analysis uncovers Coruscant as a site of comedy, not crime. The video game immerses the gamer in a playful approximation of this city-planet, while simultaneously stripping the ecumenopolis of its foreboding affect. A similar dynamic is apparent at the Mos Eisley Spaceport on Tatooine. This, the original "wretched hive of scum and villainy" in Star Wars, is sanitized through spoof and slapstick, with the morally ambiguous violence and threatening mise-en-scène of the original cinematic source material removed. These dynamics become more problematic as the game progresses to represent policing and prisons at Canto Bight, redacting state violence and stripping out the critical social justice politics of the counterpart cinematic canon. The chapter concludes by reflecting upon the consequences of these comedic representations of crime and justice in *LEGO Star Wars: The Skywalker Saga*; tracing the limits of LEGO's postmodern sensibilities as it seeks, through its disarmingly playful aesthetic, to "make light of darkness."

LEGO Star Wars: The Skywalker Saga in the lineage of Star Wars video games

Video games based on the Star Wars franchise have a long history. The first Star Wars home video games included the 1982 title *Star Wars: The Empire Strikes Back*, released on the Atari 2600 system and (one year later) on the Mattel Electronics Intellivision console, and the 1983 game *Star Wars: Jedi Arena*, which was released on the Atari 2600 only. The limited capabilities of the second-generation systems meant that the visuals and sound of these early titles could invoke only a somewhat rudimentary approximation of the events, characters, places, and weaponry of the Star Wars universe. Drawing upon ever-improving processing power multiple Star Wars video games were published across successive generations of consoles and computers in the years thereafter. These titles ranged from multi-platform titles such as *Star Wars* (1991), to the *Super Star Wars* trilogy that began a year later on the Super Nintendo Entertainment System (1992, 1993, 1994), and the X-Wing series of computer games for Windows-based computers (1993–1999). Further multi-platform titles such as *Star Wars: Knights of the Old Republic I* and *II* (2003, 2004), and *Star Wars: Battlefront I* and *II* (2004; 2005) diversified the franchise into new genres, such as the role-playing game, the massively multiplayer online role-player, and the first- and third-person shooter. Importantly, since the acquisition in 2012 of Lucasfilm, the company that produced Star Wars, by The Walt Disney Company, video games have increasingly become dedicated and important vehicles for canonical Star Wars transmedia storytelling, through titles such as *Star Wars Jedi: Fallen Order* (2019) and *Star Wars Jedi: Survivor* (2023).

In some contrast to Star Wars, video games based on original LEGO content date back only to 1995, specifically the video game *LEGO Fun to Build* released on the Sega Pico (Baker, 2013). It was not until a decade later that the first of the now six Star Wars-themed LEGO video games was released. *LEGO Star Wars: The Video Game* (2005), as an action-adventure/puzzle-platformer title, adapted events from the Star Wars theatrical releases that comprise the "prequel trilogy"—*Star Wars: Episode I—The Phantom Menace* (1999), *Star Wars: Episode II—Attack of the Clones* (2002) and *Star Wars: Episode III—Revenge of the Sith* (2005)—with some additional content adapted from *Star Wars: Episode IV—A New Hope*. Robert Buerkle (2014) recognized that, while *LEGO Star Wars: The Video Game* was ostensibly a video game for children, it had undoubted transgenerational appeal and set the tone for future installments in the series. For Buerkle (2014, p. 123),

> The basic premise of the games is simple: the *Star Wars* saga retold in comic fashion, acted out by animated LEGO minifigures. Familiar *Star*

Wars settings are depicted via LEGO pieces, with much of the landscape able to be destroyed in a shower of bricks—bricks which can sometimes be reconfigured into new LEGO objects.

Frans Mäyrä (2015, p. 91) further summarized the gameplay style of *LEGO Star Wars: The Video Game*,

> The ability to manipulate characters who are famous from movies and other media in the format of playable, animated Lego minifigurines creates also a distinctive parodic style that pervades Lego games. Rather than focusing on realistic simulated violence, these games provide opportunities for playfully anarchistic smashing of animated Lego toy characters and surroundings.

Mäyrä (2015) further remarked how violence in the narrative of the Star Wars canon that was possibly less appropriate for small children—such as Luke Skywalker's hand being severed by Darth Vader—was treated humorously in animated cutscenes and not offered as playable content. The success of *LEGO Star Wars: The Video Game* in both substance and style spawned further LEGO-based Star Wars multi-platform video games, including *LEGO Star Wars II: The Original Trilogy* (2006), *LEGO Star Wars: The Complete Saga* (2007), *LEGO Star Wars III: The Clone Wars* (2011), and *LEGO Star Wars: The Force Awakens* (2016). *LEGO Star Wars: The Skywalker Saga* updated, refined, and expanded this highly successful formula; appealing to a wide range of gamers.

Methodology

The methodology of this chapter was inspired by Giddings and Kennedy's reflective account of "not being very good at *LEGO Star Wars*" (Giddings & Kennedy, 2008). They conducted a micro-ethnography of the 2005 PlayStation 2 release of *LEGO Star Wars: The Video Game*. In the course of their research they played *LEGO Star Wars* for around one hour, recording the on-screen action and events, as well capturing video and audio content of themselves as they played through the game during this time, before subjecting short "game events" to in-depth and reflexive analysis (Giddings & Kennedy, 2008). The research for this chapter, however, diverges from Giddings and Kennedy's approach in two ways. First, this chapter explicitly treats *LEGO Star Wars: The Skywalker Saga* as a multimodal text that can be subjected to critical discourse analysis. Critical discourse analysis has, in recent years, diversified and developed towards a multimodal approach that moves beyond the traditional focus on language, especially in its written form (Wodak & Meyer, 2009). Multimodal critical discourse analysis seeks not only to broaden the interest of the research program beyond language but also to both engage and denaturalize visual communication, revealing how images are constitutive in being both produced by and in reproducing dominant ideologies and power structures in society (Atkinson, 2023). This chapter extends further the multimodality of critical discourse analysis, foregrounding the value in exploring the visible and audible manifestations of ideology, as well as surfacing those hidden structures and narratives that both prompt and limit the possibilities for politics in play. Second, in contrast to the single video game play session analyzed by Giddings and Kennedy, this chapter explored *LEGO Star Wars: The Skywalker Saga* more expansively and in greater detail.

Data was collected from a total of 117 dedicated gameplay sessions of the "deluxe edition" of *LEGO Star Wars: The Skywalker Saga* on the Nintendo Switch.[2] The style of gameplay session for this study was a period of single player, offline gameplay by the researcher. Each session lasted for an average of 28 minutes and each session was separated by a minimum of at least 30 minutes. These 117 dedicated gameplay sessions were spread over two research stages. In this first stage, each of nine episodic levels (each based on a corresponding Star Wars movie title) was played for 11 sessions, resulting in 99 dedicated gaming sessions. The purpose of this research stage was to complete the game in full, gaining a holistic understanding of the structure and mechanics of the game, as well as to identify relevant encounters with, and representations of, crime and justice. Following the data collection process used by Giddings & Kennedy (2008), across these 99 sessions I recorded video of on-screen gameplay and video and audio of myself as the "gamer." These audiovisual data from the initial 99 sessions of gameplay were imported into the qualitative data analysis software package NVivo 12. Coding was undertaken across all content, focusing on aspects of gameplay that related to the broad and interlinked fields of crime and justice.

Based on the thematic analysis of these 99 sessions (Braun & Clarke, 2021), and having completed the game as comprehensively as possible, three case-study locations were chosen for further analysis in a second research stage: Coruscant and the underground Uscru District; the Mos Eisley Spaceport on Tatooine; and Canto Bight, Cantonica. The criteria for the selection of these locations were on the basis that they particularly disclosed, across a diverse range of gameplay environments from across each of the three trilogies, the use of humor to depict issues of crime and justice. Having been identified as a case-study site each location was subject to a further six video game play sessions (18 in total), adopting the same data collection technique as stage one. This allowed for the further in-depth analysis of each setting. These data were also imported into NVivo 12 and again subject to coding and thematic analysis. The following sections, presented chronologically as they were played across the video game, detail the findings of this overall research design.

Crime-as-Comedy on Coruscant

The city-planet of Coruscant features across several episodes of the Skywalker saga. This multi-layered world is first encountered in *LEGO Star Wars: The Skywalker Saga* in *Star Wars: Episode I—The Phantom Menace*, but is of particular interest to this chapter in its depiction of crime in *Star Wars: Episode II—Attack of the Clones*. The narrative introduction to *Attack of the Clones* in the video game begins with a cutscene recreation in LEGO of the opening scene of the movie. This scene is a terrorist attack on the starship of Padmé Amidala, herself a member of the Galactic Senate, as she arrives on Coruscant. While the movie depicts this violent attack and its consequences in some detail—with a catastrophic explosion, material destruction, mass causalities, blood, and death—*LEGO Star Wars: The Skywalker Saga* plays this scene for laughs. The video game replaces the young and somewhat bloodied female victim of the movie with an elderly male LEGO figure who overacts his own "death scene" while ironically referencing Stanley Kubric's *Spartacus* (1960). Again in contrast to the movie, those affected by the terrorist blast in the video game are shown to be unharmed and only "playing" dead in the scene.

This comedic treatment also extends to a subsequent attempt on the life of Senator Amidala on Coruscant in *Attack of the Clones*. This second attempted assassination of Padmé in the movie involved a bounty hunter deploying two poisonous arthropods against her as she slept in her quarters. In the cinematic release the sight of these slithering creatures in the dark and quiet quarters of the senator, creeping towards her face, was sinister and unsettling. *LEGO Star Wars: The Skywalker Saga*, however, re-creates the scene comedically in a cutscene. The arthropods in the video game are present, but not seeking to poison Padmé. Instead they are seen to precariously position an anvil above the senator as she sleeps. This use of a comedic prop more commonly seen in the Warner Brothers cartoons of the 20th century removes any potential horror or threat from the scene. The anvil in the video game does not drop on Padmé, and even if it was to do so the consequences of this trope as it plays out in classic cartoons are never fatal.[3] Beyond the comedy of these cutscenes, issues of crime and justice on Coruscant are also encountered in both mainline gameplay and side missions, particularly in the city-planet's underworld Uscru District.

Playing through the Uscru District in the video game allows the player to descend from the surface level of Coruscant—with its architecture and environment encoded with political, economic, and religious power—to move deeper down into the planet's physical and metaphorical underworld.

In contrast to the surface level, the Uscru underworld is devoid of natural light, instead adopting an aesthetic of neon signs, strip lighting, and towering holographs. Just as the movie offers a brighter interpretation of the classic cyberpunk city seen in the visual iconography of *Blade Runner* (1982) so *LEGO Star Wars: The Skywalker Saga* further intensifies this aesthetic style. Many of the bright neon signs in the video game are written in Aurebesh, the stylized bespoke alphabet of the Star Wars universe, and when translated indicate the illicit nature of the Uscru District. The "Outer Rim Arcade" evokes the disorderly system far from Coruscant. "Hutt's Headgear" namechecks the franchise's most infamous gangster Jabba the Hutt. The "Correllian Cantina" draws attention to planet Correllia, the homeworld of Han Solo that became penetrated by crime syndicates. A long neon-lit Aurebesh tickertape circles above the streets, encouraging those below to "Report All Suspicious Activity." There are thus indications of securitization at play here, but one has to look quite deeply at the Uscru environment to literally de-code the signs.

The gameplay experience at the Uscru District is typical of the wider game and, indeed, previous LEGO Star Wars installments. Free roaming around large hub areas is encouraged, including through side missions, puzzles, and challenges, with the aim of collecting LEGO studs and Star Wars-styled "kyber bricks."[4] Taking the opportunity to diverge further from canonical storytelling, side missions in the Uscru District are light and amusing, and largely work to diminish any danger inherent in both the particular setting itself and the wider Star Wars universe. The "Crime Dining" quest, for example, simply involves tracking down diners who have left a local restaurant without paying their bill. Crime is rendered as minor and inconsequential. The "Dancing with the Star Wars" side mission is silly even beyond the pun-laden title. The quest here begins on the streets of the Uscru District with the player encountering a very minor canonical character, a female alien Rodian named Greeata Jendowanian. Greeata is dancer for a band known to have performed for Jabba the Hutt. She is new to Coruscant, broke, and seeking work. Reducing her previous exposure to the galaxy's most notorious organized crime syndicate as a simple matter of health and safety at work she remarks,

> Greeata Jendowanian: That whole business at Jabba's palace really opened my eyes. I was lucky to get out alive! I will never underestimate the importance of a safe working environment again . . .

Helping her involves meeting with the owner of the Outlander Club to ask if he can give her a job as a dancer. The Outlander Boss, however, is conveniently "out of town," visiting the owner of the Mos Eisley cantina. Tracking him down at the infamous "hive of scum and villainy" on Tatooine only results in finding that he is elsewhere, at a self-styled "shindig" of the "High-Class Club Owners" on the planet Takodana. Upon locating him there, the player finds that his help is conditional on creating a party atmosphere with some "banging tunes." The player must use Jedi Force powers to make by-standers dance for the Outlander Boss, at which point he declares that the player is a "party animal" and that the dancing job is Greeata's to take. This is fun and frivolous, but also works to de-render the Uscru District as a site of risk or danger. Coruscant becomes place of comedy, not of crime; immersing the gamer in a playful approximation of this city-planet while simultaneously stripping the city of its foreboding affect. Despite presenting Coruscant as an expansive free-roam environment to explore, *LEGO Star Wars: The Skywalker Saga* dilutes the cinematic city, reducing its engagement with crime and justice to the trivial and obfuscating to gamers the complexities of the urban experience.

Sanitizing Violence on Tatooine

Tatooine is the classic desert planet of the twin suns first seen in the 1977 cinema release *Star Wars*. In this movie the character Obi-Wan Kenobi refers to the planet's Mos Eisley Spaceport as a "wretched hive of scum and villainy." Given the infamous reputation of this location in Star Wars, and its wider resonance in popular culture, Mos Eisley presents a logical case study for this chapter. Tatooine features across several episodes of the cinematic Skywalker saga, but when played in sequential timeline order in *LEGO Star Wars: The Skywalker Saga*, as per the research design for this chapter, the specific settlement of Mos Eisley is first encountered in *Star Wars: Episode IV—A New Hope*. The in-game playable protagonists here during the first playthrough are Luke Skywalker and Old Ben Kenobi. The introduction to Mos Eisley in the video game begins with a LEGO cutscene recreation of Kenobi's aforementioned warning to Luke on the dangers of this spaceport settlement. What follows is, in some contrast to the movie, a light-hearted representation of Mos Eisley largely devoid of serious danger. The city is shown, for example through the presence of LEGO stormtroopers manning checkpoints, as securitized by the Empire; however, any threatening consequence of state violence is removed. LEGO Twi'leks boogie around a beatbox as Kenobi outlines the nature of the supposedly hostile local environment to Luke, and Jawas jive at the entrance to an infamous cantina ostensibly frequented by criminals and smugglers.

The playable video game scene inside this cantina is largely true to the layout and aesthetic of the corresponding movie, but the narrative differs. As a further cutscene exposition plays out, the background violence—fighting and blaster-shooting between the LEGO characters frequenting the cantina—includes a LEGO Rodian character standing on the head of a misplaced broom only to be hit square on the nose by the broom handle.[5] The violence here is slapstick; humorous and inconsequential, with little prospect of any lasting harm to anyone present. The omission of serious violence here again contributes to a more comedic and light-hearted tone in comparison to the cinematic source material. In particular, the game features a re-imagining in LEGO of the confrontation in the cantina between the intergalactic smuggler Han Solo and the Rodian bounty hunter Greedo.

The original 1977 movie famously depicts a conversation between Solo and Greedo in a dark recess of the cantina, which culminates in Solo pre-emptively shooting and killing Greedo before the Rodian can respond. *LEGO Star Wars: The Skywalker Saga*, in contrast, plays this scene comically, almost directly copying the comedic beats of a shootout scene in the 1991 movie *The Naked Gun 2½: The Smell of Fear*. The video game scene shows Solo and Greedo ducking at opposite ends of a short table and popping up from their positions of cover to shoot their laser blasters waywardly at one another. This ends not in Greedo's death, but with his laser blaster jamming and Solo physically throwing his own blaster a short distance to hit Greedo on the head. Greedo walks off glumly, while Solo celebrates exuberantly in a classic LEGO style. Through this scene *LEGO Star Wars: The Skywalker Saga*, as a video game paratext, works to sanitize conflict and removes morally ambiguous violence.

Representations of crime and justice at Mos Eisley are further developed through the numerous side missions to be played through. Seven of the 140 side missions in *LEGO Star Wars: The Skywalker Saga* begin at Mos Eisley. These Mos Eisley side missions, particularly those centered in and around the cantina, become further sources of the sanitization of violence, with such acts reduced to inconsequential fun. As such they offer a further interesting study of "dark play"—understood as the engagement with video game content, themes, or actions that may be considered problematic, subversive, controversial, deviant, or tasteless, and which may be transformed in the act of play (Linderoth & Mortensen, 2015)—beyond the core canonical content of the video game.

The "Baba Bar Brawl" side mission, for example, allows a minor alien Aqualish character named Ponda Baba, who had his arm severed by Obi-Wan Kenobi in the cantina in the movie *A New Hope*, to return with a new arm and an offer to team up for a "Good old fashioned Cantina brawl." The subsequent chaotic play has the tone of a school playground scuffle, with the background character "Local Ruffian" screaming "Fiiiiiight!" The violence does not depict death or lasting harm. Victims of the side mission are instead simply shown to be dazed, with shining stars and glowing musical notes circling around their heads as they dizzily sway. In fact, the most consequential crime committed at the cantina, represented in the side mission "End of the Road for Modal Nodes?," is the cantina band having their instruments stolen by some "music hatin' punks." The mission encourages the player to recover the instruments via series of off-world space battles. Even here, however, there is sanitization at play: the offending "punks" are bounty hunters, reduced in the game to partaking in petty theft and speaking in humorous dialogue. Playing through the side missions on Mos Eisley disarms the town and sanitizes of the reputation of this settlement as a "wretched hive of scum and villainy."

Policing Race and Parodying Prisons at Canto Bight

The third case-study site of this chapter is the Monte Carlo-inspired city of Canto Bight, on the desert planet Cantonica. Canto Bight features as a setting in the theatrical release *Star Wars: Episode VIII—The Last Jedi* and is playable as such in *LEGO Star Wars: The Skywalker Saga*. Upon a first playthrough the in-game playable protagonists at Canto Bight are the Rebel Alliance heroes Rose Tico and Finn. In the movie *The Last Jedi* Rose and Finn, two high-profile rebel heroes very demonstrably portrayed by people of color, are subjected to the unprovoked use of electro-shock stun prods by officers of the Canto Bight Police Department, all of whom are ethnically white. During this scene, which takes place in the opulent casino, Rose and Finn suffer this police violence prior to them being told they are under arrest for a parking violation.[6] Given that the movie was released in 2017, four years on from the beginning of the Black Lives Matter movement (Rickford, 2016), this particular depiction of police violence in Star Wars cinema presented an important site of critical politics. Indeed, given the significant and very public "racist backlash" from some elements of the fandom to the casting of John Boyega, as Black British actor, to the role of Finn in *Star Wars: Episode VII—The Force Awakens* (Hodge and Boston, 2018) the Canto Bight arrest scene can be further read as a deliberate choice to engage positively with a progressive political movement.

In the video game, however, as part of a cutscene that progresses the gameplay narrative, the encounter between our rebel heroes and the police is reinterpreted in a fashion that strips the cinema scene of its critical politics. Rose and Finn are instead simply physically grabbed, restrained, and arrested by the LEGO officers, with no weapons used. The officers in this particular cutscene are ethnically white, as per the movie, but the video game subsequently diversifies the wider cohort of Canto Bight police officers in gameplay to incorporate officers of color. Previous studies have indicated how the inclusion of Rose and Finn in Star Wars storytelling is acknowledged as representative of the shift in the franchise towards a more ethnically diverse cast of characters (Booy, 2021). The diversification of the cast of Canto Bight police officers in the video game, however, presents a more problematic politics; with the consequence of diminishing *white* police violence against people of color. This signals a significant redaction in *LEGO Star Wars: The Skywalker Saga*, stripping out the critical social justice politics of the counterpart movie.

Despite differing depictions of the arrest, in both the movie and the video game Rose and Finn are subsequently taken to the Canto Bight Police Department Jail for incarceration. In the movie the Canto Bight jail is a somewhat flat and perfunctory functional holding pen for prisoners. The same location in *LEGO Star Wars: The Skywalker Saga*, however, is instead reimagined as a site for multi-level gameplay and playful political commentary. A circular succession of cells, with broad arched doorways that are barred from top to bottom, form the interior circumference of the jail, more fully evoking Panoptic architecture and a techno-Victorian aesthetic. Supervising police officers are housed in a secure central control tower from which they outwardly surveil prisoners in the surrounding cells, including through two CCTV monitoring stations. The first playable action here in the video game begins with an audio address that is broadcast to those individuals detained in the facility. This address cheerily announces,

PUBLIC ADDRESS SYSTEM: Attention. Those prisoners who are asking what time check out is; we would like to remind you that this is a jail, not a hotel. Thank you.

Political and media discourses in the United Kingdom and the United States around the stereotypical tropes of the prison as a "holiday camp" or a "country club" have been foregrounded and explored by James Treadwell in his own analysis of the carceral video game *Prison Architect* (Treadwell, 2020). Treadwell (2020, p. 190) remarked,

It would appear that there are those members of the public (and particularly the right-wing tabloid news media) that seemingly want and indeed appear to expect prisons to feel like nineteenth-century institutions of severe and unremitting punishment. Obviously, within such austere regimes, there is no place for PlayStation. In prison architect terms, they do not want the rehabilitative parts, they want guard towers and riot cops.

LEGO Star Wars: The Skywalker Saga lampoons and subverts such societal stereotypes by juxtaposing the claim that the jail is "not a hotel" with the aforementioned techno-Victorian aesthetic and the actions of both the police officers (who act as prison guards) and the prisoners themselves.

In both the movie and in the video game the officers guarding the jail quietly engage in a card game to pass the time. However, in the video game they also excitedly bounce on trampolines in their central quarters. The gleeful comments from the guards here include,

GUARD: Trampoline, you're the best pal a guy could ask for.
GUARD: If my pa could see me bounce now! Woo!

Playing as Rose and Finn in the jail causes a mass prison riot, and one that is well-received by the prisoners in the gameplay narrative:

PRISONER: RIOT! YEAH!
PRISONER: I love a good riot!
PRISONER: Oh boy! I'm gonna do me a whole buncha new crimes!

Even here, however, the presence of the protagonists as escapees and the impending riot does not prevent one guard from continuing to enjoy bouncing on his trampoline. In contrast to the video game depiction of police and prison officers, research evidences a strong commitment of each to their job through either a "sense of mission" (Bowling et al., 2019) or a "desire to make a difference" (Arnold, 2016). Similarly, the depiction of prison riots as opportunistic, straightforward fun runs contrary to existing research on the topic. Carrabine (2005), for example, emphasizes the pejorative nature of the term "riot" itself, the complex precipitating factors to any such disturbance in a prison context, and the broader issues of the production and maintenance of a given social order. In the video game, therefore, Canto Bight presents a complex and perhaps contradictory representation of the politics of crime and justice through comedy; willing to erase police violence while subsequently parodying policing and the prison.

Crime, Justice, and the Consequences of Comedy in *LEGO Star Wars: The Skywalker Saga*

The preceding analysis points to the ways in which *LEGO Star Wars: The Skywalker Saga* "makes light of darkness" in its choice to eclectically and eccentrically re-write the politics of crime and justice in Star Wars. It does so knowing its own cultural status, and with a clear understanding of its position as a metatext within a transmedia franchise that has multigenerational appeal. In this sense the video game may be seen to exhibit LEGO as both a product and an expression of postmodernism (Konzack, 2014; Lueth, 2017) and extend the "gleeful postmodern irony" that characterizes recent LEGO superhero media (Martin, 2020). In its treatment of crime and justice, from Coruscant to Canto Bight, *LEGO Star Wars: The Skywalker Saga* discloses key themes of postmodernism: from playful juxtaposition and reinterpretation of existing narratives and cultural icons; through meta-references and reflexive self-awareness; and—particularly through its side missions—towards a disruption of the linearity of the franchise canon. An overall consequence at play here, however, particularly impacting upon younger players, is an element of historical erasure.

As a video game with transgenerational appeal *LEGO Star Wars: The Skywalker Saga* will be played through, and its intertextual narrative read differently, by different generations of players. Each generation will have their own particular awareness of Star Wars, dependent on their previous engagement with the wider transmedia franchise. The aforementioned Han and Greedo scene, for example, will be viewed contrastingly by adults who saw *Star Wars* in the cinema upon its original 1977 release and understand the controversial dilemma of "who shot first" as compared to children today who may simply wish to play the latest LEGO video game and know very little about Star Wars, perhaps beyond the contemporary pop culture phenomenon of "Baby Yoda" in *The Mandalorian* (Freeman & Smith, 2023). A child playing *LEGO Star Wars: The Skywalker Saga* is not necessarily likely to have seen *A New Hope*; with the video game thus operating to effectively erase the morally ambiguous violence presented in the movie. The stripping away of previously complex issues of crime and justice—or its reframing as inconsequential comedy—therefore matters precisely *because* this video game is likely to attract younger players. Moreover, it is also important to consider that, on balance, *LEGO Star Wars: The Skywalker Saga* may simply not be particularly clever in its comedic reinterpretation or erasure of the politics of crime and justice.

The proclivity towards postmodernism in LEGO is often well-received by critics and adult audiences; many of whom will particularly laud the self-aware and sometimes cynical humor of the LEGO movies as a contemporary pop culture phenomenon. This comedic style is almost entirely replicated in counterpart LEGO video games, including the LEGO Star Wars series. James C. Taylor (2022, p. 88), however, has remarked upon how such postmodern encounters, at least as they are apparent in superhero cinema, have important limitations:

> Through intertextually engaging with past forms, postmodern parody exposes the ideological positions that their representations inscribe, reflexively critiquing histories of representation. Yet postmodern parody's critical edge is compromised . . . due to postmodern texts being produced in the same institutions as the texts they are targeting, which engenders forms of complicity with the institutions.

This tension may explain in part, for example, the contradictions apparent at Canto Bight. On the surface, given the subversion and provocative postmodern irony of the wider LEGO franchise in cinema (see Martin, 2020), the Canto Bight Police Department Jail and its guards work to offer a comedic but critical reflection on contemporary penal practice. This is achieved through the caricature of the lazy and disengaged guard alongside the satire of media and political discourses that depict the prison as cozy and comfortable and prisoners as violent and unruly. Alternatively, one may also convincingly argue that the depiction of prisons and the police in the video game works to humanize the powerful criminal justice actors at play; thereby perpetuating a conservative ideology that may align with the dominant worldviews of both the LEGO company and Disney as global megacorporations, each with a stake in validating and perpetuating existing systems of power and control (Mazzarella & Hains, 2019). Overall, the comedic treatment of crime and justice in *LEGO Star Wars: The Skywalker Saga* works to both censor and sanitize these issues; compounded by the video game's disarmingly playful aesthetic. In "making light of darkness," therefore, *LEGO Star Wars: The Skywalker Saga* is a profoundly political text, and one with important consequences through both its exposure and erasure of crime and justice issues to a diverse demographic of gamers.

Notes

1 *Star Wars* was retroactively named as *Star Wars: Episode IV—A New Hope* in April 1981.
2 Additionally, for the purpose of comprehensiveness, the analysis for this chapter also engaged with all available downloadable content (DLC) character packs that were released between April 5 and May 4, 2022.
3 In the classic Road Runner cartoons, for example, Wile E. Coyote fails in such attempts to crush his avian nemesis, and survives even when his elaborate traps inevitably backfire on him (Cohen, 1975).
4 Side missions in video games, sometimes called sidequests, are mini-missions that deviate from the larger in-game narrative, allowing players to complete a small series of tasks often to obtain or unlock additional skills, characters, attributes, or gameplay areas. Side missions are prevalent in *LEGO Star Wars: The Skywalker Saga*, with 140 playable across the game.
5 This slapstick scene—which acts as an homage to the recurring fate of *The Simpsons* character Sideshow Bob (Roberts, 2019)—works to usurp and subvert any lingering threat from the "villains" in the cantina.
6 The role of the Canto Bight Police Department is to ensure "public safety," but particularly the safety and security of the visitors spending money at this destination, and to maintain a "relaxing atmosphere" in the resort (Hidalgo, 2017).

References

Arnold, H. (2016). The prison officer. In Y. Jewkes, B. Crewe, & J. Bennett (Eds.) *Handbook on prisons* (pp. 265–283). Routledge.
Atkinson, C. (2022). Security politics, crisis, and techno-securitisation in Star Wars: From the Fall of the Jedi to the Reign of the Empire. *Contemporary Social Science*, 17(5), 501–516.
Atkinson, C. (2023). Deception: A critical discourse analysis of undercover policing and intelligence operations in *Star Wars: The Clone Wars*. *Journal of Policing, Intelligence and Counter Terrorism*, 18(1), 95–111.
Baker, K. (2013). *The ultimate guide to classic game consoles* [ebook]. eBookIt.com.
Buerkle, R. (2014). Playset nostalgia: *LEGO Star Wars: The Video Game* and the transgenerational appeal of the LEGO video game franchise. In J.P. Wolf (Ed.), *LEGO studies: Examining the building blocks of a transmedial phenomenon* (pp. 118–152). Routledge.

Black, R.W., Tomlinson, B., & Korobkova, K. (2016). Play and identity in gendered LEGO franchises. *International Journal of Play*, 5(1), 64–76.

Booy, M. (2021). *Interpreting Star Wars*. Bloomsbury Academic.

Bowling, B., Reiner, R., & Sheptycki, J. (2019). *The politics of the police*. Oxford University Press.

Braun, V., & Clarke, V. (2021). *Thematic analysis: A practical guide*. Sage.

Carrabine, E. (2005). Prison riots, social order and the problem of legitimacy. *The British Journal of Criminology*, 45(6), 896–913.

Cohen, M.S. (1975). Looney tunes and merrie melodies. *The Velvet Light Trap*, 15, 33–37.

Freeman, M., & Smith, A.N. (2023). *Transmedia/Genre*. Palgrave Macmillan.

Giddings, S., & Kennedy, H.W. (2008). Little Jesuses and *@#?-off robots: On cybernetics, aesthetics, and not being very good at *Lego Star Wars*. In M. Swalwell & J. Wilson (Eds.), *The pleasures of computer gaming: Essays on cultural history, theory and aesthetics* (pp. 13–32). McFarland & Company.

Goggin, J. (2017). "Everything is awesome": The LEGO movie and the affective politics of security. *Finance and Society*, 3(2), 143–158.

Hidalgo, P. (2017). *Star Wars: The Last Jedi the visual dictionary*. Dorling Kindersley.

Hodge, D.W., & Boston, J. (2018). The racism awakens. In K. Derry & J.C. Lyden (Eds.), *The myth awakens: Canon, conservatism, and fan reception of Star Wars* (pp. 74–91). Cascade Books.

Hunting, K. (2019). The man behind the mask: Camp and queer masculinity in *LEGO Batman*. In R.C. Hains & S.R. Mazzarella (Eds.), *Cultural studies of LEGO: More than just bricks* (pp. 297–319). Springer International Publishing.

Kaser, R. (2023). December 2022 NPD: Holiday sales boost otherwise slow year. *Venture Beat*. https://venturebeat.com/games/december-2022-npd-holiday-sales-boost-otherwise-slow-year/

Kennedy, L. (2021). "Whenever there's trouble, just yelp for help": Crime, conservation, and corporatization in *Paw Patrol*. *Crime, Media, Culture*, 17(2), 255–270.

Konzack, L. (2014). The cultural history of LEGO. In M.J.P. Wolf (Ed.), *LEGO Studies: Examining the building blocks of a transmedial phenomenon* (pp. 1–14). Routledge.

Lee, J.R. (2020). *Deconstructing LEGO: The medium and messages of LEGO play*. Springer International.

Linderoth, J., & Mortensen, T.E. (2015). Dark play: The aesthetics of controversial playfulness. In T.E. Mortensen, J. Linderoth, & A.M.L. Brown (Eds.), *The dark side of game play: Controversial issues in playful environments* (pp. 3–12). Routledge.

Lueth, D. (2017). The reality of LEGO: Building the apocalypse. In W. Irwin & R.T. Cook (Eds.), *LEGO and philosophy: Constructing reality brick by brick* (pp. 153–162). Wiley.

Martin, D. (2020). Reanimating the dark knight: Superheroes, animation and the critical reception of *The Lego Batman Movie*. *Animation*, 15(1), 93–107.

Mattes, A. (2019). Everything is awesome when you're part of a list: The flattening of distinction in post-ironic LEGO media. In R.C. Hains & S.R. Mazzarella (Eds.), *Cultural studies of LEGO: More than just bricks* (pp. 73–95). Springer International.

Mazzarella, S.R., & Hains, R.C. (2019). "Let there be LEGO!": An introduction to *Cultural Studies of LEGO*. In R.C. Hains & S.R. Mazzarella (Eds.), *Cultural studies of LEGO: More than just bricks* (pp. 1–20). Springer International.

Mäyrä, F. (2015). Little evils: Subversive uses of children's games. In T.E. Mortensen, J. Linderoth, & A.M.L. Brown (Eds.), *The dark side of game play: Controversial issues in playful environments* (pp. 82–99). Routledge.

Rafter, N., & Brown, M. (2011). *Criminology goes to the movies*. New York University Press.

Rickford, R. (2016). Black Lives Matter: Toward a modern practice of mass struggle. *New Labor Forum, 25*(1), 34–42.

Roberts, A. (2019). *A philosophy of humour*. Springer International.

Taylor, J.C. (2022). Postmodern parody in animated superhero cinema. In L. Piatti-Farnell (Ed.), *The superhero multiverse: Readapting comic book icons in twenty-first-century film and popular media* (pp. 87–104). Lexington Books.

Treadwell, J. (2020). "Gaming the system?" The merits, myths and realities in understanding Prison Architect: Security, rehabilitation and violence as represented in the world's bestselling carceral video game. In C. Kelly, A. Lynes, & K. Hoffin (Eds.), *Video games crime and next-gen deviance: Reorienting the debate* (pp. 175–199). Emerald.

Wilczak, A. (2021). Radical criminology and *Star Wars*. In S.E. Daly (Ed.), *Theories of crime through popular culture* (pp. 219–238). Springer International Publishing.

Williams, D. (2022, April 21). "Lego Star Wars: The Skywalker Saga" is Lego's bestselling game to date. *New Musical Express*. https://www.nme.com/news/gaming-news/lego-star-wars-the-skywalker-saga-is-legos-best-selling-game-to-date-3209723.

Wodak, R., & Meyer, M. (2009). Critical discourse analysis: History, agenda, theory and methodology. In R. Wodak & M. Meyer (Eds.), *Methods of critical discourse analysis* (pp. 1–33). Sage.

Wolf, M.J.P. (2018). Adapting the Death Star into LEGO: The case of LEGO set #10188. In S. Guynes & D. Hassler-Forest (Eds.), *Star Wars and the history of transmedia storytelling* (pp. 169–185). Amsterdam University Press.

8

FIGHTING FIRE WITH FIRE

Disco Elysium, Hard-boiled Detective Noir, and Procedural (In)justice

Edward L.W. Green

Humans have long been fascinated by crime stories. As Yardley, Kelly, and Robinson-Edwards state, "A subject of popular fascination, representations of crime have been drawing audiences since at least the times of the Greek and Roman dramatists" (2019, p. 505; Biressi & Bloom, 2001; Turnbull, 2014). Criminologists have similarly been fascinated by "true crime" narratives (Linnemann, 2015; Yardley et al, 2019; Linnemann, 2022). Cultural criminologists, in particular, have taken seriously the content of such narratives as well as their cultural, political, and economic contexts (Ferrell et al., 2015, p. 63; Linnemann, 2022). Similarly, criminology has long considered the role of the police in the cultural imaginary, exploring the complex relationship between police culture and behavior (including deviance and brutality), mediated representations of the police, and public perceptions of the police (Marina & Marina, 2023).

An underexamined domain of "true crime" or police detective stories are video games, a medium unique in its ability to pull in its audience through interactive storytelling. Criminologists have only recently begun examining videogames to understand how such artistic works portray or reflect reality and create emotional responses through narrative and environmental ambiance (Steinmetz, 2018; Skott & Bengtson, 2021; Steinmetz & Petkovsek 2022). Perhaps no game has become more synonymous with the hard-boiled detective genre than developer ZA/UM's *Disco Elysium*.[1] The hard-boiled detective genre can be described as a rough, callous, and often self-destructive detective with a violent but overall good moral code.

Disco Elysium, released in 2019 on PC and a "Final Cut" which added voice acting for consoles in 2021, is a roleplaying game that combines true crime, detective stories, and science-fiction genres to provide a rich site for

DOI: 10.4324/9781003346869-8

criminological analysis regarding the framing of police work, trauma, and disillusionment. The game is set in a fictional, dystopian, rundown city rife with crime, political conflict, and eroded or altogether dismantled social institutions. The protagonist of *Disco Elysium*, Harry Du Bois, is a hard-living detective who, at the outset of the game, wakes up with amnesia during a murder investigation. While the challenge of the game surrounds a "whodunit" mystery, much of the game's intrigue and peril are rooted in moral dilemmas, self-doubt, and, ultimately, the contradictions of conducting police work in a broken society. In this manner, the game engages in the "essential subject matter of criminology—the manufacture of meaning around issues of crime, transgression, and control" (Ferrell et al., 2015, p. 87) by exploring the conflicts and complications of doing justice work in a hostile, morally fraught, gritty, urban environment.

This chapter examines representations of policing in the dystopian world of *Disco Elysium*. It first considers how policing intersects with the gameplay mechanics and science-fiction setting of *Disco Elysium*. The analysis then turns to consider how the narrative of the game presents the player-character, a detective, with moral dilemmas and how these dilemmas reflect those that confront real-world police officers. First is the moral dilemma of bravery which concerns the demand that officers confront instances of human awful while suppressing their emotional reactions and trauma. The second dilemma concerns the fact that police work often requires that officers take sides, sometimes in ways that can have significant political consequences. Finally, *Disco Elysium* portrays the moral dilemma of policing that officers must sometimes make difficult decisions concerning the interpretation and presentation of truth.

Before delving into the analysis, however, this chapter reviews the genre of hard-boiled detective narratives to provide context for the analysis. Specifically, this chapter considers how scholars have analyzed the popular genre of crime fiction the hard-boiled detective novels turned into film noir movies of the 1940s. This chapter then explains the methodological approach used herein to make sense of the complex interactive and narratological elements of the game.

The Hard-Boiled Detective Genre

To understand *Disco Elysium*, it is first necessary to understand the literary traditions from which it draws many of its themes and narrative conventions which include detective stories and, specifically, the "hard-boiled detective" genre. A key feature of detective stories is that they typically feature a brilliant, fastidious, and sometimes peculiar detective capable of seemingly supernatural feats of deduction (Featherstone, 2014). Prominent examples include Edgar Allan Poe's Auguste Dupin (1841) and Arthur Conan Doyle's Sherlock Holmes (1887–1927). Relatedly, these stories also heavily fictionalized the state of scientific methods of the late 19th century, mythologizing the kinds of tools and capabilities available to detectives of the time.

The hard-boiled detective genre builds from prior detective stories and introduces grittier and darker plots, settings, and characters. Featherstone (2014, p. 277) notes that a key element that characterizes hard-boiled detective stories is that they revel in urban realism, set within grim and decaying cityscapes riddled with poverty, lawlessness, and crime, especially murder (see also: Yardley et al., 2019). They are dark settings that mirror the stories' protagonists—the hard-boiled detectives themselves. The *good* guys have to be as tough and often violent as the *bad* guys. Consider, for instance, Dashiell Hammett's (1929) *The Maltese Falcon,* which was set in a dark, perilous, and seemingly lawless urban setting which provides the backdrop for the activities of Sam Spade, a hard-nosed, hard-drinking, misogynistic sleuth. Hard-boiled detective stories such as *The Maltese Falcon*, *The Thin Man*, and *Red Harvest* were likely influenced by Hammett's brief experience working for Pinkerton Detective Agency (a prominent real-world private detective agency), where he learned about stakeouts, paperwork, and informal violent and/or illegal justice often involving an investigative ethos where the means justify the ends versus the other way around—catching the "bad" guy. Indeed, a key characteristic of the hard-boiled detective is that they are willing to get their hands dirty (i.e., use violence and means outside the law) to achieve justice.

The hard-boiled detective genre gained new life in the post-World War II era with readers who had endured the horrors of global mechanized war and suffered the brutal effects of the Great Depression, a period "defined by systemic economic and ecological failure, and horrific economic hardship; it was lived out by many as a time of profound drift" (Ferrell, 2018, p. 83). During these historical conditions, gritty urban realism of a transient, diverse, and unequal society became the chaotic world for street vigilantes with a moral code toward narratives of anti-heroes. In other words, the reader would empathize with outright violence toward the greater good. These narratives had a backdrop of class consciousness yet just as often as color blindness or outright dehumanization of ethnic or foreign characters. Hollywood during the 1940s turned many of these hard-boiled detective novels into motion pictures which brought a now easily recognizable aesthetic to the detective genre—*film noir.*

As the new iteration of the hard-boiled detective genre, film noir featured ordinary characters who broke the law and found themselves at odds with the growing state apparatus. The environment of the gritty urban area becomes a story device for critiquing ideas of political ideologies, social justice, and state injustice. In this manner, Broe (2003) argues that the film noir was shaped by changing social conditions and reflected a lens of class, crime, and a growing neoliberal state apparatus that had emerged following The New Deal to manage an increasingly disenfranchised working class. At the same time, film noir stories have been argued to uphold the status quo by featuring down-on-their-luck White characters at the top of the social order or what Broe (2003) describes as the sympathetic fugitive outsider, yet creating a sense of who is worthy of stepping outside the law to help. This would be especially true of the White female victim within both hard-boiled detective novels and early film noir. The 1950s saw a shift in the telling of crime and detective stories as the power of labor waned and the Cold War began in earnest (Broe, 2003). This period saw the production of police procedural films and television shows which depicted White male police in a more sympathetic light (i.e., shows like *Dragnet*).

As indicated, crime and detective stories—including the hard-boiled variety—often rely on various character archetypes which are, unfortunately, often entangled with racial and gendered stereotypes. For instance, most of the protagonists of these stories are White men. The genre wouldn't prominently include a Black protagonist until 1990 when Walter Mosley published *Devil in a Blue Dress* which features Easy Rawlings, an African American detective in Los Angeles in 1948. In addition, racial stereotypes feature prominently in depictions of crime and victimization in these stories, which often rely on what Webb (2021) terms "danger narratives" framing crime as acts committed along racial lines, with non-Whites preying on Whites (especially White women). These narratives tend to overemphasize the threat of interracial crime and violence while simultaneously underemphasizing or overlooking the terror and oppression being visited upon communities of color (which were substantial during this period). While she examines mostly true crime narratives, Webb's insights can easily be applied to the hard-boiled detective genre as its portrayals of crime and criminal organizations are similarly racialized, painting crime and victimization as largely stratified along both racial and gender lines.

Additionally, hard-boiled detective stories often heavily rely upon certain two-dimensional representations of women, who tend to be either someone to save, a "damsel in distress," or someone to be saved from, a *femme fatale,* an attractive female who masterminds an advantage by using chivalry as a shield to manipulate the otherwise helpful (and often overbearing but gullible) men in her life. One notable exception to this dichotomy is what Masten (2018) calls the "*femme fiable,*" or dependable woman. Effie Perine from Hammett's *The Maltese Falcon* is one example of a strong and competent woman in hard-boiled detective literature. These characters exist as the reliable assistant to the detective and, importantly, rarely constitute a love interest for the male protagonist. Masten (2018) argues that the *femme fatale,* such as the antagonist Brigid O'Shaughnessy in *The Maltese Falcon*, helps to drive the plot and to support the importance of, "stronger female characters such as Effie," the assistant and reliable sidekick (p. 31). This essentialized gender dichotomy nonetheless reinforces a social order between men and women through narrative.

Though it has evolved over time, the core elements of the hard-boiled detective genre remain relatively static. Involved is a pessimistic and grim view of human nature, the idea that order is tenuously maintained by well-meaning though flawed police officers, a view that justice sometimes must be achieved outside the confines of the law (and sometimes through dirty means), and formulaic character archetypes that rely on various racial and ethnic stereotypes. As such, any contemporary medium that draws from the genre must grapple with the underlying politics of the genre. As will be explored, *Disco Elysium* pulls from the genre to make commentary on policing and *doing* justice in the context of a broken society in a manner more nuanced than its predecessors.

Methodology

Cultural criminology explores, among other things, narratives, media representations, and entertainment commodities (such as video games) as pathways to examine deeper problems of control, resistance, crime, and deviance. As Yardley and colleagues (2019, p. 504) explain, "criminological study has moved beyond the traditional positivism of treating crime and its representation as separate and discrete to acknowledging that the representations are themselves locales of knowledge, sites where meanings are performed and challenged" (see also Carrabine, 2008; Wakeman, 2014). Involved is a fluid-yet-systematic approach tailored to the particular cultural phenomenon in question and the data available (Ferrell et al., 2015).

To begin, several influential detective books and short stories were read to understand traditional detective tropes that permeate *Disco Elysium*. These include Poe's (1841) *The Murders in the Rue Morgue*, Hammett's (1929) *The Maltese Falcon*, Raymond Chandler's *The Big Sleep* (1939), and Walter Mosley's (1990) *Devil in a Blue Dress*. While Poe's detective is more decorum-oriented and measured, the rest of these stories feature heavy drinking, philandering, and violent (when the situation calls for it) male detectives attempting to solve crimes and thwart criminals—flawed heroes doing their best in fundamentally dysfunctional worlds, where average police fail. These novels are often referred to as critically acclaimed and influential books within the hard-boiled detective genre of crime novels.

The analysis of *Disco Elysium* itself involved playing the game twice (> 100 hours of gameplay logged). Such extensive engagement was necessary to try out different decision paths throughout the game. The player can choose what kind of police officer Harry is as explained later. Given that the game is interactive and offers players choices that have consequences within the internal logic of the systems of the game, exploring some of these paths is warranted. *Disco Elysium* is a lengthy game, in which a single play-through for entertainment alone can take up to 50 or more hours.

Much of the game is examining an area and interacting with items, buttons, characters, animals, and so on. Point-and-click controls offer a slower but more thorough—even ponderous—means of narrative interaction, much like the kinds of methodical work needed for good police investigative work. Nevertheless, the game was designed with keyboard and mouse controls (Personal Computer) and I played through the Nintendo Switch (Console) version of the game, which uses a game controller. The game control was initially clunky, yet the point-and-click nature of the game quickly became part of the process of investigation and worked within the antique aesthetic of the world itself.

While playing the game, extensive notes were taken and key quotes were transcribed. Relying on inductive content analysis, themes that manifested throughout the game regarding the perils and pitfalls of policing in the world of *Disco Elysium* were considered as well as how the mechanics and world-building in the game structure the role of the police, and how the game reflects moral dilemmas confronting real-world police. The characteristics of the tough, traumatized, heavy drinking, misogynist who solves crime with an off-beat moral code are also visible in some real-world police research literature (Velazquez & Hernandez, 2019).

Policing in *Disco Elysium*

The beginning of *Disco Elysium* immediately places the player in the role of a flawed, broken, hard-boiled detective. The game opens with a black screen slowly dissolving into an impressionistic painting initially introducing two inner voices: the "ancient reptilian brain" and the "limbic system." These voices, among others introduced through the game, provide an internal dialog that helps convey the internal turmoil facing the player-character. After the voices provide exposition, the blackness disappears and the player takes control of Harry DuBois as he regains consciousness in a dilapidated hotel room, suffering amnesia after a long alcohol- and drug-addled bender. In these opening moments, the player is taught the fundamental controls of the game as the player-character attempts to piece together who they are and what is happening. The player quickly learns certain key plot details: (1) a murder occurred approximately seven days ago and (2) the player-character is a police detective who has been on the scene for the past three days. Additional background information is uncovered as well—that, since arriving on the scene, the main character racked up significant debt, drank heavily, offended the locals and, at some unknown point in the past, was left by his wife. Like all other details, however, the player is unsure of the temporal order of these traumas.

Nary a single element of *Disco Elysium* is untouched by the politics of policing. In fact, there are too many examples to cover in a single analysis. As such, this analysis is necessarily selective. To begin, an important first step in analyzing representations of the police in *Disco Elysium* is to detail how policing is situated within the mechanics (controls and interface) of the game and its setting. Specifically, this analysis conveys how the mechanics and setting of *Disco Elysium* convey the difficulties of doing police work in a broken society. Finally, this analysis considers how narrative interactions presented throughout the game convey specific moral dilemmas of policing that parallel the moral dilemmas facing real police officers.

The Game Mechanics of *Disco Elysium*: Moral, Political, and Psycho-analytical Decision Trees

Thematically, *Disco Elysium* is firmly rooted in detective and crime fiction. Its gameplay structure and mechanics, however, are situated in the tradition of "roleplaying games." For this reason, it is worth taking a momentary departure to explain this unique genre of video games which features its own mechanistic and narrative conventions. Roleplaying games, like *Disco Elysium*, are a type of video game where the player embodies a character making decisions and interacting with an environment and non-player characters which often includes character growth or discovery throughout the adventure/game. Another way to think about roleplaying video games is that they are like early "choose your own adventure" books that ask readers to make choices and then guide them to different plot elements and endings based on those decisions. In roleplaying games, the success/failures of those choices are randomized based on the character's numerically based attributes. The earliest roleplaying video games, dating back to the 1970s (i.e., Colossal Cave Adventure by Will Crowther between 1975–1977), were text-based in the medieval-fantasy genre and were heavily inspired by analog tabletop roleplaying games like Dungeons & Dragons. Since this time, roleplaying video games have branched out into a variety of genres including science fiction, fantasy, post-apocalyptic, survival horror, and crime, which include hardboiled detective and film noir aesthetics.

Though other games have trodden such ground, *Disco Elysium* is relatively unique as the thematic conventions of hard-boiled detective stories remain uncommon in roleplaying video games. Of course, this is not to say that *Disco Elysium* is a one-to-one parallel of the genre. Notably, the film noir aesthetic—rooted as it is in high-contrast black-and-white visuals—is reinterpreted through a pastel-colored oil-painting aesthetic. The player can choose to be ethical, violent, or continue being a raucous drunk—depending on how you play the game—such choices are part of the most immersive aspects of roleplaying games in general. Yet in *Disco Elysium*, those decisions really make a difference in the play experience and ultimately what kind of police officer Harry, the detective becomes. Much of the dialog occurs on an existential level within the protagonist's thoughts about himself. Much of the on-screen text stems from internal monologues from the main character's personality constructs.

The game mechanics of Disco Elysium themselves can be viewed as a kind of commentary on police work. Exploring themes like morality and demoralization, the player-character begins the game at their lowest point. Failing tasks results in a loss of morale. If too much morale is lost, it's "game over," though the main character does not die as occurs in most video games but, instead, quits policing and fades toward personal moral collapse. Such a trajectory parallels the dynamic evinced among real-world police officers who regularly suffer from burnout and fatigue, a theme revisited later in the analysis that seems intrinsic to doing justice work. Further, when the player fails to succeed in an important choice, the game expresses the demoralization of the main character through his inner voice, such as "Volition" stating, "Despair creeps in, getting fat on your weakness. Whatever noble intentions you once had as a police officer—it's eating them all up now."

In addition to drawing from conventions and mechanics of the roleplaying genre, the controls of the games are rooted in point-and-click adventure games. Point-and-click adventures are an early form of storytelling games with origins in full-text-based games in the mid-1980s and 1990s. Users would literally use their mouse to click around an environment on a screen to find clues and solve puzzles. Though point-and-click games are still being produced in contemporary times, their mechanics are antiquated to the point of nostalgia. Yet this tried and tested historical game design fits into the alternative universe of *Disco Elysium* as its design feels as though it should have come out in the past, not too far from when the game world would have splintered off from the real world; perhaps at some point during the end of the Cold War of the late 1980s. While the game control feels somewhat dated compared to contemporary video games, the aesthetic and art direction of *Disco Elysium* blends into an immersive interactive experience; this is especially true given the investigative nature of the game.

The Setting of *Disco Elysium:* The World of Revachol

Disco Elysium engages in *environmental storytelling*, a term used to refer to the fact that many of the details about the plot, characters, factions, and other elements are not overtly handed to the player but, instead, require them to interact with the world and piece together the lore. In this game, the environment services provide a backdrop that contextualizes the politics of policing and justice work. The game takes place in the fictional world of Revachol, during the fictional time of the "xx50s," 50 years after a major revolution to overthrow a monarchy for a communist system, which is now in disrepair and crumbling after being crushed by corporate-dominated capitalism. Specifically, *Disco Elysium* is set in the impoverished neighborhood of Martinaise, a marginalized ghetto of dock workers, drunks, bigots, and an environment of structural neglect that tends to blame outsiders, foreigners, and corporations.

The world of Revachol is mired in intense political conflicts. The story doesn't progress far before the player is beset with a variety of factions with each representing a different political theory. While the primary plot surrounds "The Hanged Man," the murder that the detective, Harry Du Bois has been assigned to investigate, it is through these political intrigues that we get to know both the world of Revachol and the neighborhood of Martinaise. The ethnicities of Revachol are made up but follow similar real-world ethnicities such as Eastern and Western countries.

The Estonian author and lead game designer, Robert Kurvitz, wrote over 1 million words of dialog for the game by detailing the history, philosophy, and politics of Revachol through character interactions and the environment itself. As mentioned, it is learned that Revachol experienced the overthrow of a monarchy through a communist revolution 50 years prior to the game. This communist project failed and is now giving way to neoliberal capitalism, or the governance model empowering for-profit corporations to do what traditional governments have traditionally done such as social welfare and services such as criminal justice. Much of the game is focused on navigating competing factions who all want to use the situation created by or involving the murder for their own agendas.

Because *Disco Elysium* is a roleplaying experience, the player gets to choose how Harry, the detective interacts with the world, politics, ethics, and his own mental health within the game. Yet it quickly becomes apparent that however you navigate the game, the detective will have little effect on changing the world itself but he does affect how justice will be served and his decisions demonstrate the kind of police officer he is. In this manner, the very act of attempting to do something such as solve a murder requires that the police—in this case chiefly represented by Du Bois—navigate the larger political struggles endemic to Revachol.

For instance, the player is quickly mired in the class politics that pervade the larger mega-city, outside of Martinaise, which is largely segregated by class. There are middle-income boroughs that are described through interactions with characters, yet you never go to or visit them. The entirety of the game takes place in Martinaise. This is where the setting is part of the narrative and plot. Through graffiti, characters scattered around Martinaise, and events that Harry must navigate, such as the labor strike by dock workers that creates an environment of gate-keepers and interest groups (corporation, labor union, non-affiliated citizens, and the police department) that the player has to appease to conduct the murder investigation. The narrative of the game is intertwined with environmental storytelling in the way that the player examines the neighborhood, itself.

Environmental storytelling and its effects on the detective can be found early in the game. The player comes across a public trashcan with, "Fuck the Police" written on it. The player must interact with the message, which can hurt or heal the morale of Harry, depending on both player choices but also the random roll of the dice. The environment is riddled with political and philosophical statements and stances concerning how to make sense of crime, policing, and the contradictions of personal expectations, failures, and doing justice more broadly. This moment of interacting with political messages can literally cause Harry to quit policing, hence ending the game. These types of interactions can lead to opportunities for morale failure, using excessive amounts of alcohol and drugs, or treating the residents more violently. For our purpose of this chapter *doing* justice means how the detective goes about solving the crime, through professionalism, heavy-handed street justice, or empathetically with the residents of the neighborhood more broadly. These approaches to "doing justice" dovetail into the observed trauma of real-world policing, a subject to which this analysis now turns.

Policing Dilemmas in *Disco Elysium*

Up to this point, the chapter has largely focused on representations of policing as evinced through gameplay mechanics and the setting. The current section, however, turns from a purely representational analysis to consider how the story and interactions that occur in the game present three moral dilemmas to the player that mirror the real-world challenges of policing. The first dilemma concerns the enactment of a culture of stoicism among police officers, where they confront terrible situations while facing demands to control their emotional reactions to said situations. The second dilemma is that the very nature of police work requires officers to take sides and such decisions by officers can have significant political ramifications. Finally, *Disco Elysium* portrays the moral dilemma of policing that officers must selectively choose which truths to embrace and express.

Dilemma #1: Maintaining Composure and Internalizing Trauma

One facet of the game that parallels real-world policing is that *Disco Elysium* conveys a culture of stoicism among officers. Near the beginning of the game, the player meets their investigative partner, Kim Kitsuragi, and, together, they make their way to the dead body they have been assigned to investigate, "The Hanged Man." As the player approaches the body the text reads, "There he still is—looking right through you with his White eyes. The body below is entirely dedicated to that corpse smell. Emitting it is *all* it does now." The player has three initial choices. The first response is, "God . . . what is that? Why is it so bad?" The second choice is a legendary endurance test that states, "Let go of your nose without throwing up." The third choice is to, "Turn away [leave]." Having retrieved some ammonia to help with the smell, I try the second choice of letting go of my nose to examine the body. When I fail the test, the text reads, "The ammonia only makes it worse! The combination forces tears out of your ducts. You manage to keep it in once . . ." The text continues, "The second time—not so much. When the vomiting is done your cheeks are wet with tears." Your partner quickly offers you some consolation, "Are you okay, officer?" He pats the detective on the back in a reassuring way. Kim then states, "You're facing tough odds here. It's aggravated further by alcohol withdrawal." At this point in the game, the detective must investigate elsewhere or choose, "This is bullshit. I don't wanna do this anymore. I don't wanna be a cop." If this option is chosen, Kim tells you to "get your shit together" and suggests talking to the locals. In other words, get to work. This type of stoicism is reinforced throughout the game between Harry and his partner, Kim. This ethos of bravery is a well-established cultural phenomenon within real-world policing.

There is a growing body of literature and research on the effects of police officer's exposure to both perceived and real traumatic experiences (Velazquez & Hernandez, 2019; Kleim & Westphal, 2011; Gershon et al., 2009). Just like some of the more eccentric behaviors of Harry Du Bois—the detective in *Disco Elysium*—first responders, those who are first to traumatic incidents and the first to interact with victims, have been the subject of research generally associated with posttraumatic stress disorder (PTSD), major depressive disorder, and drug and alcohol abuse (Kleim & Westphal, 2011). For police, specifically, long periods of work-related stress punctuated with exigent emergencies put officers at a higher rate of cardiovascular disease in addition to severe depression. Further, "police stress is also associated with maladaptive and anti-social behavior, such as problem drinking and hyper-aggressiveness and violence, both on and off the job" (Gershon et al., 2009, p. 276). While these behaviors are also part of the fictional traits of hard-boiled detective movies and novels they also translate directly to the literary mechanics in *Disco Elysium*. The connection here is the reality of these tropes in the mental health concerns for real-world police officers.

Violanti (2004) observes predictors of police suicide ideation, especially without family support, which can be exacerbated by high divorce rates. In *Disco Elysium* much of the detective's deepest sources of depression was the loss of his wife. Harry's partner, Kim is also consistently working to support and remind the detective that he is good at being a detective which, also comes with warnings against drinking and drug taking. Albeit much of the support comes in the form of telling him to "get his shit together" and that there is work to be done. This kind of stoic support plays an important role of support for the detective as it pushes them forward, but it may also simultaneously engender a stigma toward perceived weakness and mental health issues in general.

The experience of trauma and its subsequent mental health issues is exacerbated by the well-established stigma that discourages officers from seeking mental health care—they are supposed to be tough and brave, not needing such help (Corrigan 2004). The amnesiac beginning in *Disco Elysium* offers a mechanism for the game to allow player choice in which to determine what kind of detective Harry Du Bois is in *Disco Elysium*, it allows the player to discover divorce, heavy drinking, drug taking, and violent impulses or tendencies consistent in both hard-boiled detective tropes and police mental health research. The stoic sub-culture of policing also makes seeking help for mental health more challenging. These mental health issues and associated stigma may also work against procedural justice and community relations.

Trauma and depression also come with self-stigma. As police are quick to trust professional instincts, which develop through both perceived and real threats, signs of mental illness are stigmatized. Stigmatization from others may turn inward and manifest as self-stigma. Corrigan (2004) reports that "research shows that people with mental illness often internalize stigmatizing ideas that are widely endorsed within society and believe that they are less valued because of their psychiatric disorder" (p. 618). In other words, there is a kind of self-loathing that can occur which may only further compound the consequences of trauma and prevent individuals, including officers, from seeking help. These sets of mental health associations, exposure to both perceived and real violent situations, and substance abuse create a kind of negative feedback loop within the profession of policing.

Dilemma #2: Police Work Often Necessitates Taking Sides

Another corollary of real-world policing presented in *Disco Elysium* is the fact that doing justice often means taking a side (or, if one portends neutrality, that itself is a stance in favor of the status quo). For instance, another major character that serves as either an enemy or ally, depending on how you play the detective, is the local union boss. During a particularly important part of the investigation, the player goes to him for information concerning Harry's lost badge and gun due to his drunken tirade. The union, however, also functions as a local gatekeeper, thus either facilitating or hindering police work. It is also worth noting that Harry's murder case leads him to investigate the dock worker's strike. Evrart Claire, the union boss responds when asked about the labor strike, "Harry, there is no strike, only war. Class war. Or, in business terms: *a dawn raid*. Or wait . . ." He pauses to rub his chin. "Is that when you still *pay* them something? Because we won't do that." This is a particular part of the story wherein the player begins to shape which *side* Harry is on philosophically. As an arbiter of justice, the player—through Harry—must make decisions about what justice will look like and who will be the beneficiary. Will they subvert the union and support the interest of the upper classes? Or will they support the worker's union?

Other interactions similarly present the player with an opportunity to decide how they will implement justice as police officers in a fractured world. Police are arbiters of the status quo, and, as a result, their role in political conflicts shapes citizens' perception of their legitimacy and whose interests they protect. Yet, this doesn't mean that they have to act as cudgels for the state—they can build relationships with the public and, as a result, gain a deeper understanding of the context in which they operate. For instance, the polarizing politics of the revolution from a half-century in the past is witnessed between two old men in the game. Rene and Gaston were childhood friends but enemies during the revolution. As young men, they fell in love with the same woman, Jennie. She fell in love with Rene, who was a war hero for the king during the revolution. Gaston was a "communard" (thinly veiled communist), or a revolutionary. Eventually, after a few days into the investigation, Rene dies. Gaston reminisces:

> We've hated each other our entire lives. So much in fact that . . . He falls silent and looks at you, eyes filling up with tears. He continues, "Yes. I . . . I loved that angry prick. He didn't deserve it, but I did." He wipes his eyes with a sleeve. "You know what his last words to me were?" Gaston recalls, "In Guillaume's [the overthrown monarch] time you'd have been shot without a trial. That's what he said to me." The old man gathers himself and wipes his eyes again. "He lived a cunt and he died a cunt. Let's leave it at that."

Rene was a right-wing monarchy loyalist and Gaston was a left-wing revolutionary. Yet they both survived the revolution and grew old as friends. It is through interactions with the residents of the Martinaise neighborhood, in the world of Revachol, that the story and history of the setting make themselves known. Through the interaction with Gaston, Harry gains a deeper insight into the community's struggles—knowledge the player can use when making decisions about the kind of police officer Harry is and where his sympathies lie.

Between the lack of faith of the residents and his own troubled past (loss of his partner), Harry has opportunities to act sympathetic to one interest group or another. During his quest to put his own life together, *Disco Elysium* becomes a game that not only is about saving Harry's personal, professional, and philosophic life, but also about the ramifications of police decision-making in a world of political conflict, power struggle, and loss of self-dignity.

Dilemma #3: You Can't Handle the Truth

A final example dilemma that echoes contemporary police work is the problem of truth—specifically, when is it appropriate to tell the truth and when is it necessary to withhold it? Consider, for example, an interaction with a local bookstore owner. While investigating the murder and gaining rapport with the locals the detective meets Plaisance, who believes that her building is cursed by a ghost and that is why her bookstore business is doing poorly—rather than a failing economy. After investigating the building for her you discover that there is another secret business, a dice maker (this scenario is an homage to the tabletop roleplaying roots of the computer roleplaying genre) in the building whose business is booming. After discovering this secret occupant and returning to Plaisance, your inner endurance voice asks you, "Before you say anything, ask yourself. Is the woman really able to *withstand* the truth?" Your logical inner voice asks, "The narrative she's built herself—it does need tearing down." Your inner composure voice states, "She's squeezing on the pendant too tight. A drop of blood in her palm . . ." Finally, your inner suggestion states, "Just don't say you don't have *any* answer yet. The uncertainty is killing her." The detective then has several response options including lying to maintain her superstition, telling her that her troubles are simply due to the ups and downs of capitalism, or some combination of the two. This outlines the gray area of truth that police work often necessitates.

The moral dilemma presented here is relatively simple—perhaps even obvious—but one that has significant implications. The police investigate and, by investigating, gain some amount of power through the knowledge that they accumulate. Part of this power manifests in what they do with this knowledge (e.g., make an arrest) and some through what they divulge. Often, police detectives are reluctant to give information about an ongoing investigation out of fear of compromising their case. Yet, the withholding of information may also be conducted toward leverage for their inquiry. For instance, they may withhold details about a crime to avoid hurting victims and survivors. In more nefarious cases, however, details may be withheld to preserve police power and to protect fellow officers—a product of the "code of silence" that pervades many police cultures (Alpert et al., 2015). Control over such knowledge also gives police command of the prevailing narrative, allowing them to shape public and political discourse surrounding criminal and police activities. Thus, officers routinely face a significant moral dilemma when to tell the truth and determine what kind of truth to tell.

Conclusion: The Ending of *Disco Elysium*

A quote near the beginning of Ferrell's (2018) book *Drift*, blurs the real and the imagined of cultural research and applies in this video game analysis. Cultural criminology captures some inherent tendencies of crime stories in general. Concerning the uncertain and illicit circumstances that lead to acts defined as a *crime*, much like the central murder MacGuffin, or the plot device in *Disco Elysium*:

> In any case, all such trajectories remain entangled in the messy course of human history and likewise remain contested and compromised in the practice of everyday social life. Because of this, the notion of a historical moment's trajectory is probably most useful when thought of not as some sort of teleological determinism but as a narrative device by which certain stories can be told, or perhaps an analytic metaphor by which certain historical tendencies can be understood.
>
> *(Ferrell, 2018, p. 5)*

It does seem as though someone either politically benefits or progresses their interests through a tale or trauma of horror in *Disco Elysium*. Whether it's the local informal authorities, such as the "Hardy Boys" (a gang that looks out for the locals) in Martinaise, or the enculturated need for state intervention and the *real* police. Gilman-Opalsky (2016, pp. 221–222) describes real-world social-order maintenance policing in a manner which equally captures the war-torn world of Revachol:

> Those who condemn the revolts actually love them because they get to condemn a violence that justifies the violence they defend, the violence they love. Critics of revolt do not, therefore, fear the violence, but rather the transformative potentialities of revolt, its abolitionist and creative content.
>
> *(as quoted in Linnemann, 2022, p. 193)*

While Gilman-Opalsky is describing the horror that is the history of real-world policing narratives, it also captures the central political tensions in *Disco Elysium*.

Harry Du Bois is depressed and addicted to substances and full of self-doubt, his whole existence is wrapped around his profession of being a detective. It is up to the player as to what kind of detective Harry is during the game. Yet throughout the story, Harry Du Bois is no doubt afraid mostly of his trauma, his addictions, his depression, or more simply—himself. These traits can be seen in hard-boiled detective novels and movies, but also in the emerging literature concerning first responders in general, and specifically police officers. *Disco Elysium* plays with this very sentiment as experienced by the player through the inner voices of Harry Du Bois, the hard-boiled detective.

A portion of the ending of *Disco Elysium* can be read below. When pressed to report his week on this case with detective Harry Du Bois, Kim Kitsuragi reports:

> Well . . . He pulls up his collar. "The drinking, the gun-losing, also los-ing the badge—that's all true. Although he has *not* been drinking on the job this week." Kitsuragi continues, "Then there's the . . . self-flagellation issue. He likes to apologize—profusely. Making it sound like he's guilty of at least first-degree murder. It's not a good communication strategy for an officer, It's . . . It's worrying. Especially considering his political views. Detective Du Bois is—as you may know—a Mazovian socio-economist. He wants to liquidate the ruling class. Which—again—for a police of-ficer . . . is a little odd."

I ended up playing a fairly chaotic yet good cop through both play-throughs. I tried to be ethical but always willing to engage in minor criminality, fire with fire if you will, to gain bigger results or mitigate risk—and an arguably ethical detective. Despite playing both the proverbial left and right-wing in-terest groups against one another, I tried to maintain a professional approach to the investigation itself but role-played a hard-living addict in recovery—who copes through smoking cigarettes like a freight train.

Video games and crime stories certainly don't always prepare folks for empathy toward the mentally ill, the victim, the perpetrator, or those do-ing justice. Crime stories—real or imagined—and video games, as narratives use traditional tropes to create an emotionally charged ambiance to elicit a sense of verisimilitude and often reify prejudice reflective of the real world. More so than novels or movies though, a video game offers the player some choice about their character's personal philosophy and ethics. As prompted and limited as dialog options are, *Disco Elysium* allows the player to play more of a Gonzo reporter, a corrupt and violent detective, or attempt to navi-gate the game as a damaged, but "good cop." These stories, like real crime narratives, are never really explicit in context between deontological [intent] decisions or the teleological [outcomes] impacts of crime control amidst the ethical puzzle of "doing justice." *Disco Elysium* allows a player to get right in the middle of complex social and political philosophy, interact with a rather diverse and boldly motivated dramatis personae of a cast—dressed up in hard-boiled detective tropes—and perhaps survive the emotional labor, trauma, and futility of *doing* justice in a forgotten ghetto of a made-up place called, Revachol.

Note

1 The author would like to thank Kevin Steinmetz and Carl Root for their editorial remarks and insights regarding this chapter.

References

Alpert, G.P., Noble, J.J. & Rojek, J. (2015). Solidarity and the code of silence. In R.G. Dunham & G.P. Alpert (eds.) *Critical issues in policing: Contemporary readings* (7th ed.) (pp. 106–121). Waveland Press.

Biressi A., & Bloom, C. (2001). *Crime, fear, and the law in true crime stories.* Palgrave.

Broe, D. (2003). Class, crime, and film noir: Labor, the fugitive outsider, and the anti-authoritarian tradition. *Social Justice, 30*(1), 22–41.

Carrabine, E. (2008). *Crime, culture and the media.* Polity.

Chandler, R. (2002 [1939]). The big sleep. In *Collected stories* (pp. 1–198). Alfred A. Knopf.

Corrigan, P. (2004). How stigma interferes with mental health care. *American Psychologist, 59*(7), 614–625.

Ferrell, J. (2018). *Drift: Illicit mobility and uncertain knowledge.* University of California Press.

Ferrell, J., Hayward, K., & Young, J. (2015). *Cultural criminology: An invitation* (2nd ed.). Sage.

Gershon, R.R.M, Barocas, B., Canton, A.N., Li, X., & Vlahov, D. (2009). Mental, physical, and behavioral outcomes associated with perceived work stress in police officers. *Criminal Justice and Behavior, 36*(3), 275–289.

Gilman-Opalsky, R. (2016). *Specters of revolt.* Penguin Random House.

Hammett, D. (2000 [1929]). The Maltese falcon. In *The Maltese Falcon, the thin man, red harvest* (pp. 5–225). Alfred A. Knopf.

Kleim, B., & Westphal, M. (2011). Mental health in first responders: A review and recommendation for prevention and intervention strategies. *Traumatology, 17*(4), 17–24.

Linnemann, T. (2015). Capote's ghosts: Violence, media and the spectre of suspicion. *British Journal of Criminology, 55*(3), 514–533.

Linnemann, T. (2022). *The horror of police.* University of Minnesota Press.

Marina, P., & Marina, P. (2023). *Human rights policing: Reimagining law enforcement in the 21st century.* Routledge.

Masten, K. (2018). Cherchez la femme: A good woman's place in hard-boiled detective fiction. *Clues: A Journal of Detection, 36*(2), 29–39.

Mosley, W. (1990). *Devil in a blue dress.* W.W. Norton & Company.

Poe, E.A. (2009 [1841]). The Murders in the Rue Morgue. In *The first detective: The complete Auguste Dupin stories.* Oakpast.

Skott, S., & Bengtson, K. S. (2021). "You've met with a terrible fate, haven't you?": A hauntological analysis of carceral violence in Majora's Mask. *Games & Culture, 0*(0), 1–21.

Steinmetz, K.F. (2018). Carceral horror: Punishment and control in *Silent Hill. Crime Media Culture, 14*(2), 265–287.

Steinmetz, K.F., & Petkovsek, M.A. (2022, Online First). Perilous Policing: An analysis of the Resident Evil series. *Critical Criminology, 31*(1), 1–20. http://doi.org/10.1007/s10612-022-09640-1

Turnbull, S. (2014). *The TV crime drama.* Edinburgh University Press.

Velazquez, E., & Hernandez, M. (2019). Effects of police officer exposure to traumatic experiences and recognizing the stigma associated with police officer mental health: A state-of-the-art review. *Policing: An International Journal, 42*(4), 711–724.

Violanti, J.M. (2004). Predictors of police suicide. *Suicide and Life-Threatening Behavior, 34*(3), 277–283.

Wakeman, S. (2014). "No one wins. One side just loses more slowly": The Wire and drug policy. *Theoretical Criminology, 18*(2), 224–240.

Webb, L. (2021). True crime and danger narratives: Reflections on stories of violence, race, and (in)justice. *The Journal of Gender, Race & Justice, 24*, 131–170.

Yardley, E., Kelly, E., & Robinson-Edwards, S. (2019). Forever trapped in the imaginary of late capitalism? The serialized true crime podcast as a wake-up call in times of criminological slumber. *Crime Media Culture, 15*(3), 503–521.

ZA/UM. (2021). *Disco elysium: The final cut* [Nintendo Switch]. Iam8bit.com. https://discoelysium.com/

9

TO SERVE AND PROTECT FROM BEHIND THE MASK

Miles Morales in *Marvel's Spider-Man* and *Marvel's Spider-Man: Miles Morales*, Policing, Justice, and Representation

Christina Fawcett and Steven Kohm

Video games are participatory sites of cultural reflection and potential social critique. The player's involvement in the avatar's actions, choices, and narrative progression mean that we cannot remain neutral: we do not watch the story in a detached fashion, but take control, and thus responsibility, for our character's actions. As we address in an earlier analysis of *Batman: Arkham Asylum*:

> The participatory element drives the player's investment, as the actions of the game generate emotional experience. [. . .] T]hese games implicate players in the action, making visceral the emotional, philosophical and psychological dimensions of the experience of crime and punishment that may be neglected in scholarly criminological discourses.
>
> *(Fawcett & Kohm, 2020, p. 267)*

The significance of games asking for our participation, our investment, in a protagonist using excessive violence in state-sanctioned vigilantism, means we have a culpability in those actions. Emotional investment is a powerful tool of persuasion, as the action of play involves us in the values and ideals that the game espouses (Flanagan & Nissenbaum, 2014). Sicart (2014) argues that play, as a multifaceted and complex subject, is a means of accessing and exploring, even in frameworks like a video game:

> Play is finding expression; it is letting us understand the world and, through that understanding, challenging the establishment, leading for knowledge, and creating new ties or breaking old ones. But ultimately whatever we do in play stays with us. Play is a singularly individual experience—shared,

DOI: 10.4324/9781003346869-9

yes, but meaningful only in the way it scaffolds an individual experience of the world. Through play, we are in the world.

(p. 18)

Video games, while traditionally understudied in popular criminology, offer participatory experiences that place users at the center of legal and extralegal criminal pacification and make video games rich spaces for popular criminological analysis. *Marvel's Spider-Man: Miles Morales* functions as one such text, situating the player as Miles, who is training as a new Spider-Man navigating corporate crime, private policing, surveillance, racial marginalization, and extralegal vigilantism. Players are offered an immersive space to experience, and contend with, the complex relationships between police and Black peoples, the surveillance state, and the privatization of policing through the lens of a comic superhero narrative.

We undertake a popular criminological analysis of crime and criminality, law enforcement and surveillance, as well as race and policing in *Marvel's Spider-Man: Miles Morales*. As popular superhero media, the game is imbricated in traditions of crime, vigilantism, and law enforcement that subvert the game's potential for societal critique. In representing complex interrelated issues of justice, the game functions at times to critique race and policing, while simultaneously reifying traditional law-and-order values and vigilantism in superheroes (e.g., Phillips & Strobl, 2013). Miles embodies a tension between his racialized identity and his work as an extralegal member of the policing body. The game troubles our understanding of either position as primary because Miles is driven both by a love of his community and family, and a need for justice. While critiquing the limited visibility and efficacy of the police, the game promotes invasive privatized surveillance; while disregarding the social roots of crime, criminal etiology is grounded in conspiracies, corporate interests, and gang-warfare. The game's potential as a critical countervisual (e.g., Fawcett & Kohm, 2020) is undermined by a narrative that steadfastly serves existing systems of power.

Following a brief plot synopsis of *Marvel's Spider-Man* (2018) and *Marvel's Spider-Man: Miles Morales* (2020), our popular criminological analysis unfolds in four parts. First, we analyze the representation of crime and criminality in *Miles Morales*, linking cultural representation to scholarly theory, demonstrating that the game centers exceptional criminality while sidelining mundane crimes. Second, we examine the representation of technology, surveillance, and the privatization of policing and social control, arguing that the game provides limited space for critical and subversive takes on these troubling trends in late modern criminal justice. We then move to an analysis of race and player projection, critically assessing the way the game represents and places the player within depictions of race and criminal justice in America, providing both subversive and mainstream engagements with these critical issues. Finally, we examine the representation of police visibility in the game, arguing that, despite its subversive potential, ultimately the game is ideologically complicit in upholding current political and social arrangements that devalue Black and Brown lives.

Plot Synopsis

Marvel's Spider-Man (2018) and *Marvel's Spider-Man: Miles Morales* (2020) follow the story of Peter Parker meeting his eventual protégé and newest Spider-Man: Miles Morales. While the 2018 game positions the player predominantly as Peter, some scenes are played as Mary-Jane or Miles. Peter works to stop Martin Li, also called Mr. Negative, and Dr. Octavius, or Doc Ock, as they release a bioweapon and mastermind a jailbreak at The Raft—a high-security carceral facility for supervillains. In the chaos of disease and disaster ravaging the city, Peter enlists Mary-Jane and Miles to track down villains, find a researcher to make a vaccine, and take care of vulnerable people at F.E.A.S.T. (Food, Emergency, Aid, Shelter and Training). Mary-Jane discovers a secret research lab in Mayor Osborn's penthouse and unknowingly carries a genetically engineered spider back to F.E.A.S.T. where it bites Miles. We first play Miles when his father, police officer Jefferson Davis, receives a commendation for helping Spider-Man track the Demons, a criminal gang working for Mr. Negative. The Demons attack the ceremony, killing Jefferson and knocking Peter unconscious. We navigate Miles through the aftermath of the attack. Miles focuses on stealth, and his self-designed hacking-app, to navigate high-stress situations; he is bitten near the end of the game, and the story wraps with a cut-scene of Miles revealing his powers to Peter, and Peter sharing his secret identity in return.

Marvel's Spider-Man: Miles Morales opens with Miles in training. Nearly a year after the first game's events, Peter and Miles escort a prison transport returning escapees, including the supervillain Rhino, back to The Raft. Rhino escapes, freeing the other prisoners, and Peter and Miles subdue him and leave him in the custody of Roxxon Energy's private security forces. Peter leaves for an investigative trip and gifts Miles his own Spider-suit—complete with knee and elbow pads—and training modules around the city. On his way home, Miles interrupts The Underground breaking into Roxxon Plaza. The conflict between Roxxon and The Underground drives the game's narrative, as Miles navigates between the seemingly law-abiding corporation and the gang-cum-terrorists. Miles and his best friend Ganke set up the Friendly Neighborhood Spider-Man app to engage the public, inviting requests for help; the first request comes from Miles's estranged Uncle Aaron when The Underground disrupts the train system. Miles thwarts their attempted sabotage, and later theft of Roxxon's new energy source, Nuform; his bioelectricity renders Nuform unstable, causing a catastrophic bridge explosion.

During the attempted heist, Miles discovers The Underground leader, the Tinkerer, is his middle-school friend Phin. This friendship gives Miles an avenue to infiltrate The Underground, as encouraged by his Uncle Aaron, who is also the thief the Prowler. Aaron's life of crime and Phin's position as a terrorist situates Miles between law and crime, family and friends. Miles must navigate his own sense of justice and right in the conflict between destructive economic interests and anti-corporate terrorism. In the next section, we undertake a popular criminological analysis to interrogate the way game represents the "causes, consequences, and remedies for crime, and the relationship of these ideas to academic discourses about crime" (Kohm, 2017, para. 1).

Crime and Criminality in Marvel's New York

The world of Spider-Man, like other superhero stories of the past 50 years, focuses on law enforcement in extremis: superheroes require supervillains. Ordinary crime and criminals cannot provide a real challenge to aliens, mutants, or humans bitten by radioactive spiders. While early superhero comics of the 1930s featured Superman breaking in to see the Governor to stop a wrongful execution, intervening in domestic abuse, or stopping a kidnapping (Siegel, 1997), more extreme antagonists quickly appear. Batman's 1940 debut features a jewel-thief who poisons his victims, leaving a rictus-grin to emulate his own: the Joker (Kane, 1940). The rise of nemeses and supervillains meant that superheroes shifted focus away from ordinary street crime toward more complex and damaging issues of justice, including terrorism and corporate crime. *Miles Morales* continues this trend. Focused on corporate crime and terrorism, otherwise serious, violent, or street-level felonies become minor distractions. Miles can intervene in muggings, break-ins, and car-jackings, as alerts pop into the head's-up display indicating a crime in progress. However, intervention is optional: Miles does not need to help, and after violently subduing the perpetrators, he leaves them to be handled by police. As gameplay, the excitement is the fight, not guarding unconscious or webbed-up perpetrators until police process them for lawful arrest. The game creates a run-and-gun approach to crime management, as Miles, and thus the player, shows no concern for justifiable force, bodily harm, or the safety of the individuals he subdues. Day-to-day policing is sidelined, as Miles focuses on the exceptional criminality of terrorist gangs and corporate criminals.

The two major criminal threats are the protest-terrorist-group, The Underground, and Roxxon Energy—in particular, its militarized police force and corrupt head of Research and Development, Simon Krieger. The Underground and Roxxon offer very different articulations of exceptional criminality and provide the game's primary conflict. The Underground blends futuristic technology—programmable matter weapons and masks provided by the Tinkerer—with ripped jeans and the graffiti aesthetic of 1990s rave-culture: a "glow-stick army." The Underground are not ideologically motivated; rather, they follow the Tinkerer's goals to make a name for themselves. This articulation of crime for fame, or crime to disrupt the malaise of modern life, links to cultural criminology's exploration of the existential foreground of transgression (Ferrell, 1992), viewing crime as a reaction to institutionalized boredom in late modernity (e.g., Ferrell, 2004; Ferrell et al., 2015; Steinmetz et al., 2017) or a quest for socially-mediated recognition (Yar, 2012). The Underground's desire for notoriety is apparent in Miles's visit to their central base in Fisk Tower, which sits empty after Wilson Fisk—the Kingpin—was arrested in *Marvel's Spider-Man*. The notorious building is full of rave music, neon graffiti, and large video screens broadcasting The Underground's news-coverage: focused on their mediated image, The Underground appear caught up in their own press. Phin explains that their campaign against Roxxon and Krieger is in exchange for "Notoriety. They want to be so well-known, they can get away with anything." Members of The Underground echo these sentiments, declaring their need to "establish dominance," "show this city what power really looks like," and "grow that rep [. . . by] focusin' on PR." Locating the etiology of crime in the quest for media coverage provides a popular criminological instantiation of Yar's (2012) contention that "instead of asking whether 'media' instigates crime or fear of crime, we must ask how the very possibility of *mediating oneself* to an audience through self-representation might be bound up with the genesis of criminal behaviour" (p. 246).

The second major criminal threat engaged by Miles is corporate crime. Roxxon Energy and Simon Krieger, head of Research and Development, embody this threat as Nuform energy, touted as a new low-emission energy source, turns out to be unstable and toxic. Miles uncovers Roxxon's corporate malfeasance, greed, and corporate greenwashing that threatens New York and beyond. Miles uncovers Krieger's willful endangerment of lives in favor of corporate profits before discovering Krieger works with notorious convicted criminals Rhino and Prowler. Krieger's behavior crosses from corporate greed to sociopathy, as he knowingly plans to build reactors across New York that can cause illness and death. Roxxon's militarized security forces are a constant antagonist to Miles, appearing almost robotic in full body-armor, gloves, and helmets. This visual form echoes the logic of corporate industrial capitalism, as each member of the security forces is a nameless, faceless, interchangeable cog in the security apparatus. This anonymous corporate policing contrasts with Miles's grassroots community crime fighting via his friendly neighborhood app. While both embody private, extralegal policing, players are encouraged to view private superhero vigilantism positively because it appears to respond to community need rather than supporting corporate greed.

Miles can uncover additional organized corporate criminal harm in Harlem. Spider-Man's nemesis Kingpin, arrested early in *Marvel's Spider-Man*, coordinates robberies and sabotages F.E.A.S.T.'s water and sewage systems to devalue, and then purchase, the properties from his jail cell on The Raft. The White criminal-businessman uses legal and illegal pressures to drive the people of Harlem from their homes, businesses, and shelters. His plan to devalue and purchase the Harlem properties speaks to the corrupting forces of late modern capitalism and gentrification, as well as the social pressures these create in underserved and minoritized populations. In this way the game positions ordinary crimes, such as robberies, as part of a larger system of manipulation and criminal enterprise. Kingpin's involvement with street-level crime reframes the usual causes of crime as a strategic, more nefarious process. Yet, while offering a potentially critical focus on corporate crime often lacking in conventional crime media (Linnemann & Jewkes, 2017), the game's critique is blunted by positioning a supervillain at the head of corporate malfeasance—individualizing the far more insidious legal and structural process that give rise to the damaging and at times criminal actions of corporations (e.g., Bakan, 2004).

These large-scale criminal organizations, be they terrorist or corporate, give Miles and the player a clear focus: to eliminate the exceptional criminality of Roxxon, The Underground, and Kingpin. These nefarious criminal enterprises are positioned as clear threats to Miles's community and the people of New York. While necessary for the closed-world narrative line of the game, this popular criminological framing reifies existing ideas about crime as predominantly organized, strategic, and personified by evil individuals. The centrality of these evil criminal masterminds forgives Miles's violent approach to criminality, suggesting that beating and webbing up street-level thugs is a necessary treatment of the symptoms of the larger disease of crime. The player can participate in Miles inflicting grievous bodily harm because the game sets his actions as a greater good. Further to this normalizing of violence, the game also asks player to participate in Miles's use of invasive electronic surveillance, which is likewise positioned as necessary to fight exceptional forms of supervillainy.

Technology, Surveillance, and Policing

The mechanics of gameplay not only limit our engagement with the nuance and complexity of crime, but also facilitate sweeping and uncritical surveillance. The mapping systems and integration of Miles's suit with a grassroots app gives us sweeping access to the digital city and its people: a way that players can target goals, tasks, and errands, as well as navigate from one side of New York to the other. These surveillance technologies are powerful, providing community empowerment, as the people of Harlem have a new non-police response to abuses and threats. The game also provides a potential critical countervisual of unchecked private and for-profit access to people's information. Here, we address how the game articulates tools of surveillance, showing them working both ways: corporations and communities can both deploy cameras and tracking for their own aims.

As a technological superhero, with both powers and a keen scientific mind, Spider-Man has a capacity to design and build his own gadgetry, associating him with surveillance and hacking. A Spider-Man newspaper comic is said to have inspired the electronic monitoring of offenders in the United States in the early 1980s, unwittingly ushering in "a new era of social control" (Koulish, 2015, p. 85; see also Burrell & Gable, 2008).[1] Technologically mediated "policing" appears in the game through the Friendly Neighborhood Spider-Man (FNSM) app. Designed by Ganke, the app enables New Yorkers to request Spider-Man's help. App tasks are cued through the game, with periodic reminders. Tasks range from finding a lost cat, tracking thieves stealing from local shops, or posing for a photo. Because players must navigate the map to respond to app tasks, citizens seeking help provide geo-tagging or give Spider-Man access to their GPS. This voluntary access to personal data is alarming, suggesting real-world issues of data surveillance and even commercialization. Ganke jokingly suggests incorporating ads: "I know you said no to ads before, but maybe we could reconsider . . . ." While the FNSM app is ostensibly not for monetization, glimmers of revenue still appear at the edges of this altruistic venture. Targeted advertising or third-party cookies open app-users to nearly invisible forms of digital surveillance. As a central aspect of gameplay, the app casually elides the surveillance issues of civilians giving permission to be tracked by Spider-Man: they exchange their privacy for Spider-Man's extralegal help.

Marvel's Spider-Man and *Miles Morales* reflect shifting attitudes toward state and private surveillance. Normalized surveillance, rendered necessary by game map mechanics, extends the pro-surveillance movement that Spider-Man has undertaken in recent years. As Schänzel (2021) notes, the anti-surveillance storyline of Issues 105–107 move to a more permissive and surveillance-friendly character in modern Marvel Cinematic Universe storylines (p. 253), eventually asking the player to participate in widespread, unwarranted surveillance (p. 255). Peter's technological acumen and relationship with Captain Watanabe get him access to the state surveillance apparatus, which he then gifts to Miles in the form of a first official Spider-Man suit. As the player takes on the mantle of Miles Morales, rather than police-collaborator Peter Parker, we see the tools of surveillance inverted, centering the potential for community-based policing and the power of the neighborhood watch: the game provides space to critically reflect about the potential of surveillance as a tool of both care and control (Wise, 2016).

While Peter may tap illegally into police scanners, Miles and Ganke's FNSM app illustrates conceptual shifts in late modern crime prevention and policing. As Garland (2001) observed some two decades ago, late modern criminal justice is increasingly characterized by a third governmental sector occupying "an intermediate, borderline position, poised between the state and civil society, connecting criminal justice agencies with the activities of citizens, communities and corporations" (p. 170). Police are now just one of many players in a field that includes private security and citizens encouraged to become active participants in policing, increasingly through technologically mediated forms of neighborhood watch (e.g., Lub, 2018; van Steden & Mehlbaum, 2021; Wood & Thompson, 2020). The FNSM app is a popular criminological representation of a digital neighborhood watch where the community can report problems or ask Spider-Man directly for help. While the app is open across New York, most requests come from Harlem. Miles assists shop-owners and local artists, as well as the F.E.A.S.T. shelter: people that don't traditionally have safe relationships with police. Miles helping predominantly racialized, unhoused, and poor communities illustrates the problems and prospects of late modern crime control and the increasing use of surveillance and technologically mediated forms of privatized crime prevention.

The game positions civilian surveillance as a response to systemic violences and corporate abuses by suggesting an inverted panopticon—what Mathiesen (1997) dubbed the "synopticon"—a viewer society in which the many watch the few (see also Doyle, 2011). The synopticon appears in the game when civilians pull out their phones when Spider-Man is threatened by Roxxon (discussed in detail below). The cut-scene includes a shot of a phone screen recording the events: we are momentarily positioned as the woman recording. Roxxon Security demands she stop, but in their full masks and body-armor, each member of the team is functionally unidentifiable. Instead of threatening personal legal culpability, by recording Roxxon Security's actions, the civilian is impugning an arm of the corporate body. Synoptic surveillance reverses the camera with the people in power watched by the citizen, rather than Foucault's image of the central authority surveilling the population. Revealing the security force's actions is an attempt to disempower them: recording their actions is the community's technological response to Roxxon exercising authority far beyond their corporate ambit. The economic and political control of Krieger and Kingpin demands a grassroots response, albeit a digital one. This grassroots resistance to oppressive power is foregrounded as players take on the perspective of a racialized young man in the post Black Lives Matter era, as we address in the next section.

Race and Player Projection

Issues of crime and surveillance are brought to the fore more readily through player investment, which games can create through different tools of emersion. Sensory experience can magnify story and emotional investment to create participation. While a first-person avatar offers the player projection into a digital space, third-person gameplay creates balance between player and character (Crick, 2011). In *Miles Morales*, our protagonist's identity is fundamental: Miles's age and race are important to the story. A game with the tagline "Be Greater. Be Yourself," centering a young, racialized man is important. We engage the story through the eyes of a young Afro-Latino to ensure we stay conscious of that body. As such, game alerts and interruptions keep us aware of how wired in Miles is in his suit, using tactile and audio tools to provide physical cues.

Haptic feedback can help create character immersion in place of first-person perspective. While third-person perspective limits embodiment, the game playfully addresses how the physics of swinging through the city would make first-person play fundamentally uncomfortable: Ganke jokes when he first starts piggybacking on Miles's mask-visor: "I can see everything you see. How are you not puking all the time?" The game instead uses tactile response, as the controller buzzes, vibrates, or pulses to create sensations that reflect the screen. When Miles discovers his bioelectricity early in the game, small speakers in the PlayStation controller crackle while internal servos pulse to simulate electricity in our hands. The sparking sensation brings us into the strange, unfamiliar, and growing empowerment Miles experiences. This physical engagement draws us into our avatar to encourage projection on a personal and cultural level. Embodiment in a game about race, crime, policing, and vigilantism is paramount, as the game asks players to project into a young Afro-Latino hero. This projection is a challenge, as players of all ages, races, and genders are positioned with a minoritized body that is regularly over-policed and threatened by state and corporate violence. We are encouraged to share Miles's struggles to claim his identity and position in Harlem, in New York, and in the Spider-Man mask.

Video games in North America are typically associated with White middle- and upper-class households but Mills (2022) contends that the link between video games and whiteness is outdated, even though avatars are still predominantly White. Pew Research Center's 2017 report on video gaming in the United States found that 41% of White respondents said they played often or sometimes, while 44% of Black respondents and 48% of Hispanic respondents said the same (Brown 2017). Players should see themselves in games, but attempts to center Black or Latinix protagonists can face pushback, or use harmful stereotyping. Leonard (2003) argues that video games' capacity to reiterate and legitimize stereotypes makes them a powerful and dangerous form of media. Digital storytelling can unpack and contest stereotypes, or engage in what Leonard calls "High-Tech Blackface" (p. 5). While he looks at the minstrelsy bound up in the articulation of Black athletes in sports games, the latent issue of representation for players of color also provides "its primarily white creators and players the opportunity to become black" (p. 5). *Miles Morales* appears a sign of change to come; yet, these issues of character and voice remain complex, as authenticity and identity are central to engaging with complex subjects such as policing, surveillance and crime.

Miles's first appearance in 2011's *Spider-Man: Ultimate Fallout* #4 was a fight-scene that echoed the inexperience and youth of early Peter Parker; Miles wears a Spider-Man Halloween costume, removing his mask in the final panel to reveal his race. Carter (2022) notes this panel was not a surprise:

> Unfortunately, that was less a "reveal" than a confirmation of previously reported information. The story revealing Miles and his half-Black, half-Hispanic background first ran in USA Today, and was followed by a storm of praise and outrage of the new character before he had appeared in a single panel.
>
> *(p. 5)*

Miles developed in different authors' hands, featuring or downplaying different aspects of his heritage; comics are, after all, collaborative serials. Jason Reynolds' (2018) *Miles Morales: Spider-Man* young adult novel examines the School-to-Prison Pipeline and the policing of Black students. Miles clashes with his White history teacher who romanticizes the Civil War. As Worlds and Miller (2019) explain:

> Miles has an emotional reaction when he eventually challenges Mr. Chamberlain's assertion that enslaved people should be "grateful" to their masters, which causes Mr. Chamberlain to tell Miles to "put a muzzle on . . . this anger of yours" (117). Mr. Chamberlain's response reflects dangerous and unexamined views White teachers hold about Black youth that lead to higher rates of disciplinary action taken against Black students.
>
> *(p. 46)*

The novel uses a supernatural plot involving a Confederate zombie controlling Miles's teacher to unpack the larger issue of racially-biased school punishments leading to incarceration. Miles's race and identity are fundamental to the character across different media, as Mills (2022) argues that centering the Black and Brown context changes the expectations of the game's projection and identification:

> The game has no white character (other than the barely present Peter Parker and the CEO villain) to which an imagined white gamer is supposed

to "relate." By existing in a space where blackness and brownness is the norm rather than the exception, the game creates an "other" space. Spanish Harlem becomes a mestizo futurist place that "dare[s] to imagine a world not dominated or defined by whiteness."

(p. 46)

Player projection into an Afro-Latino protagonist is an important part of shifting media representation. The game lets us not only imagine a world where whiteness is not a central and driving force, but to participate in that space as its hero.

Miles's Latino heritage, which was lost in early issues of *Ultimate Fallout*, is highlighted in-game through conversations with his mother—these Spanish interjections appear translated into English if the player has subtitles on. Moving between languages is often personal, or a term of affection, as he tells his mother he loves her in Spanish. Miles carries his mother's last name rather than his father's to distance himself from the threats of Uncle Aaron's criminal life. Miles's name and voice highlight his Latino heritage as a marker of home and safety. This audibility reinforces cultural visibility, as the Puerto Rican flag features in the Morales apartment and throughout Harlem. This signifier draws attention to the many cultures and communities that make up New York and, metonymically, America. While Miles's biracial body is a key part of his identity, it is not one that we appropriate: we are not playing racial clichés or trying on a lived experience. Daley (2020) notes that:

> Miles Morales is by no means a stereotype. He isn't walking around low-riding, saying the N-word or using a gun. [. . .] Despite the game not mentioning police brutality or COVID-19, *Miles Morales* still offered respect to what's going on in the real-world with a Black Lives Matter mural and a black and gold 'Pride' suit.
>
> *(paras. 13, 30)*

The game balances racist realities and fantasy escapism from systemic violences facing Black people in North America and beyond. Yet the game's representation of police and crime fail to contend meaningfully with systemic threats to Black lives. As one reviewer noted, if the game wants to be engaged with socially and politically relevant issues "it's going have to do a better job of addressing the way things actually are rather than how we want them to be" (Pulliam-Moore, 2020, para. 14). Miles's dual heritage of two minority populations in the United States means that his identity matters, particularly as it ties to his unique abilities.

In a pivotal game moment, we see Miles's Blackness and vulnerability to militarized policing laid bare. The Underground attempts to steal Nuform by robbing a truck crossing Braithwaite Bridge: an imagined location in

New York. While trying to stop them, Miles's bioelectricity destabilizes the Nuform and causes an explosion that destroys the bridge; Miles is left fighting both The Underground and Roxxon forces while trying to rescue people. This high-tension scene challenges players with difficult navigation and quick-time events, using ludic stress to bring us into Miles's emotional state. While the haptics keep us physically connected to Miles's fight, the responses and movement amplify our stress as Miles faces Roxxon. Miles's suit is damaged, with rips and tears showing his skin: while his mask stays in place, his young voice and Black skin are on display. After rescuing everyone, Roxxon forces approach as the game shifts to a cut-scene: a hypoludic tool that takes away player control. We, as player, experience disempowerment with Miles. A Roxxon soldier radios through his helmet: "We've got eyes on the other Spider-Man, please advise." After a moment's pause, he answers "Copy" and the forces all raise their guns. The civilians react with anger, vocally defending Miles and one raises her phone to record the scene. Roxxon Security immediately turns menacingly to the civilian and demands "You! Put that phone away, now!"; the scene shows the woman's perspective, featuring the screen, with Roxxon Security filling the shot and Miles in the background in a "hands up, don't shoot" stance. This is a scene we have all seen before: a young Black man backing away from raised weapons wielded by overly-militarized police forces.

While Sable International threatened Peter in *Marvel's Spider-Man*, it took place in empowering playable combat sequences; here, Miles stands still with a ripped suit and raised hands in a cut-scene we cannot control. The order to shoot comes from someone who does not see or hear that Miles is a young Black man; however, Miles standing in front of these guns shows literal systemic violence. Miles cannot fight back like Peter; instead, he stands fixed and wholly vulnerable. The cut-scene shows a close shot of Miles's mask, before moving to his perspective. The designers mediate the horror by defocusing the encroaching forces and diverting our attention to Miles's hands—our hands, in this moment. We watch them begin to disappear before the scene cuts to shots of and around Miles. His camouflage enables him to swing away, while our immersion in Miles ensures we understand the threat, and his impossible escape. Miles gets home and offloads his anxieties to Ganke; the two then redesign his suit in a montage intercut with him running through the city in a music-video-action-sequence. This musical cut-scene celebrates Miles as a Black Spider-Man, in a black and red suit that highlights his identity apart from the original Spider-Man; "While seemingly a superficial change, the surface reflects a deeper exploration of his identity and values" (Mills, 2022, p. 46). We are asked to recognize the importance of the character-position of a young Black Latino man in contemporary America.

Because this is a superhero fantasy, Miles, and thus the player, can escape this horrific scene. Instead of playing out as interactions between young

Black men and police frequently do, Miles escapes by turning invisible, while the bystanders accuse Roxxon of pushing him off the bridge. Relying on super-powers to ensure his safety raises the troubling specter that without inhuman abilities, a young Black man's life would be lost to a private police force. Miles, once safely away, reflects on the horrific hypocrisy of the public face versus corporate brutality: "What happened to Roxxon being 'here for us'?! They were going to shoot me! They didn't even listen." Ganke, who remains wired in through Miles's suit, asks "Are you okay?," to which Miles can only say "I don't know." This destabilizing moment points to a naiveté on Miles's part, but a reasonable one: he had no reason to believe that private security would shoot someone who saved lives on a collapsing bridge. This scenario is equally disturbing for players invested in superhero mythologies, that tell us that heroes are functionally innocent. As Scott (2022) discusses in his reading of Black Superheroes:

> the superhero is constitutively white insofar as whiteness is defined by, and is the offer of, innocence. To be or to have innocence is to be free of guilt, and to be free of guilt is to be constitutionally insulated from the consequences of harmful actions. [. . .] The fusion of innocence versus guilt with whiteness versus blackness has of course been accomplished in history with all the vicious obsessive determination that our political, economic, educational, and cultural institutions could have brought to bear on that project.
>
> *(pp. 101–102)*

Players are confronted with Roxxon's treatment of the young superhero because we have been taught that superheroes bear the innocence inherent in cultural whiteness. Miles's Black body, costumed or not, remains threatened with state- or corporate-sanctioned violence. We may be shocked, but perhaps shouldn't be, as Miles's Blackness is fundamental to his character.

Miles's powers of electricity and invisibility are established in the *Miles Morales: Ultimate Spider-Man* comic series. While invisibility comes as inherent camouflage for Miles, his bioelectricity, called venom, is a result of experimentation by Dr. Doom. Each power speaks to Miles's reality as a Black man in America. His camouflage, moving through spaces unseen, echoes Ralph Ellison's *Invisible Man*. While there are only sparing narrative parallels, like each character winning a scholarship and having stories situated around Harlem, the language of visibility or invisibility of the Black man in America is key; Ellison builds on earlier writers like W.E.B. Du Bois to show how invisibility is itself an act of violence: an erasure from society. Miles's invisibility, particularly as first deployed in the game, instead offers safety: he only survives Braithwaite Bridge because he can disappear. The second power that differentiates Miles from Peter is his venom punch; in the game, his

bioelectricity activates when fighting Rhino. The comics show this ability resulting from experimentation, which evokes the exploitative and abusive history of medical experimentation on African American men. One of the most
famous, the Tuskagee syphilis study, ran from 1932 to 1972 and knowingly
deprived African American participants of medical treatments, only stopping
due to public outcry against the ethically unjustifiable actions (CDC, 2021).
However, the horrors of experimentation are stripped from the game; the
bioelectricity instead appears when Miles heroically steps in when Peter is
badly injured. While the game does not have the narrative space to contend
with this dark history that underpins Black peoples' interactions with the
medical systems, situating camouflage in a moment of corporate-sanctioned
violence does raise issues of race and its resulting abuses in a game about
law and order, justice, and right. Miles's unique powers are fundamentally
grounded in his Blackness. However, while grappling with issues of racialized (in)justice, the public police remain largely invisible or at best relegated
to the sidelines in the game, an absence with ideological implications that we
address next.

Policing and Police Visibility

Comics in the United States were heavily shaped by the Comics Code Authority (CCA) (Phillips & Strobl, 2013), with wholesalers and distributors
frequently requiring the CCA seal. A moral panic about comics contributing
to rising crime and deviance led to the CCA's founding in 1954 (Adkinson,
2008, p. 244). This self-regulatory body was a de facto censor with firm
rules about promoting pro-social messages and omitting antisocial and ta-
boo elements, similar in ideological effect to Hollywood's infamous Hays
Code (Rafter, 2006). The CCA was intentionally ideological because it was
"designed to control how creators portrayed agents of hegemonic order"
(Adkinson, 2008, p. 245). The CCA code focused on justice as a primary element of hero-comics and crime stories, declaring the criminal justice system
beyond reproach while demanding comics focus on the pursuit of wrongdo-
ers rather than the perpetration of crime:

1) Crimes shall never be presented in such a way as to create sympathy for
   the criminal, to promote distrust of the forces of law and justice, or to
   inspire others with a desire to imitate criminals.
2) No comics shall explicitly present the unique details and methods of a
   crime.
3) Policemen, judges, government officials, and respected institutions shall
   never be presented in such a way as to create disrespect for established
   authority.
4) If crime is depicted it shall be as a sordid and unpleasant activity.

5) Criminals shall not be presented so as to be rendered glamorous or to occupy a position which creates the desire for emulation; and
6) In every instance good shall triumph over evil and the criminal punished for his misdeeds.

(Adkinson, 2008, p. 246)

Lee and Ditko's Spider-Man series challenged the CCA with the young, flawed hero's more macabre origin of a spider-mutation and distance from policing and criminal justice. So, while the comics technically adhered to the code insofar as the criminals were unsympathetic and Peter worked to apprehend them, Spider-Man is far from a traditional protagonist; unlike the authoritative scientist Mr. Fantastic, or journalist Clark Kent, Peter Parker was a student who struggled to make ends meet. Lee and Ditko advanced a more socially conscious agenda in Spider-Man's interactions with criminals—some of whom were redeemable and remained unpunished—police, justice, and civil disobedience (Adkinson, 2008).

Marvel left the CCA in 2001, but Peter's formation under the 1960s guidelines shaped his original powers and responsibilities. Miles's first appearance in 2011 puts his character outside the CCA restrictions, while still reflecting the code's traditions. The games articulate the characters in new and accessible ways, but remain fundamentally bound up in terms of law and order. *Marvel's Spider-Man* frequently positions Peter as a police-ally, as Captain Watanabe asks Peter to fix police surveillance towers, provide back-up during a prison riot, and investigate Kingpin construction sites and Prisoner Outposts after the riot and escape. Peter jokingly responds in a persona, Spider-Cop, which leans into noir-tropes of a loner cop who plays outside the rules. Peter helps apprehend Kingpin, stops Mr. Negative's shock-troops attacking police-stations, and otherwise works hand in glove with the police. This partnership leaves the player fully complicit with law-and-order ideology.

Miles Morales situates Miles's experiences with the police wholly differently. Miles's father Jefferson Davis, an officer in the Police Department of New York (PDNY), is killed in *Marvel's Spider-Man*; Jefferson's death leads to Peter mentoring Miles before Miles is bitten and transforms. Early in his own game, Miles can reflect on his mantle at home, which features his father's portrait and a folded flag; he quietly says: "I'm going to make you proud, Dad." The police are largely absent from gameplay, more akin to environmental elements than characters. For example, when Miles intervenes after The Underground plant bombs around the rail tracks in Harlem, the police at the scene shoot at The Underground but have no impact in combat. When combat ends, the police point their weapons at the unconscious Underground members and Miles cannot interact with these officers. As Dockterman (2020) notes, the police's relationship with Peter or Miles is fundamentally different: "To its credit, Insomniac did realize that Miles can't have the same relationship with the police as Parker, a white man" (para. 6). When Miles tries to help with an investigation, he is chased from the crime scene. The police refuse his help, responding with aggression: "This is an active crime scene. Back off, or I'll take you in for obstruction." Their language is dismissive, calling him "the kid," saying Spider-Man was "irresponsible" to leave Miles to protect New York, and minimizing his repair of the subway lines: "at least he's doing some good, I guess." They distrust his youth, rather than his race, which they don't reliably know. However, Miles knows his race, and Mills (2022) argues it shapes his actions:

> how Miles responds to wrongdoing reflects the realities of Spanish Harlem's history with the police. In one side quest, Miles wants to investigate a kidnapping that is cordoned off as a crime scene. However, aware that he is a vigilante and a Black Puerto Rican one at that, he knows he cannot just stroll up to the evidence; the player must distract the officers and use Miles' invisibility to complete the investigation.
>
> *(p. 47)*

The officers disparaging Miles are wearing full riot gear in an echo of Roxxon's dehumanized security forces, thus situating both as part of the same repressive law-enforcement system. Their response to Miles, even when he is masked and costumed, requires him to navigate around systems that would silence him. This opaque representation of race is nevertheless ideological: the game recognizes the necessity of Miles's different relationship with police without engaging in direct criticism of institutionalized racism within the police or in American society more generally.

Removing police from much of the gameplay leaves Miles facing a private law-enforcement antagonist: Roxxon Security. While we may recognize the appropriate limitations of privatized policing in an American city, Roxxon's actions echo Sable International: in *Marvel's Spider-Man*, Mayor Osborn brings in a private militia to stem the terrorist threat in the city. This private security force sets up checkpoints across the city—ostensibly to stop Mr. Negative and the Demons, but also to pursue Spider-Man. The extrajudicial security positions Peter in a combat triangle, as he drops into fights between the Demons and Sable International forces, fighting both sides at once. *Miles Morales* provides a similar triangle, with Miles facing both Roxxon and The Underground. The Underground appear human, with visible race and presenting gender, while Roxxon forces, in full metal gear, are only male voice-actors: the removal of race and uniform gender presentation means they are interchangeable cogs in a system of security. Their actions do not demonstrate personality or agency, but are an extension of the corporation. Their authority in public spaces serves corporate interests.

Echoing the long abandoned CCA code, the replacement of public police with Roxxon, or Sable International, enables the games to show the hyper-militarization of policing without directly demonizing the police. This careful threading of the needle attempts to play both sides, as Peter is friendly with the police and Miles is the son of a fallen officer. Laying out, but not engaging with, complex issues of justice appear throughout the game, as Schänzel (2021) points out:

> By all appearances, the game appears deeply unwilling to grapple with the morally ambiguous behaviors it mandatorily bestows upon the player, nor ask players to critically consider the repercussions of their reliance on such surveillance technology to enact such violence against their anonymous victims.
>
> *(p. 257)*

Spider-Man's complicity with the legal system and its surveillance shifts in *Miles Morales* where the police appear at best vestigial and at worst rude. The invisibility of the police as a force for good is important in the game, as Miles receives a gift from the community in front of a large Black Lives Matter mural. As Miles's costuming is a powerful signifier of his Blackness and community, these suits "aren't simply elements of authentic representation, but rather pieces of iconography that identify him as someone who lives in—and loves—his community" (Carter 2022, para. 18). He can wear a suit that reflects who he is both for and in his community. While Spider-Man's extralegal policing ties him to New York's police, Miles's role is parallel to, if not wholly separate from, the public police. Instead of facing the complexity of Miles's position as a young Afro-Latino and son of an officer, Insomniac choses omission:

> . . . why Miles would rather avoid police—or why Harlem residents might turn to him rather than the cops—is never stated outright, and players might have different expectations for how the game ought to handle unspoken moments of tension. A Black player who has grown up approaching police with caution because of racism in our criminal justice system might immediately understand what's going on, whereas a white player might need these more subtle plot points spelled out for them because they've have [*sic*] had a radically different experience with the police.
>
> *(Dockterman, 2020, para. 7)*

Dockterman (2020) contends this silence on complex subjects creates different experiences, as players who engage in Miles's world do so from their individual perspectives. This silence and relative absence of police gives Miles a space to exist as a young Black man without the harassment or threat of

police violence: a kind of fantasy space. As that fantasy does not confront
or acknowledge the institutionalized racist violence of the police, the game is
thus ideologically complicit in upholding current political and social arrangements that devalue Black and Brown lives.

Conclusion

Popular criminology explores spaces where popular culture and criminology "interpenetrate and cross fertilize one another" (Rafter & Brown, 2011,
p. 2). Popular criminological depictions of crime and the criminal justice
system center emotion, allowing a vicarious experience of the sensual aspects of crime: "its adrenaline rush, pleasure, desperation, anger, rage, and
humiliation" (Rafter & Brown, 2011, p. 5). Video games offer a particularly
immersive encounter with the affective, emotional, and sensual dimensions
of crime and justice. Video games like *Marvel's Spider-Man: Miles Morales*
offer potentially transformative spaces that facilitate critical and reflective
engagements around crime and policing in diverse communities in America
and beyond. While the game reflects cultural, critical, and green criminology
in the way power manifests in crime at the community level, much of the
critical potential is blunted by the game's foreclosure on issues like corporate
malfeasance and racial justice. Moreover, the game naturalizes and neutral-
izes the oppressive power of surveillance and private forms of policing by
presenting these as potentially community driven and benign. While players might disapprove of the faceless, robotic Roxxon Security forces, Miles's
technologically-driven surveillance app appears to support community watch
in marginalized communities like Harlem that suffer from both under and
over policing. Thus, the same forces that militate against social justice in
communities of color—surveillance and privatization—are offered as ways
for communities to fight back. Similarly, depictions of corporate crime, environmental injustice, and institutionalized racism in policing appear throughout the game, but avoid and subvert serious criticism in deliberate silences
that permit the game to project a fantasy about a racialized superhero who
provides an effective alternative to dysfunctional systems of police and criminal justice.

Popular criminology may reflect, refract, and at times even contest current understandings and practices of justice while reaching much larger
audiences than academic criminology and scholarly discourse. However,
our analysis of *Marvel's Spider-Man: Miles Morales* suggests considerable
continuity with earlier depictions of superhero justice that uphold broader
ideological underpinnings of contemporary society. Crime—even when
perpetrated by corporations—is the work of villainous individuals, and
vigilantism grounded in violence and omnipresent surveillance provide justice for community members who rely on superheroes working outside the

constraints of the law. Transposing tried and true themes to racialized and socially vulnerable communities in Harlem does little to sharpen the critical potential of popular culture to reveal social injustice and call for much needed reforms. *Marvel's Spider-Man: Miles Morales* provides a potent fantasy of justice that sits uneasily within contemporary social movements and the growing awareness of racialized injustice in America today.

Note

1 New Mexico State Judge Jack Love was inspired by a 1977 Spider-Man newspaper comic, in which Kingpin used a bracelet to monitor the whereabouts of Spider-Man. Love thought an electronic monitoring bracelet could reduce overcrowding in jails, so he approached several electronic companies with the idea. He convinced Michael Goss, a computer salesman, to build a prototype, which was tested by Love in the early 1980s, and the US Department of Justice funded an evaluation by Criminologist Walter Niederberger. See Koulish<> (2015) and Burrell and Gable (2008); see also https://www.esquire.com/news-politics/news/a2164/spiderman022007/ and https://www.nytimes.com/1984/02/12/us/electronic-monitor-turns-home-into-jail.html

References

Adkinson, C.D. (2008). The Amazing Spider-Man and the evolution of the Comics Code: Case study in cultural criminology. *Journal of Criminal Justice and Popular Culture*, 15(3), 241–261.

Bakan, J. (2004). *The corporation: The pathological pursuit of profit and power*. Free Press.

Brown, A. (2017, September 11). Younger men play video games, but so do a diverse group of other Americans. *Pew Research*.

Burrell, W.D., & Gable, R.S. (2008). From B.F. Skinner to Spiderman to Martha Stewart: The past, present and future of electronic monitoring of offenders. *Journal of Offender Rehabilitation*, 46(3–4), 101–118. https://doi.org/10.1080/10509670802143342

Carter, R. (2022, May 27). How Miles Morales grew from a legacy Spider-Man into his own unique hero. *Popverse*. https://www.thepopverse.com/miles-morales-legacy-spider-man-marvel

CDC. (2021, April 22). The Tuskagee Timeline. *Centers for Disease Control and Prevention*. https://www.cdc.gov/tuskegee/timeline.htm

Crick, T. (2011). The game body: Toward a phenomenology of contemporary video gaming. *Games and Culture*, 6(3), 259–269. https://doi.org/10.1177/1555412010364980

Daley, D. (2020, November 26). Spider-Man: Miles Morales fights for inclusivity in games. *Mobile Syrup*. https://mobilesyrup.com/2020/11/26/spider-man-miles-morales-editorial/

Dockterman, E. (2020, November 10). *Spider-Man: Miles Morales* could've tackled police reform head-on. Instead, the cops are almost entirely cone. *Time Magazine*. https://time.com/5907872/spider-man-miles-morales-police/

Doyle, A. (2011). Revisiting the synopticon: Reconsidering Mathiesen's "The Viewer Society" in the age of web 2.0. *Theoretical Criminology*, 15(3), 283–299. https://doi.org/10.1177/1362480610396645

Fawcett, C., & Kohm, S. (2020). Carceral violence at the intersection of madness and crime in Batman: Arkham Asylum and Batman: Arkham City. *Crime, Media, Culture, 16*(2), 265–285. https://doi.org/10.1177/1741659019865298

Ferrell, J. (1992). Making sense of crime: Review essay on Jack Katz's *Seductions of Crime. Social Justice, 19*(2), 110–123. http://www.jstor.org/stable/29766697

Ferrell, J. (2004). Boredom, crime and criminology. *Theoretical Criminology, 8*(3), 287–302. https://doi.org/10.1177/1362480604044610

Ferrell, J., Hayward, K., & Young, J. (2015). *Cultural criminology: An invitation* (2nd ed.). Sage.

Flanagan, M., & Nissenbaum, H. (2014). *Values at play in digital games*. MIT Press.

Garland, D. (2001). *The culture of control*. University of Chicago Press.

Kane, B. (1940). *Batman #1*. DC Comics.

Kohm, S. (2017). Popular criminology. In N. Rafter and E. Carrabine (Eds.), *Oxford research encyclopedia of crime, media, and popular culture*. Oxford University Press. https://doi.org/10.1093/acrefore/9780190264079.013.158

Koulish, R. (2015). Spiderman's web and the governmentality of electronic immigrant detention. *Law, Culture and the Humanities, 11*(1), 83–108. https://doi.org/10.1177/1743872111433376

Leonard, D. (2003). "Live in your world, play in ours": Race, video games, and consuming the other. *Simile: Studies in Media & Information Literacy Education, 3*(4), 1–9. https://doi.org/10.3138/sim.3.4.002

Lub, V. (2018). Neighbourhood watch: Mechanisms and moral implications. *British Journal of Criminology, 58*(4), 906–924. https://doi.org/10.1093/bjc/azx058

Marvel's Spider-Man. Playstation 4. (2018). Insomniac Games.

Marvel's Spider-Man: Miles Morales. Playstation 5. (2020). Insomniac Games.

Mathiesen, T. (1997). The viewer society. *Theoretical Criminology, 1*(2), 215–234. https://doi.org/10.1177/1362480697001002003

Mills, R.M. (2022). A post-Soul Spider-Man: The remixed geroics of Miles Morales. *The Black Scholar, 52*(1), 41–52. https://doi.org/10.1080/00064246.2022.2007345

Phillips, N., & Strobl, S. (2013). *Comic book crime*. NYU Press.

Pulliam-Moore, C. (2020). Miles Morales reforms Spider-Man's relationship with the police when it needs to be abolished. *Gizmodo*. https://gizmodo.com/miles-morales-reforms-spider-mans-relationship-with-the-1845575036

Rafter, N. (2006). *Shots in the mirror: Crime films and society*. Oxford University Press.

Rafter, N., & Brown, M. (2011) *Criminology goes to the movies: Crime theory and popular culture*. NYU Press.

Schänzel, D. (2021). Spider-Man, the panopticon, and the normalization of mass surveillance. In L. Piatti-Farnell (Ed.), *The superhero multiverse: Readapting comic book icons in twenty-first-century film and popular media* (pp. 249–260). Lexington Books.

Siegel, J., & Schuster J. (1997). Action comics #1. In B. Kahan (Ed.), *Superman: The Action Comics Archive vol. 1* (pp. 1–14). DC Comics.

Scott, D. (2022). *Keeping it unreal: Black queer fantasy and superhero comics* (Ser. Sexual cultures). NYU Press.

Sicart, M. (2014). *Play matters* (Ser. Playful thinking). MIT Press.

Steinmetz, K., Schaefer, B., & Green, E. (2017). Anything but boring: A cultural criminological exploration of boredom. *Theoretical Criminology, 21*(3), 342–360. https://doi.org/10.1177/1362480616652686

Van Steden, R., & Mehlbaum, S. (2021) Do-it-yourself surveillance: The practices and effects of Whatsapp neighbourhood crime prevention groups. *Crime, Media, Culture* (online first). https://doi.org/10.1177/17416590211041017

Wise, M. (2016). *Surveillance and film*. Bloomsbury.

Wood, M.A., & Thompson, C. (2020) Crime prevention, swarm intelligence and stigmergy: Understanding the mechanisms of social media-facilitated community crime prevention. *The British Journal of Criminology, 61*(2), 414–433. https://doi.org/10.1093/bjc/azaa065

Worlds, M., & Miller, H. (2019). *Miles Morales: Spider-Man* and reimagining the canon for racial justice. *English Journal, 108*(4), 43–50.

Yar, M. (2012). Crime, media and the will-to-representation: Reconsidering relationships in the new media age. *Crime Media Culture, 8*(3), 245–260. https://doi.org/10.1177/1741659012443227

10

CYNICISM IN POLICE SIMULATION

A Case Study of *Beat Cop*

*James Popham, Andrea Corradi, Michael Ouellet,
Sarthak Pal, Chris McDiarmid, Jocelyn Booton
and Michelle Goodridge*

The police and policing are common figures in contemporary entertainment media. The spectrum of tasks typically referred to as "police work"—inclusive of car chases, crime scene investigations, writing tickets, and generally enforcing public moralities—provides alluring subjects for coverage in virtually all forms of media (Dowler et al., 2006). Despite this breadth of attention, the police are often unimpressed or even hostile toward the media and its coverage of their work, and have stated concerns to researchers about the glamorized framing of investigations and even the potential to undermine their operations through false allegations (Nix & Pickett, 2017; Huey & Broll, 2012). These tensions have contributed toward an incomplete image of police work in the media that undervalues the everyday realities of policing and the importance of this work (Chermak et al., 2006; Mustafaj & Van den Bulck, 2021).

Moreover, as representatives of the state, the police and their activities are often subject to contextual investigation by the media in a manner reflective of current events (Herbert, 2006). While the critical examination of the police in a popular forum plays a significant role in driving public discourse about their legitimacy, the media prioritizes volatile event-driven framings of the police based on newsworthiness rather than institutional-level critique (Lawrence, 2000). This strategic approach to media coverage drives increased consumer engagement; however, its emphasis on negative stories and the sensational contributes toward public cynicism about policing (Cappella & Jamieson, 1997). While some have argued that police agencies have at least partially retaken control of the messaging about their work through 21st-century technologies like social media and consultations with production

DOI: 10.4324/9781003346869-10

firms (e.g., Bullock, 2018; Walsh & O'Connor, 2018), contemporary presentations of policing often retain this cynical framing in connection to culturally significant events like the murder of George Floyd, the Black Lives Matter movement, and the Ferguson protests (Mustafaj & Van den Bulck, 2021; Moule et al., 2018; Dowler & Zawilski, 2007).

Our chapter is premised on the assumption that interactive long-form technologies like video games provide an outlet for presenting police work in an alternative and unconventional manner (Levan & Downing, 2022). In light of this, our chapter focuses on a contemporary police simulation videogame (*Beat Cop*), assesses the game's plot, dialog, interactions, and mechanics, interrogates the game's messaging about police work. The game positions the player as a disgraced police detective who has been demoted to street patrol and must re-learn the basics of foot patrol police work. These lessons, plus ongoing plotlines, manifest as a series of in-game challenges that affect the player's progress through *Beat Cop's* storyline.

We begin with an exploration of existing research about the connection between police and media coverage, leading into our proposition that the nature of video games provides an opportunity to present the police and police work in an interactive format. We follow with a qualitative investigation of the gameplay in *Beat Cop* focusing on its presentation of police work as understood by game players. Our findings indicate that much of the gameplay is centered on unavoidable, negative interactions that reinforce a sense of cynicism in players, specifically around policing. The game heavily rewards corruption and toxic behavior, and at times makes illegal or violent activities inescapable. Overall, we found that the game forms an antagonistic view of policing that it perpetuates through systems of rewards, challenging the player's ability to choices about what type of police officer they would like to be. Our chapter then concludes with a discussion of the potential reasoning behind this cynicism.

About Beat Cop

Beat Cop was created by the independent video game studio *Pixel Crow* and published by 11 bit Studios in 2017 (11 bit studios, 2023). After its initial release to personal computer (PC) systems on the Steam platform, *Beat Cop* was ported to most major console systems and the Android and Apple operating systems. Marketed as a retro pixel art adventure, *Beat Cop* employs a throwback gameplay style known as point-and-click that requires the player to identify objects and characters within the game world and then select them for interaction. Much of the game space is interactive, and specific opportunities are emphasized with indicators (e.g., a set of handcuffs appears over a person who can be arrested).

Beat Cop is marketed as a policing simulator inspired by and parodying police dramas of the 1980s (11 bit studios, 2023; Steam, 2023; Taylor, 2018). As the game's developers explain:

> When we were kids we spent countless hours on watching 80s TV cop shows. We loved watching good guys kicking bad guys asses, saving beautiful women and driving muscle cars into the night. We knew they weren't true, but we didn't care. We had damn good time and that's what counted. Beat Cop is not a document about New York in the 80s. It's our tribute to all those evenings spent in front of the TV. So . . . relax, enjoy the game and don't take life too seriously.
>
> *(11 bit studios, 2023)*

To emulate these experiences, players take control of disgraced former New York Police Department (NYPD) detective Jack Kelly as he re-learns the basics of foot patrol. Kelly must navigate a fictional city block undergoing significant urban decay with a 1980s backdrop, including frequent interactions with various organized crime groups. Players are instructed to interact with the community members and merchants inhabiting the block while engaging in law enforcement tasks like traffic control and arresting shop thieves. They must also navigate Kelly's personal issues, like reconnecting with an estranged child and paying alimony bills. Each element of police and personal work influences the in-game choices presented to the player, potentially taking Kelly down a range of pathways.

The game offers nine different endings, theoretically giving players considerable autonomy in controlling the narrative outcome (11 bit studios, 2023; Taylor, 2018). This flexibility is further amplified by the game's open-world approach. Players are encouraged to explore every corner of the game's map to uncover new interactions and story sub-quests; however, in so doing they learn that they cannot be in all places at all times. Players must quickly learn to triage their options, forcing critical reflection about the consequences of their actions and fostering greater connection to the outcomes that Kelly faces (Chen et al., 2023; Aarseth, 2014; Sicart, 2020; Holl et al., 2020).

Background

Law enforcement agencies and their activities are prominent in contemporary media entertainment across various platforms. Topics ranging from crime prevention and public safety to ethical considerations form the tapestry of what is commonly termed "police work," offering captivating content for diverse media outlets (Mawby, 1999). Despite this widespread representation, a discernible tension exists between law enforcement entities and the media (Ericson, 1989). Agencies frequently express ambivalence or hostility toward media portrayals, citing concerns about inaccurate or misleading depictions that could compromise operational effectiveness (Huey & Broll, 2012). This complex relationship is further exacerbated by the media's predilection for focusing on the sensational aspects of policing, such as serial murderers or forensic investigations, often ignoring incidents that represent a more realistic portrayal of police activities and crime (Huey & Broll, 2012). This selective coverage contributes to a fragmented public understanding of the multifaceted nature of police work (Rhineberger-Dunn et al., 2016).

A significant body of criminological research has been devoted to mapping the historical development of media representations of the police and connecting them with public opinions (e.g., Surrette, 2015; Clifford & White, 2017; Herbert, 2006). For instance, Surrette (2015) outlines a history of media constructs of law enforcement starting with "lampooned" police in the silent film era (*Keystone Cops*), shifting to a procedural crime-buster treatment reflecting post-WWII interpretations of authority (*Dragnet*), to gritty construction of anti-bureaucracy "cops" following civil rights movements of the late 1960s (*Dirty Harry*), and finally as forensic experts in a post-DNA era (*CSI: Crime Scene Investigation*). Surrette (2015) argues that each of these constructs are caricatures portraying in-the-moment public perceptions of policing. For instance, Surrette (2015) argues that the "cop" framing emerged during a period of heightened awareness about urban decay and the rise of narcotics, depicting the police as soldiers in a war against crime and drugs (Peterson & Hagan, 2005).

Notably, Surrette (2015, p. 114) adds that regardless of framing, the differences between "media cops" and the actions of their real-world counterparts inevitably contribute toward public dissatisfaction and even cynicism directed at the police as they are incapable of fulfilling the imaginary roles set up for them through news and fictional media. In many cases, media producers will intentionally lean into cynicism about the police to improve the marketability of their product (Reiner, 2010). Driven by market demands, newsmakers will focus on the subjects that are known to drive engagement by eliciting emotions in the viewer or reader. This sentiment has been distilled into the commonly-heard refrain "if it bleeds, it leads" (e.g., Moriearty, 2010), emphasizing the media's preference for the extreme. While the statement infers a preference for violence, it often means greater emphasis on subjects that will raise the ire of the public, which in terms of the police can include cases of police violence/brutality alongside administrative issues like corruption and investigative failures along with a range of other transgressions (Herbert, 2006; Dowler & Zawilski, 2007; Moule et al., 2018).

Moreover, the police are often framed as a singular entity, meaning that an event occurring in one jurisdiction can influence public perceptions in a wholly remote location (Chan, 1996).

Taken from a social-constructionist lens, these machinations can drive public sentiments and define societal "problems" in a selective manner that is only loosely connected to contemporary realities (Moule et al., 2018; Surrette, 2015; Lawrence, 2000, p. 7). The overwhelming emphasis on critique then contributes toward a "spiral of cynicism" (Cappella & Jamieson, 1997, p. 10), whereby conflict-driven media invokes public discord, inspiring even greater media coverage. In general terms, authors like Lawrence (2000) and Cappella & Jamieson (1997) argue that the constant scrutiny directed at the police and their actions has established a hyper-critical and self-fulfilling media environment, leading to public cynicism about policing.

Cynical and even antagonistic media representations of the police are frequently encountered in multiple media formats (Carr et al., 2007; Reiner, 2010; Mawby,1999). A recent example occurred over the spring and summer of 2019 in response to the murder of George Floyd by Minneapolis police officer Derek Chauvin, which had been recorded on cell phones by several witnesses. Floyd's death, and the Black Lives Matter protests that it inspired, were cause for significant media coverage about the relationship between policing and embedded racial inequalities in the United States. Researchers have argued that this coverage led to historically low levels of public confidence in the police (Cowart et al., 2022).

An important note here is the amplifying effect of modern digital media. Clips taken from body-worn cameras, cell-phone videos by civilians, and their accompanying dialog are quickly transmitted across the internet through social media and then often picked up by the popular media as newsworthy events (Goldsmith, 2015; Lawrence, 2000). While these events are a legitimate and important mechanism of critique (e.g., Moule et al., 2018; Cowart et al., 2022), they also contribute toward an asymmetric relationship between the media and the police that can skew how their work is presented to the public (Ericson, 1989; Skogan, 2007; Goldsmith, 2015; Carr et al., 2007). Again, in line with the Cappella and Jamieson's (1997) spiral described earlier, the constant and international flow of critical imagery and messaging is likely to contribute toward cynicism about the police (Cowart et al., 2022).

Media, Video Games, and Policing

Like other forms of media, video games often include some representation of policing or law enforcement. Video games provide an opportunity to capitalize on the long-format and interactive modality of digital technologies to provide an immersive study of police work. Indeed, some popular video games feature police or police-adjacent figures as playable protagonists ("player characters" or "PCs"). For instance, Rockstar Games' *L.A. Noire* (2011) has players interrogate non-player characters (NPCs) and advises the gamer to consider their facial expressions and body language along with their dialog (Wright, 2017). Another police simulator, ZA/UM's *Disco Elysium* (2019), makes use of a skill tree that expands dialog options with NPCs and enriches the investigative experience; however, many perks come with both positive and negative effects for the character. Similarly, THQ Nordic's *This Is The Police 2* (2018) presents players with multiple possible sequences of events leading up to a single event, forcing them to determine which was the most likely based on various investigative techniques.

Several successful gaming franchises have attempted to provide more realistic depictions of policing that engage players in work beyond the snippets of action mythologized through popular forms of media. For instance, the Police Quest series published by *Sierra On-Line* through the 1980s and 1990s attempted to engage the player in multiple elements of police work, from locker-room banter to administrative record keeping, interspersed with moments of extreme violence and action (Juul, 2019). The third installment of Police Quest, *The Kindred* (Sierra On-Line, 1991) had a relatively open city map to explore, and several crime scene situations that required player-initiated interactions to locate evidence (Toh, 2023). To add credibility, Sierra relied on the experiences of police officers, including a former chief of police for the LAPD, in the production of these games and credited them as designers (Sierra On-Line, 1991). The initial Police Quest series, spanning the first three titles, attempted to emulate police work by taking advantage of burgeoning computer technology to develop an immersive simulation of policing.

While there are certainly examples of successful attempts to emulate police work in a digital format, we must not overlook equally prominent games that take subversive approaches to policing (Annandale, 2006; Levan & Downing, 2022). One of the most infamous cases, which garnered worldwide attention and ongoing legal battles about the effect of gaming on violent behaviors (Calvert & Richards, 2007), occurred with Rockstar Games' 2004 *Grand Theft Auto: San Andreas* (GTA:SA). The fifth iteration of the series, GTA:SA had players take control of Carl Johnson (CJ) who is drawn into the gang life in cities inspired by Los Angeles (Los Santos), San Francisco (San Fierro), and Las Vegas (Las Venturas). A corrupt police officer and his cronies takes a central role in the plot, which ultimately leads to a series of in-game citywide riots, reflecting the events that occurred in Los Angeles in 1992 following the acquittal of Rodney King's attackers (Garrelts, 2006). The plot and gameplay of GTA:SA is interwoven with numerous subversive critiques of the police, ranging from NPC police dialog that infers equal shares of incompetence and brutality, to key plot points that parody ongoing public controversies and corruption within the LAPD (Garrelts, 2006). In taking this approach,

GTA:SA leveled a series of critiques about policing that may have had lasting effect on its players (Whalen, 2006).

An interesting consideration here relates to the difference between "telling" and "playing" experienced in different video game formats (Whalen, 2006). Games like *LA Noire* and *GTA:SA*, which provide an inescapable and largely linear main plot, do not provide players with the opportunity to develop their character based on their own morality. This is notable, as previous qualitative gaming research has indicated that when given the opportunity, players will make in-game decisions based on their own moralities (Holl et al., 2020). The authors found that many gamers experienced meaningful gameplay when they could take actions that they felt reflected their own worldview (Holl et al., 2020; Weaver & Lewis, 2012). Conversely, in situations where a difficult decision must be taken, simulation game players will often neutralize and morally disengage from the harms of their actions and ascribing them to the game's plot or developer's intentions (Hartmann & Vorderer, 2010). In the context of games featuring policing, this research suggests that players will roleplay as a police officer who enforces the law according to their own moral standards, rather than taking a highly critical or consensus-based approach to play.

Method

Approach

Our method attempted to reflect Steinmetz' (2018) application of Altheide's (1987) *Ethnographic Content Analysis* to study video games. The ECA approach generally centers on "*constant discovery* and *constant comparison* of relevant situations, settings, styles, images, meanings and nuances" (Altheide, 1987, p. 68, emphasis original). For media formats like video games, which present multiple sensory experiences, ECA provides a framework for reflexive investigation of the interconnectedness between varying modes of communication. In line with Steinmetz' (2018) study, players were instructed to consider game mechanics, objectives, dialog, spaces, and plots as they emerged in *Beat Cop*. Bolstering this approach, we also incorporated a player-modeling design that adds structural prompts to influence gameplay (see Nacke et al., 2010).

Data Source

Our study uses data collected from several contributors as they played through *Beat Cop* (see Table 10.1). The game is divided into 21 chapters, each representing a day of in-game police work, each taking approximately 20 minutes to complete. In its entirety, the game takes approximately

TABLE 10.1 Demographic summary of play testers

Player	Gender	Age	System	Level of experience	Frequency	Preferred game
Z03	F	29	iOS	Beginner	Monthly	RPG
X13	M	42	XBox One	Casual	Weekly	Action/Adventure
T16	M	42	PC	Casual	Weekly	Sim
T02	F	43	PC	Beginner	Yearly	Cards
H16	M	23	PC	Competitive	Daily	RTS
N15	M	28	PS5	Expert	Daily	Sports
T15	F	37	PC	Expert	Weekly	MMORPG

6–8 hours to complete based on in-game decisions and successful completion of escalating mission requirements. The game's story is consistent across each platform it operates on. However, slight differences in control schemes were noted (e.g., differences between using a mouse to control gameplay versus a console controller).

Data collection was completed by each co-author of this study, who were provided with a copy of *Beat Cop* on their chosen platform. Each researcher was instructed to attempt three playthroughs of *Beat Cop* using different strategies. For playthrough one, team members were instructed to act as metaphorical "good cop" and take what they understood to be morally appropriate when faced with in-game decision-making situations. During their second playthrough, researchers were instructed to take on the "bad cop" role, taking the opposite approach to their first playthrough. Finally, researchers were directed to aim for "success" in their final playthrough, shifting their focus to decision-making, ensuring that *Beat Cop*'s challenges, plots, and sub-plots would be fulfilled. Each player was challenged to reach at least day seven in-game but encouraged to reach completion.

Players were instructed to journal their experiences with *Beat Cop* throughout gameplay. The game has a natural pause after the completion of each in-game day, providing an opportunity to collect notes and reflexively jot conceptual observations (Saldaña, 2021). Each player was provided with a set of prompting questions intended to direct their path of discovery. They were also encouraged to record any observations, emotions, or experiences that they felt were significant. Additionally, we collected a short biographical survey from each researcher, providing descriptive information that assisted with grounding their outputs in their levels of experience.

Analysis

Data were collated in a spreadsheet format and analyzed using the open source QualCoder qualitative data analysis software package. Coding was primarily led by two researchers (Z03, T16), which was then summarized and presented to the remaining co-authors. After seeking input and confirmation through personal experiences, a final list of thematic observations was compiled. We employed a multi-cycle coding process outlined by Saldaña (2021), commencing with in vivo and concept coding, followed by an axial process to identify prominent codes (Charmaz, 2014). The resulting emergent themes and subthemes are presented below, and selected remarks from coders were given to emphasize the underlying emotionality (Hartmann & Vorderer, 2010). While several themes were identified, we have prioritized discussing *Beat Cop's* production of cynicism through several lenses, as this was the most saturated theme amongst all players (Low, 2019). Additionally, we noted significant overlaps in gameplay experiences between "bad cop" and "success" playthroughs, so we elected to draw our data from only the "good" and "bad" instances of play.

Results

Beat Cop is organized around a deeply cynical framing of the police, policing, and the communities that they engage with. Players face a constant barrage of negative imagery and dialog that reflects a century of popular media policing tropes, primarily emphasizing their power over the public and a general sense of corruption (e.g., throughout the game, you are often provided the opportunity to plant drugs in cars). Many of the situations faced by players could be argued to reflect the systemic corruption embedded within NYPD through the 20th century; however, the game's developers claim that these are not reflections of historical record. Instead, players are immersed in a corrupt policing environment from the start and are forced to engage regardless of their moral imperative.

Cynicism in Play

While early gameplay affords some agency as they situate Jack Kelly in a community policing role, players quickly observed that the flexibility to pursue meaningful gameplay through moral engagement is undermined by the in-game encounters that direct the narrative. Key moments in the game's main plot force the player to make unsavory decisions that build toward an apathetic and ultimately cynical view of policing and the player's capacity to make a difference. For example, an early game situation forces players to shepherd a visiting Russian police officer throughout their beat. During this mission, players must bend or break laws for their guest —ultimately forcing their hand to cover up an attempted murder by the NPC. Several players complained that this was an unavoidable situation, as ignoring their directive to watch over the Russian visitor was framed as a dereliction of duty leading to a game-over screen. This experience was commonly recounted by all coders, who expressed concern and frustration.

> *Being forced to hide the body went against my player philosophy and personal morality but was integral to maintaining international peace and harmony. If it were up to me, the Russian would have been arrested.*

Cynicism toward policing is similarly embedded into *Beat Cop's* mechanics. Players sit through a squad briefing at the beginning of each in-game day, during which they are assigned daily tasks. While most tasks are not a *de facto* requirement, players are often punished with loss of pay, being berated by their superior officer, and eventually a game-over firing event if they continue to miss their tasks. Traffic citations are the most prominent of these expectations, and players are usually required to complete a certain number to satisfy their captain. This daily ticket quota forms a central element in gameplay.

Fulfillment of the often-demanding quota requirements elicited feelings of discontent amongst coders, and these feelings were most prominent during their "good cop" playthroughs. They observed that specific standards, such as writing 12 parking tickets daily, significantly detracted from what they considered more valuable police work. They noted how it deviated from their understanding of "good" law enforcement as they were not afforded any flexibility. Rather, Kelly's actions were viewed as the robotic fulfillment of daily requirements tied to in-game success measures like appeasing superior officers and earning a living. To this end, one of the game's requirements is to make regular alimony payments to Kelly's ex-wife, which start at US$300 weekly and are doubled to US$600 later in the game. Playing as a good cop, which generally meant eschewing payment opportunities and bribes offered by NPCs, presented players with inadequate means to meet these financial obligations. The only "legitimate" mechanism to earn additional income came with doubling their daily ticket quota. This requirement often disrupted attempts to focus on what players felt should be prioritized by the police:

> *Doubled my quota to ensure I would make my alimony payment; left little time for other priorities (putting out fires after the fact).*

NPC interactions tied to ticketing further impacted players' cynicism toward police work. At relatively random intervals during gameplay, players are presented with the opportunity to accept a bribe from NPCs after a ticket has been filled but before it has been administered. These interactions factored heavily into both "good cop" and "bad cop" playthroughs, leading to differing interpretations. During good playthroughs, coders faced a regular barrage of hateful language directed at their character upon declining a bribe. Beyond the explicit statements made by NPCs about the player's character, the experience left players dissatisfied with their in-game accomplishments. Additionally, several coders observed that tagging and towing vehicles elicited feelings of guilt for those affected by their actions—one player attempted to navigate these emotions by targeting only the most egregious violations, like parking in front of a hydrant:

> *I was also forced to tow people to meet objectives which thus far I have not done. I choose to only tow people parked next to fire hydrants to be fairest.*

Players experienced the ticketing system in a very different manner during their "bad cop" playthroughs. As a general observation, every player reported finding the game more enjoyable, or at least more easily completed, when they were no longer bound by their moral underpinnings. This was most clearly observed in their experiences with administering citations, as they could now allow Kelly to accept bribes and fulfill the financial requirements set out in the game. These bribes proved lucrative, allowing players to amass cash reserves that far exceeded their obligations and freeing time to engage with other game mechanics and situations.

> *I turned down a crew's offer of alliance, because I think that concentrating on money acquisition may be more important in the end and have decided that I probably have more money to make from the mafia than from the crew and definitely from the police—I can afford being docked $25 for not meeting all objectives when I take a bribe for a ticket.*

In addition to the ticketing mechanic, *Beat Cop* introduces several puzzles linking the primary plot of Kelly's redress with seemingly trivial activities, primarily tied to maintaining his position within the force (and avoiding a game-over scenario). These tasks become increasingly complex as the game progresses, requiring greater attention to game elements like timing and tools. These experiences often frustrated players as they limited their capacity to fulfill other requirements like ticket quotas. By the end of day seven on their "good" playthroughs, many players expressed concern that they could not balance the various needs presented to them—in other words, their hand had been forced, and they experienced a reduced sense of agency.

Conversely, during "bad" playthroughs, players could electively ignore virtually any side quest presented to them; in some cases, this meant that they could opt to ignore or take callous approaches to their tasks without concern for consequence. Nonetheless, this free-for-all approach contributed to the player's cynicism, this time rooted in moral disengagement from Kelly's actions. Interestingly, players' narratives shifted to third-party observations in these situations and were often framed reflexively.

The escapist element of this game affords one the opportunity to explore their darkest instincts in a venue that is free from consequence. I can't state enough how much easier, less stressful, and more fun this run was.

Cynicism by Design

In addition to novel mechanics, *Beat Cop* offers players a great deal of freedom to explore the in-game community, commencing with a required tour of the neighborhood on day one. The fictional New York City block that serves as the game's map is revealed to the player in a non-linear and exploratory fashion—they are encouraged to enter buildings, converse with NPCs, and interact with on-screen items. The map has no unlockable sections, and all its spatial/temporal elements are immediately available to the player.

For many of our coders, the exploratory design of the *Beat Cop's* map translated into immediate exposure to the cynical worldview presented by its writers. During day one, players are presented with requests from competing organized crime groups, propositions by sex workers and drug dealers, face hateful dialog from NPCs, and are introduced to a general sense of social disorganization within Kelly's beat. From this point on, the game's narrative constantly presents opportunities to corrupt Kelly's morals, encouraging the player to engage in difficult situations.

As with the discussion provided above, these challenges were often most pronounced during the "good" playthroughs. *Beat Cop's* narrative heavily relies on the tensions between Kelly's framing as a good cop fallen on hard times and the inherent advantages of embracing corrupt policing practices. These moral dilemmas were central to the game's narrative and challenged players' sense of agency in its outcomes—in many cases, dialog trees ultimately led to the same conclusion. One example that stood out to players was an interaction with an elderly NPC. For this mission they were informed through an unavoidable radio dialog that that the woman is related to a high-ranking officer and that the player *must* fulfill any requests that she makes, in this case purchasing donuts. Through the course of this interaction Kelly feeds the donuts to the woman's dog, causing it to be sick. While this experience had little-to-no bearing on the outcome of the game, several players expressed their concern that they had no option but to harm an animal.

These dilemmas were presented in a binary fashion, leaving little space for players to take their preferred course of action. In another example, several players encountered a situation during the sixth day of gameplay where Kelly intervenes in a dispute involving a man harassing a woman on the street.

After responding to her, the player quickly learns that she is a sex worker engaged with one of the local gangs, and Kelly is forced to either watch her (to ensure safety) or arrest her. Without additional options, players were forced to make an uncomfortable choice:

> *I agreed to help a woman who was having trouble outside a liquor store, but then it turned out she was a sex worker. It was difficult then to do know what to do as my options were watch her or arrest her, neither of which I should probably do. As a person, I would want to look out for her but as a cop I should arrest her. I was supposed to be "good" cop, which was unclear in this context because she hadn't committed a crime. I chose not to arrest her.*

The spatiality of *Beat Cop* also affected players' sense of agency in the game. Players often encountered a series of overlapping in-game challenges. In these situations, they were forced to prioritize some situations while letting others pass. Players faced moral tensions related to unclear game mechanics whereby the unknown consequences of their decisions could have immediate and severe repercussions that leading to end-game outcomes. As the following statements suggest, players felt frustration and, ultimately cynicism toward the work that was required of them during good cop playthroughs:

> *It takes a lot of time to look for the broken lights, which gets in the way of doing additional things. For example, I was trying to fulfill the quota when I got a call about a fire and vehicle blocking the hydrant. I had to run to deal with it, and in doing missed another situation that wound up affecting my end-game score.*

Interestingly, one player related these experiences to the practicalities of on-the-ground police work, reflecting on the decision-making processes undertaken by police in their day-to-day business (e.g., Manning & Hawkins, 1990):

> *I focused more on those [organized crime tasks] rather than policing, and my policing score did take a hit because of it, especially because I got caught taking a lot of bribes. The inability to do everything reminds me of the common perception that police are "never around when you need them."*

Again, as was noted earlier, "bad cop" playthroughs also contributed toward cynical emotionality from players, albeit in a different fashion (Hartmann & Vorderer, 2010). When players were no longer hindered by the moral imperative of good work, they found that they were still forced to engage in difficult decisions relating to community interests. *Beat Cop* features an "Alliance Meter" that quantifies the Kelly's relationship with various in-game factions—namely, the Police, the Mafia, the Crew, and the local community. Notably, it is impossible for Kelly to maintain a positive standing with all these groups simultaneously, reflecting the game's intrinsic conflicts and moral dilemmas. Actions taken to assist one faction typically come at the expense of another. For instance, aiding the Crew often diminishes standing with the Mafia and vice versa. Similarly, aligning with either criminal element tends to adversely affect the player's relationship with the Police and the local community, if not both. This structure creates an environment in which players feel pressured to prioritize one group over another, often requiring them to suspend ethical considerations in favor of meeting immediate in-game objectives or needs. In some cases, this meant full-on support for one of the groups and discarding any contravening morals:

> *I am starting to get into the mindset that I do not really mind. I am starting to get a lot more points with the crew than with the mafia also. So might focus on that more.*

For others, this meant exploiting in-game tensions for self-serving purposes:

> *Because I was a Bad Cop, I always chose the most destructive path, but playing both sides against each other was profitable and helped me manage my community relations and personal threat level.*

Ultimately, the freedom of movement in *Beat Cop* was taken to be an illusion by the coders (Aarseth, 2014). Players felt that conflicting interests reduced their agency to have Kelly perform as their idealized police officer (regardless of play style). They also found that their in-game decisions were laden with underlying pressures that were commonly embedded in violence (Denham et al., 2019). The coders generally expressed a feeling of learned helplessness, suggesting that by the end they did not feel that they had any control over the choices that Kelly made:

> *By the end of the game I didn't feel like I was actually doing anything to control its story. I was penalized regardless of which course of action I took, and people would interact with me regardless of my score. I guess this might be how police officers feel, but it left me frustrated.*

Conclusions

Beat Cop builds a unique set of mechanics extending from the banalities of police work heretofore shunned in popular media (Reiner, 2010) to develop an intersectional view of policing that considers family, social, professional, and community-based interpretations of police work, yet also faces criticism for its inclusion of racist stereotypes (Taylor, 2018). The broad range of gameplay opportunities offered by *Beat Cop* necessitate significant interactions that fill out the game's narrative and ground players in its pseudo-community policing format. Unfortunately, as observed above, these interactions tend toward a cynical framing of policing and the communities that police officers serve. While the game's creators attempted to mitigate this framing through their opening remarks that implied fantasy and hyperreal fiction, *Beat Cop*'s grounding as a policing simulator ultimately left players feeling a sense of frustration about the nature of police work and the policing occupation in general. *Beat Cop* fails to provide immersive control, instead creating a frustrating experience of rote activities that ultimately drove players down a linear path toward full-on corruption. Below, we unpack some observations about the source of this cynicism.

Why Does *Beat Cop* Frame Police Work Through a Cynical Lens?

The first suggestion that we make relates to the opening remarks offered by the game's designers. As cited above, the creators suggest that their aim was to emulate their halcyon evenings of "watching good guys kicking bad guys asses [*sic*]" in policing dramas of the 1980s (11 bit studios, 2023). The use of policing dramas as source materials provides an abstracted representation of social order that extends from hyperreal presentations of police work (Nichols-Pethick, 2012). These contextual indicators align with an era in popular media that Surrette (2015) defines as the "cops frame":

> The new cops construction portrayed the local police as aggressive, crime-fighting, take-no-prisoners, frontline soldiers in the war on crime. Far from irrelevant, they were now the combat grunts who fought crime war battles . . . Local "cops" emerge in this construction as professional, gristled soldiers engaged in pre-emptive law-and-order battles—combat-hardened street soldiers in an unpopular war. (Surrette, 2015, p. 106, quotations original)

In addition to setting up crimefighting as warfare, a common trope in this frame is the divide between the theoretical lessons imbued by the police academy and the practical realities of enforcing the law on the streets (Surrette, 2015), occasionally leading to the dramatic telling of a rogue police officer. Here the banalities of police work like aiding members of the public are typically used as plot points intended to convey a faulty criminal justice system prioritizing the wrong social issues. This framing is present in many of the shows of the era alluded to by *Beat Cop*'s creators; for example, *Miami Vice* (1984), *Hill Street Blues* (1981), and *Magnum P.I.* (1980) all employ simplified, binary oppositional frames of good versus bad, urban decay, leading to a pre-emptive administration of justice (Wayne, 2016; Surrette, 2015).

Beat Cop demonstrated many of these same principles through both plot and mechanics. Most notably, the setting for the game, a hypothetical New York City block, retrenches many of the indicators of social decay framed in cop-style programming (Nichols-Pethick, 2012). Upon commencing the game, players are immersed in a virtual space where propositions from sex workers and drug dealers are the norm, bribery is commonplace, and no entity can be trusted. Once settled in, they are faced with a constant barrage of opportunities to bend or break laws and moralities, driven by Kelly's ambition to clear his name and overlapping financial obligations. Disdain for the public is pointedly expressed in dialog, using a combination of overtly racist terminology and euphemisms to other the community members that form much of Kelly's beat. Taken as a whole, players are swiftly exposed to a dystopic setting through *Beat Cop*'s ludic approach to exploration.

Similarly, the ticketing mechanic and other diegetic elements employed in Kelly's day-to-day police work reified a cynical perspective on the positionality of police in society that was commonly presented in cop framings (Carr et al., 2007). While some in-game remarks connect the daily ticket quota with public safety, it is more often presented as a matter of course that must be undertaken by the player. The relative insignificance of traffic enforcement activities is driven home by the frequent bribery opportunities presented to players and the protagonist's indifference to their purpose. These interactions serve to trivialize an activity that is commonly viewed as a *de minimis* in the eyes of the public (Woods, 2015). Further, the onslaught of hate directed at players who chose to decline bribes reinforced this cynical framing—in effect, they were punished for choosing to focus on the details (Reiss, 1971).

Again, these in-game experiences can be connected to the contextual indicators provided by the *Beat Cop*'s developers. Procedural work like traffic duty and community policing in urban settings is often employed in crime dramas to drive home how far a character has fallen in their career (Clandfield, 2009). Not only have they been demoted from a more senior position, but the afflicted police officer is also now forced to engage with the public and enforce trivial laws. The members of the public receiving tickets are generally disposable, the pain of the fine left unconsidered, and the issuing of tickets presented as an unnecessary procedure for all involved. Illustrative examples include 1992's *Lethal Weapon 3*, *Beverly Hills Cop 2*

(1987), *It Could Happen to You* (1994), *Super Troopers* (2001), and *End of Watch* (2012) amongst others.

Finally, we also suggest that the cynical presentation of the police in *Beat Cop* may be reflective of historical situations, regardless of the developer's claim that the game "is not a document about New York in the 80s [sic]." The game's frequent allusions to structural corruption within the NYPD, as well as collusion with external organized crime groups like the Italian American Mafia and NYC street gangs align with significant and public media coverage about internal corruption in the era. This was particularly pronounced in the NYPD, which, as an organization, was forced to respond to a series of scandals throughout the 1980s and 1990s that undermined public trust in the institution (see Dombrink, 1988; Levitt, 2009; and White, 2014 for expanded detail). Indeed, the period between the 1970s and 2000 marked an era of global police reformation in response to widespread media coverage of corruption and backwoods-style policing that was prominent in many developed nations (Walker & Archbold, 2018; Lovell, 2003; Surrette, 2015). Mediated representations of this corruption have been demonstrated to have residual effects on viewers' sense of trust in policing, as demonstrated by Dowler and Zawilski (2007).

While *Beat Cop* claims to be a work of fantasy, its billing as a policing simulator paired with a more than striking resemblance to both fictional and non-fiction accounts of police corruption suggest otherwise. Players frequently observed that the corruption embedded in the game reached such a critical mass that they did not feel that they could succeed without engaging in it, regardless of moral standing. Although the narrative does not make a direct connection with factual events, even if the events in *Beat Cop* were not aligned with factual events, as stated by its developers, their alignment with popular tropes about police corruption nonetheless served to reinforce the embedded cynicism by forcing the player's hands.

Limitations

It is important to note that this chapter employs a qualitative approach that is inherently subjective. We have presented a summary of our findings from our playthroughs; however, it must be considered that these playthroughs were completed with the intent of interrogating *Beat Cop*'s discourse about policing as expressed through mechanics, dialog, and plot. Were the game to be played for entertainment's sake, as is probably the case for the game's 500,000 community members, it seems likely that many of our points would be observed. With that being said, there have been several critiques leveled at the game through popular media, notably focusing on its frequent use of hateful language (Taylor, 2018; Nother, 2019). Further, this limitation should not ignore that many people purchase games with intention, suggesting that those who play *Beat Cop* are looking for a game about policing

Second, as noted before in relation to the parody elements of the game, it is important to observe that the designers at *Pixel Crow* did not set out to develop a realistic policing simulator but rather built a game that simulated their experiences with popular media presentations of policing. Bearing this point in mind, we offer that the reader should be cautious about inferring beyond the surface-level dialog and experiences in *Beat Cop*—which is what we have attempted in our chapter. Nonetheless, it seems that there was a missed opportunity for the game's developers to provide a more robust critique of policing (see Latorre, 2015). While in-game dialog will occasionally touch upon contemporary events like the Black Lives Matter movement, the game generally does not impart much in the way of messaging about police (either pro or against). To this end we suggest that future studies of a similar nature might consider critically acclaimed properties like the *Grand Theft Auto* series, *Disco Elysium* (ZA/UM, 2019), *This is the Police* (THQ Nordic, 2016), and others that may provide a more nuanced and subversive take on policing.

References

11 bit studios (2023). *Beat Cop*. https://beatcopgame.com/#home

Aarseth, E. (2014). Ludology. In M. Wolf & B. Perron (Eds.), *The Routledge companion to video game studies* (pp. 185–189). Routledge.

Altheide, D.L. (1987). Reflections: Ethnographic content analysis. Qualitative Sociology, 10(1), 65–77.

Annandale, D. (2006). The subversive carnival of Grand Theft Auto: San Andreas. In N. Garrelts (Ed.), *The meaning and culture of Grand Theft Auto: Critical essays* (pp. 88–102). McFarland & Company.

Bullock, K. (2018). The police use of social media: Transformation or normalisation? *Social Policy and Society, 17*(2), 245–258.

Calvert, C., & Richards, R.D. (2007). Violence and video games 2006: Legislation and litigation. *Texas Review of Entertainment & Sports Law, 8*, 49.

Cappella, J., & Jamieson, K. (1997). *Spirals of cynicism: The press and the public good*. Oxford University Press.

Carr, P.J., Napolitano, L., & Keating, J. (2007). We never call the cops and here is why: A qualitative examination of legal cynicism in three Philadelphia neighborhoods. *Criminology, 45*(2), 445–480.

Chan, J. (1996). Changing police culture. *The British Journal of Criminology, 36*(1), 109–134.

Charmaz, K. (2014). *Constructing grounded theory*. Sage.

Chen, L., Dowling, D., Goetz, C. (2023). At the nexus of ludology and narratology: Advances in reality-based story-driven games. *F1000Research* 12(45). https://doi.org/10.12688/f1000research.129113.1

Chermak, S., McGarrell, E., & Gruenewald, J. (2006). Media coverage of police misconduct and attitudes toward police. *Policing: An International Journal of Police Strategies & Management, 29*(2), 261–281.

Clandfield, P. (2009). "We ain't got no yard": Crime, development, and urban environment. In T. Potter & C.W. Marshall (Eds.), *The Wire: Urban decay and American television* (pp. 37–49). Continuum.

Clifford, K., & White, R. (2017). *Media and crime: Content, context and consequence.* Oxford University Press.

Cowart, H.S., Blackstone, G.E., & Riley, J.K. (2022). Framing a movement: Media portrayals of the George Floyd protests on Twitter. *Journalism & Mass Communication Quarterly, 99*(3), 676–695.

Denham, J., & Spokes, M. (2019). Thinking outside the "murder box": Virtual violence and pro-social action in video games. *The British Journal of Criminology, 59*(3), 737–755.

Dombrink, J. (1988). The touchables: Vice and police corruption in the 1980's. *Law and Contemporary Problems, 51*(1), 201–232.

Dowler, K., Fleming, T., & Muzzatti, S.L. (2006). Constructing crime: Media, crime, and popular culture. *Canadian Journal of Criminology and Criminal Justice, 48*(6), 837–850.

Dowler, K., & Zawilski, V. (2007). Public perceptions of police misconduct and discrimination: Examining the impact of media consumption. *Journal of Criminal Justice, 35*(2), 193–203.

Ericson, R.V. (1989). Patrolling the facts: Secrecy and publicity in police work. *British Journal of Sociology, 40*(2), 205–226.

Garrelts, N. (2006). An introduction to Grand Theft Auto studies. In N. Garrelts (ed.), *The meaning and culture of Grand Theft Auto: Critical essays* (pp. 1–16). McFarland & Company.

Goldsmith, A. (2015) Disgracebook policing: Social media and the rise of police indiscretion. *Policing and Society* 25(3), 249–267.

Hartmann, T., & Vorderer, P. (2010). It's okay to shoot a character: Moral disengagement in violent video games. *Journal of Communication, 60*(1), 94–119.

Herbert, S. (2006). Tangled up in blue: Conflicting paths to police legitimacy. *Theoretical Criminology, 10*(4), 481–504.

Holl, E., Bernard, S., & Melzer, A. (2020). Moral decision-making in video games: A focus group study on player perceptions. *Human Behavior and Emerging Technologies, 2*(3), 278–287.

Huey, L., & Broll, R. (2012). "All it takes is one TV show to ruin it": A police perspective on police-media relations in the era of expanding prime time crime markets. *Policing and Society, 22*(4), 384–396.

Juul, J. (2019). *Handmade pixels: Independent video games and the quest for authenticity.* MIT Press.

Latorre, P. (2015). The social discourse of video games analysis model and case study: GTA IV. *Games and Culture, 10*(5), 415–437.

Lawrence, R. (2000). *The politics of force: Media and the construction of police brutality.* University of California Press.

Levan, K., & Downing, S. (2022). *Crime, punishment, and video games.* Rowman & Littlefield.

Levitt, L. (2009). *NYPD confidential: Power and corruption in the country's greatest police force.* Macmillan.

Lovell, J.S. (2003). *Good cop, bad cop: Mass media and the cycle of police reform.* Willow Tree.

Low, J. (2019). A pragmatic definition of the concept of theoretical saturation. *Sociological Focus, 52*(2), 131–139.

Manning, P.K., & Hawkins, K. (1990). Legal decisions: a frame analytic perspective. In S. Riggins (Ed.), *Beyond Goffman: Studies on communication, institution, and social interaction* (pp. 203–234). De Gruyter.

Mawby, R.C. (1999). Visibility, transparency and police-media relations. *Policing and Society: An International Journal, 9*(3), 263–286.

Moriearty, P.L. (2010). Framing justice: Media, bias, and legal decision making. *Maryland Law Review, 69*, 849–909.

Moule, R.K., Fox, B.H., & Parry, M.M. (2018). The long shadow of Ferguson: Legitimacy, legal cynicism, and public perceptions of police militarization. *Crime & Delinquency, 65*(2), 151–182.

Mustafaj, M., & van den Bulck, J. (2021). The media and our perceptions of the police. In H. Giles, E. Maguire, & S. Hill (Eds.), *The Rowman & Littlefield handbook of policing, communication, and society*, (pp. 213–228). Rowman & Littlefield.

Nacke, L.E., Drachen, A., & Göbel, S. (2010). Methods for evaluating gameplay experience in a serious gaming context. *International Journal of Computer Science in Sport, 9*(2), 1–12.

Nichols-Pethick, J. (2012). *TV cops: The contemporary American television police drama.* Routledge.

Nix, J., & Pickett, J.T. (2017). Third-person perceptions, hostile media effects, and policing: Developing a theoretical framework for assessing the Ferguson effect. *Journal of Criminal Justice, 51*, 24–33.

Nother, B. (2019). Beat cop has a problem, it's derogatory. *Outoflives.net.* Retrieved September 22, 2023 from https://www.outoflives.net/2019/02/05/beat-cop-has-a-problem-its-derogatory/

Peterson, R., & Hagan, J. (2005). Changing conceptions of race. In S. Gabbion & H. Green (Eds.), *Race, crime, and justice* (pp. 55–72). Routledge

Reiner, R. (2010). *The politics of the police.* Oxford University Press.

Reiss, A.J. (1971). *The police and the public.* Yale University Press.

Rhineberger-Dunn, G., Briggs, S.J., & Rader, N. (2016). Clearing crime in primetime: The disjuncture between fiction and reality. *American Journal of Criminal Justice, 41*, 255–278.

Saldaña, J. (2021). *The coding manual for qualitative researchers.* Sage.

Sicart, M. (2020). Playing software: The role of the ludic in the software society. *Information, Communication & Society, 23*(14), 2081–2095.

Skogan, W. (2007). Asymmetry in the impact of encounters with police. *Policing and Society, 16*(2), 99–126.

Steam (2023). Beat Cop. Retrieved October 13, 2023 from https://store.steampowered.com/app/461950/Beat_Cop/

Steinmetz, K.F. (2018). Carceral horror: Punishment and control in Silent Hill. *Crime, Media, Culture, 14*(2), 265–287.

Surrette, R. (2015). *Media, crime, and criminal justice* (5th ed.). Nelson.

Taylor, I. (2018). The art of failing: What 11 bit Studios learnt from Beat Cop. *Games Industry.biz.* Retrieved September 19, 2023 from https://www.gamesindustry.biz/the-art-of-failing-what-11-bit-studios-learnt-from-beat-cop

Toh, W. (2023). The player experience and design implications of narrative games. *International Journal of Human–Computer Interaction, 39*(13), 2742–2769.

Walker, S.E., & Archbold, C.A. (2018). *The new world of police accountability.* Sage.

Walsh, J.P., & O'Connor, C. (2018). Social media and policing: A review of recent research. *Sociology Compass, 13*(1), e12648.

Wayne, M.L. (2016). Post-network audiences and cable crime drama. *Northern Lights: Film & Media Studies Yearbook, 14*(1), 141–157.

Weaver, A.J., & Lewis, N. (2012). Mirrored morality: An exploration of moral choice in video games. *Cyberpsychology, Behavior, and Social Networking, 15*(11), 610–614.

Whalen, Z. (2006). Cruising in San Andreas: Ludic space and urban aesthetics. In N. Garrelts (Ed.) *The meaning and culture of Grand Theft Auto: Critical essays* (pp. 143–161). McFarland & Company.

White, M.D. (2014). The New York City Police Department, its crime control strategies and organizational changes, 1970–2009. *Justice Quarterly, 31*(1), 74–95.

Woods, J.B. (2015). Decriminalization, police authority, and routine traffic stops. *UCLA L. Rev., 62*, 672.

Wright, E. (2017). Marketing authenticity: Rockstar games and the use of cinema in video game promotion. *Kinephanos: Journal of Media Studies and Popular Culture* 7(1), 131–164.

INDEX

For Product Safety Concerns and Information please contact our EU
representative GPSR@taylorandfrancis.com Taylor & Francis Verlag GmbH,
Kaufingerstraße 24, 80331 München, Germany

Printed and bound by CPI Group (UK) Ltd, Croydon, CR0 4YY

08/06/2025

01897008-0008